Europe-Asia-Pacific Studies in Economy and Technology

Titles in the Series

Manfred Kulessa (Ed.)
The Newly Industrializing Economies of Asia

Theodor Leuenberger (Ed.)
Technology Transfer to Technology Management in China

Barna Tálas
Economic Reforms and Political Reform Attempts
in China 1979 - 1989

Theodor Leuenberger
Martin E. Weinstein (Eds.)

Europe, Japan and America in the 1990s

in the 1990s

Cooperation and Competition

With 5 Figures

Springer-Verlag Berlin Heidelberg New York
London Paris Tokyo Hong Kong
Barcelona Budapest

Professor Dr. Theodor Leuenberger
University of St. Gallen
Department of Economics
Bahnhofstraße 8
CH-9000 St. Gallen, Switzerland

Professor Dr. Martin E. Weinstein, Director
The Mansfield Center
The University of Montana
Missoula, MT 59812, USA

ISBN 3-540-55856-X Springer-Verlag Berlin Heidelberg New York Tokyo
ISBN 0-387-55856-X Springer-Verlag New York Heidelberg Berlin Tokyo

© Springer-Verlag Berlin · Heidelberg 1992
Printing in Germany

Printing: Weihert-Druck, Darmstadt
Bookbinding: Buchbinderei Kränkl, Heppenheim
2142/7130-543210 - Printed on acid-free paper

Contents

The Trilateral Concert:
Indispensable but not Sufficient

Martin E. Weinstein and Theodor Leuenberger

It is gratifying to look back and note that this book on the future of European Community (EC)-Japan-United States relations had its origins in a meeting in Berlin, in September 1989, which was sponsored by the Japan-German Center in Berlin. That meeting, which took place before the Soviet Union was transformed into a group of independent states, before Germany was unified, before the Balkans drifted into civil war, and before the United States, Germany and Japan found themselves in a global credit crunch, took an unusually foresighted, realistic point of view. As a result, the articles in this book appear to be more relevant and significant in the summer of 1992, than they did when the plan for their research was conceived, and the issues which they address are likely to become more important and in some cases more urgent, as we approach the turn of the Twenty First Century.

The long-term, fundamental question facing the human race is whether we will be able to solve the problem which the British economist William Stanley Jevons posed for the United Kingdom more than a century ago. Jevons noted that while industrialization and the use of steam energy fueled by coal had enriched his country and caused an enormous increase in its population, British coal deposits were being depleted, while the population continued to grow. He saw that this would create an unstable and eventually unsustainable imbalance between dwindling, non-renewable mineral resources and population. Although we have learned to tap many more non-renewable resources since Jevon's time, the basic dilemma he posed now applies on a global scale. If we are to avoid unmanageable over-population of the planet, resource depletion and the ensuing economic collapse and famines, the human race, in the coming century, must make the transition from non-renewable to renewable resources as the basis for industrial society, and we must find a way to limit population.

In order for these fundamental technological, industrial and social questions to be resolved, we must avoid a repetition of the wars which ravaged the first half of the Twentieth Century, and reach higher levels of global cooperation than were possible during the forty years of the Cold War. The relations between the Europeans, Japanese and Americans will be crucial to this process, because these people, although they total less than 20 percent of the human race, produce and control approximately 70 percent of world economic production, and dominate world trade and finance. They also produce the most advanced science and technology, and possess or have the potential to possess the most powerful military forces. Finally, as the leading users of energy and resources, their success or failure in making the transition to a sustainable, viable ecology will create the framework and set the path for the future of the poorer, industrializing nations.

In short, the cooperation of the leading industrialized countries, or the formation of an effective European-Japanese-American trilateral, global concert system is a necessary condition for the future viability and well-being of humanity. *But it is not, in and of itself, a sufficient condition.* The 80 percent of the human race that does not live in Europe, Japan or the United States, clearly must also learn to see its future in long-term, global perspective. If their aspirations for political self-determination and industrialization are not to lead to economic collapse, war and ecological disaster, the Russians, Eastern Europeans, Chinese, Indians, Arabs, Africans and Latinos will also have to accept responsibilities that reach beyond their own borders and the traditional, narrow concepts of national or ethnic self-interest.

The Internal Problems of the Trilateral

Before the reader tackles the articles in this book, which focus on the relations between the Europeans, Japanese and Americans, it is worth noting that the centrifugal forces which seem to be pushing the world toward a three bloc system as opposed to a global economic system, have their origins in the internal problems which have come to the fore in the early 1990s, especially in the United States, in Germany and in Europe.

Despite the collapse of the its Cold War adversary, and despite its quick military victory against Iraq in the Gulf War in the spring of 1991, the United States is in many respects the most internally troubled of the trilateral. Although the United States is still the best endowed of nations in terms of mineral resources, arable land and technology, it has worked itself into a painful economic corner. In contrast to the leading international powers of the past, which usually suffered from what Paul Kennedy called "imperial over-stretch", meaning that military commitments exceeded economic resources, the United States has been undermining its economic future by "consumer over-stretch", a condition in which government and private households consume more than the American economy produces, go increasingly into debt to pay for their consumption, and fail to make sufficient capital investments to meet their future productivity and consumption needs.

The roots of this problem can be traced back to colonial times, but they can be seen most clearly in the context of American history since the Great Depression and World War II. Following those historical benchmarks, American government officials and economic planners gravitated toward the belief that the most effective way to keep their economy growing and prosperous was to maintain a high level of demand, especially consumer and government demand, even if this meant generating greater and greater debt. There was so much American capital accumulated during World War II, that it seemed in the 1950s as though Americans had a bottomless reservoir of savings upon which to draw. Of course, that was an illusion. By the 1970s and 1980s, when it was becoming clear that America had expended its own capital, Americans were able to avoid this reality because there were enormous amounts of first, Arab oil money, and then Japanese surplus capital eager to invest in the United States. Unfortunately, these generous foreign loans and investments went largely into United States government debt and into private consumption, and were not used to adequately modernize and expand American productive capacity. Consequently, in the 1980s and 1990s, manufacturing productivity growth in the United States has been much lower than in Japan or in the European Community, the transportation and communications infrastructures and the urban centers have sadly deteriorated, and for the time being, there are simply not adequate funds available either in the United States or abroad to quickly correct these deficiencies.

These rather simply stated economic problems are only understandable, however, in the broader context of what are probably deeper and even more intractable philosophical issues. Ultimately, the failure to save and to invest adequately, and the willingness to go irresponsibly into debt, have their root in an idealism and romanticism that have relieved Americans of the need to submit to the disciplines and sacrifices that are intrinsic to the human condition. The conquest of the western frontier, the incredible productivity and wealth generated by Henry Ford's assembly line, and the heady, relatively easy American victories in World Wars I and II, led too many Americans to believe that they had a special, privileged place in the universe-exempt from the strictures of economic common sense and the penalties of self-indulgence.

These economic and philosophical problems are turning the attention and energy of the American government and people inward. If this turning inward leads to a realistic reassessment of values and behavior, it will benefit America, the trilateral and the world. There is disturbing evidence, however, that the turning inward could lead to xenophobia and protectionism. These are the dangers that must be guarded against.

Although they were events of great promise, the collapse of the Soviet Union in 1990 and 1991, and the sudden, unexpected unification of Germany, have also generated profound problems for the integration and the future development of the European Community. First of all, the costs of integrating East Germany into the Federal Republic are straining the German economy, and are generating excessive debt and worrisome inflation in what until now had been the model European economy. The problems attendant to unification have also led to a grass-roots reaction among German voters, and indeed, a noticeable number of voters throughout the European Community, who doubt the advisability of pushing ahead with the Maastricht Treaty creating a unified European banking and currency system.

At the same time that this grass-root reaction has at least temporarily weakened Germany and left it prey to internal strains and divisions, many of Germany's neighbors have also become suspicious and fearful of the long-term economic and political implications of unification. Memories of earlier attempts to unify Europe — the last one within living memory — have been refreshed by the appearance of a unified, populous, dynamic Germanic state in the heart of Europe. Consequently, in Britain and in France, there is a greater and almost palpable reluctance to move toward European integration with the speed and energy that were visible 3-4 years ago. Although opposition has appeared among politicians and the media, the Euro rebels have remained in a minority. Hopefully, German unification will proceed successfully, and by the time the dust settles early in the next century, the integration and expansion of the European Community will have regained its momentum.

Of the trilateral partners, Japan is probably the least troubled by internal difficulties. Although the property and financial speculations of the late 1980s have been followed by a government policy of deliberate tightening and deflation, the basics of the Japanese economy still appear sound. The high capital investments of the 1980s make it more than likely that Japanese industries will be productive and internationally competitive through the 1990s. Although society and politics are not free of strains and problems, Japan is relatively intact and effective. Japan's problem is that while it will probably continue to be the most productive and competitive of the trilateral partners, it is not large enough or powerful enough to lead the trilateral. Moreover, even if Japan were prepared to lead, there is no inclination on the part of Americans or Europeans to accept Japan in a leadership role, even though lip service is frequently paid to this idea. As Takakazu Kuriyama, the former Vice Minister of Foreign Affairs and now Ambassador to Washington, has frequently pointed out, the GNP ratio of America, the European Community and Japan is roughly 5-5-3. This ratio puts Japan into the trilateral, but leaves it the smallest of the economic giants.

As a result of its position in the 5-5-3 trilateral, Japan is still in a basically reactive posture. It does take whatever limited initiatives it can to strengthen free trade and maintain an open global system, but at the same time, Japanese leaders do not think that they can do much to resolve America's or Europe's problems, and they are aware that these problems are pushing the world toward a three bloc system. Consequently, the Japanese are attending carefully to their relations with their Asian neighbors, directing ever larger investments into this region, and are hedging against the undesirable contingency of having to live with a protectionist North American Free Trade Area and with an economic Fortress Europa.

The Insufficiency of the Trilateral

Although the internal problems of the trilateral require serious attention, and will not be solved without great efforts, there is a better than even chance that business and political interest groups in Europe, Japan and America that have a stake in an open, international economy, will block the swing toward protectionism and a three bloc system and prevent the trilateral from disintegrating. In this case, the prospects for world order and for successful global economic development and ecological viability will be dramatically improved, but not assured. The future of mankind probably rests ultimately upon the shoulders of the 80 percent of the world's people, who now produce and consume less than 30 percent of the wealth, and who are determined to get richer and more powerful by industrializing.

Russia and China epitomize the basic questions that have to be dealt with by the developing economies. Together they hold more than a billion and a half people, almost a quarter of the human race. Both are nuclear powers. Both have ravaged their societies and ecologies in unsuccessful efforts to rapidly industrialize within the framework of totalitarian, Marxist states. If Russia and China can find a way to make the transition to workable, viable industrial societies, the second major component of the human future will have been fitted into place. Europe, Japan and America can maintain open world trading and financial systems, and can contribute technology and limited investments (relative to the size of the Russian and Chinese economies), but ultimately the Russians and the Chinese have to restructure their societies in such a way that their people can become confident that enterprise and work will be rewarded, and not confiscated by the state or by corrupt officials.

This is an enormous task, and one that is not completed or guaranteed for the future even in the most developed states. Somehow, the Russians and the Chinese must create legal structures and economic institutions that will enable their people to create wealth without generating massive and intolerable injustice and corruption, and without destroying our planet. Clearly the difficulties they face are far greater than those faced by the trilateral. This essay is not an appropriate place to analyze the tasks of successful Russian and Chinese development, except to note that without a successful trilateral to look toward as a model, as a market, and as a source of technology and capital, the task before the Russians and Chinese looks almost impossible.

Conclusion

Although realism requires us to acknowledge the limits of the trilateral's power and role in a diverse, messy world, it also leads us to understand how indispensable the success of the trilateral is to the mankind's future, and it sets clearly before us the tasks that must be accomplished. First, the Europeans, the Japanese and the Americans must put their own houses in good order, without falling prey to xenophobia and protectionism. Secondly, they must preserve the open global financial and trading systems that have been the foundation of their economic and political viability and success during the last four decades. Finally, they must learn to do what can be done to help the rest of the human race to industrialize. They must be patient, persistent and positive in their efforts, without deluding themselves or the developing countries into believing that foreign assistance can be more than a critical but ultimately marginal element in their successful development.

Part I

European Perspectives

The Japanese Challenge for Europe: Ambiguous Relations

Thilo von Brockdorff
Secretary General
Japanese German Center Berlin

Twice in history the relations with Europe were of major importance to Japan: in the 16th and in the 19th century. In both cases the relations were positive and negative. The first question to be answered here is how this historic background reflects the present day relations between Japan and Europe. The second and perhaps more interesting question, however, is what importance does Japan hold for Europe of today.

Historical and Geopolitical Background

Japan's insular position has since old times shaped the minds of the Japanese people; on the one hand they felt unique, on the other hand, threatened by outside powers. This position has given the respective rulers the possibility to close up the country to outsiders or open it gradually just as they wished. Thus Japan was secluded from the outside world from the beginning of the 16th up to the middle of the 19th century. During this time, Japan could develop its unique characteristics, which prevail even today.

This period of seclusion was preceded first by the contact with Europe through Portuguese Jesuits and later through Spaniards. The first phase of this encounter was quite successful: The Europeans brought new sciences like mathematics and physics and many other notions of the European civilization (including the knowledge of producing arms). Yet in the end, when the Spaniards demanded from the Japanese that they take over the entire package of European civilization and threatened to send the Armada if they failed to comply, the Japanese rulers reacted adversely: they banned foreigners from the Japanese islands and persecuted all Christians. Nonetheless, the things they had learned from the Europeans were incorporated, however, into their own culture.

In 1853 Japan re-opened itself to the world, giving in to available pressures, mainly because they had learned from the example of China in the opium-war that seclusion was no longer a guarantee against being colonized. Hence they studied with great enthusiasm Western societies and used whatever seemed necessary to them. They adopted many elements of Western civilization and industrialization, although not with the aim of becoming Westerners, but rather in order to conserve their own identity and independence. In this second phase of contacts with Europe, however, relations were not always friendly. At the end of last century Russia, France and also Germany sided with China rather than with Japan, leading to Japan's entry into World War I on the side of the Anglo-Americans. Then in the 1930s the USA opposed Japan's China policy, leading to Japan's siding with the Axis powers and opposing the British, Dutch and French in the Asian Pacific theater.

After World War II or the "Pacific War" Japan felt quite isolated in its region. Economic reconstruction and the development of a strong export capability under the security umbrella of the USA seemed to be the only recipe for survival in an unfriendly neighborhood. This pattern of behavior, which is not very compatible with international cooperation and regional integration, somehow still seems to be there. Having barely any raw materials of its own, Japan depends on long and vulnerable lifelines for its imports of raw materials and towards its export markets. The only way Japan could contribute to the security of these lifelines, not having the military means, was to 'buy' security through extensive development aid aimed at the stabilization of the countries along these lifelines — the so-called 'comprehensive security'.

There was little that Europe could contribute in this situation. Europe for Japan was nothing more than a far away market with little if any relevance to Japan's security. And the same was true vice versa: Europe concentrated its efforts on its security arrangement, i.e., NATO and the European integration in the EC. Japan was widely considered as merely a developing country which through copying had managed to produce some cheap products of acceptable quality in a few specific fields.

These views underwent a drastic changes in the 1970s, when Japan managed to cope with the oil crisis in a much better way than its Western partners. Japan, which by now already had managed to conquer some markets, e.g. cameras, accepted the challenge of the energy crisis and achieved the production of cars with a much lower consumption of fuel; at the same time, Japan recognized the importance the consumers now attached to middle class cars. This perception brought about its success on the U.S. car market.

Now Japan was accepted as a full member of the club of the industrialized countries and hence was invited to take part as one of the seven members in the economic summits which started in the mid-1970s.

Regional Constraints and Responsibilities

The European Community (EC), which started in London and grew from 6 to 9, and then to 12 member states, overcame internal crises in the 1980s by deciding upon the formation of a political and financial union and beginning plans toward the integration of the common market. The question was, however, how an integrated Europe should react to threats from the outside : Should it close its market to outsiders in such cases, hence becoming a 'fortress Europe', or should it remain open even at the risk of losing some of its markets to non-member countries or their companies? Although there is a generally accepted policy to keep the market open, there are still those who think that in the case of threat to whole branches of industry and the respective jobs, the community should have the option of protecting its economy against such massive disruptions.

The situation in Asia is completely different from the one in Europe; most countries are still developing economies, although a few of them developed into 'newly industrialized countries' in the meantime. Nevertheless even there one finds tendencies towards creating some kind of regional cooperation, the most concrete being the Association of Southeast Asian Nations (ASEAN). New forms of cooperation were sought between the mainland and island-states of the Asia-Pacific region by businessmen and officials, because it was obvious that intra-regional trade was on the rise and that many of these countries showed considerable growth rates. One of the politically important questions in this connection was which role Japan should play in this context and which would be played be the USA.

Japan itself, even though it is the main trading partner and investor of these countries, always tried to maintain a politically low profile, because in many Eastern and Southeastern countries the memories of the Pacific War are still fresh. Economically Japan is the leading country in the region. This is accepted as long as the USA play the counterpart role in regional cooperation. It is not necessary to define these roles precisely, because the Asia-Pacific cooperation is realized in a very pragmatic way, far from being institutionalized. But here I must add a word of caution: Europeans and especially Germans tend to judge international organizations by their form of institutionalization, but in Asia — as history shows — pragmatic solutions have prevailed and have worked quite successfully. One should therefore not underestimate the importance of these initiatives in the Asia-Pacific sphere. The question of the future therefore will be: How will the Asian-Pacific economic group, the EC and eventually the North American Free Trade zone, which is beginning to develop between the USA, Canada and Mexico, coexist?

Political Relations vis-a-vis Eastern Europe

Japan and Germany were both neighbors — directly or indirectly — of the former USSR. Nevertheless, this constellation did not constitute an element of cooperation between Europe and Japan until the 1980s. When in the context of the double track decision of NATO about INF weapons the USSR considered dislocating SS20 missiles from the European to the Asian theater, a direct link was established, because a reduction of tensions in Europe would have meant an increased threat in Asia. The triangular relations between Europe, Japan and North America were hereby activated, resulting in the declaration of the summit of Williamsburg in the summer of 1983, stating the need for triangular solidarity. Only global solutions of disarmament and detente were decreed as acceptable. The then prime minister of Japan, Nakasone Yasuhiro, stated that Japan considered itself a member of the community of the West , and new ways to deepen the relations in this triangular framework were looked for. One of the results of this policy has been the creation of the Japanese German Center Berlin (JGCB).

The relations between Japan and the Soviet Union have never been very intense, the main stumbling block being the question of the four islands (or island-groups) north of Hokkaido, the so-called 'Northern Territories', occupied by the USSR and claimed by Japan. Without the solution of this problem there cannot be a peace treaty with Japan, and without a peace treaty Japan does not want to conclude a treaty for the protection of investments. Hence intensification of economic relations here depends on the solution of political problems. Some movement concerning this question seemed to become possible when Gorbachev visited Japan in April 1991, but the disintegration of the USSR dashed all these hopes.

It is obvious that the reform and reconstruction of Eastern Europe, including the former USSR cannot be achieved without the help of Japan, the only remaining net capital exporter now that the USA has become a capital importer and Germany needs to use its capital for its own unification. The former Japanese Prime Minister Kaifu stated Japan's principal willingness to support the reforms in Eastern Europe in a speech held at the JGCB in January 1990, but little substantial help followed. Japan complies with the decisions of the economic summits concerning the Russian states, but what really is needed is substantial financial, economic and technical help from Japan. Some people think for instance that the Japanese should be interested in the conversion of the military industries of the former USSR as well as in the exploitation of its deposits of raw materials. So far, however the answer one gets in this connection is that serious feasibility studies must be carried out first, before one could visualize such cooperation. In fact, all appeals by Western statesmen and diplomats for a more intense Japanese engagement in Eastern Europe seem in vain as long as the key problem of the Northern Territories is not solved. And this has to be tackled now with the Republic of Russia.

Bilateral Trade-Issues

The growing imbalance of trade with Japan has alarmed the USA as well as the Europeans. This imbalance was caused in part by the success of Japanese exports and in part by relatively low Japanese imports of consumer and industrial goods. On the one side it was claimed that Japanese exports were successful because of their strategy of 'laser beaming', i.e., concentrating on a few selected products and even using dumping practices to conquer these markets. On the other side it was claimed that the Japanese market was closed for imports of manufactured goods.

The Japanese therefore aimed at opening their market and fostering internal growth. The result was that in the second half of the 1980s the balance of Japanese external trade was continuously reduced and the imbalance with the USA was stabilized. In 1991 this trend came to a halt: Several factors led to a reduction of the internal growth rate in Japan and hence to an increased interest in exports. However, these exports now tend to focus on East Asia and Europe, with Eastern Germany as the main new market. At the same time, imports from Europe fell off, because there were less investments in production and luxury goods. This trend causes new anxieties about a renaissance of the 'Japanese threat', this time concentrated on Europe rather than on the USA. The result is the strengthening of the position of those within the EC who call for increased protectionist measures.

The Japanese argue that the Europeans do not try hard enough to enter the Japanese market. They may indeed have a point here. The Japanese market is extremely competitive, maybe the toughest in the world. Costs for offices and warehouses are extremely high. It is very difficult to find the right personnel, and then there is also the language barrier. But obstacles which a foreign investor meets in Japan (excluding of course the language barrier) have to be overcome also by Japanese firms themselves, when trying to penetrate a new market or sector. It is however well known, that once one has succeeded in establishing oneself there, the chances for profits are remarkably good. Furthermore, once a product has been accepted by the Japanese, it has very good prospects in the Asia-Pacific market!

The problem thus is that Europeans these days seem extremely occupied with the integration of the European common market and the Germans with their unification, so that few energies are left in order to attack at the same time the Far Eastern markets.

Technological Cooperation or Dominance

Apart from the concerns about trade imbalances there are new and perhaps more basic concerns being voiced about the imbalance in technological innovation. The head of the planning staff of the German foreign office, Konrad Seitz, has issued a book with the title 'The Japanese-American Challenge' and subtitled 'Germany's HiTech Industry is Fighting for Survival'. He claims that in most of the modern key technologies like information and biotechnology, but also in new fields like new materials, space technology and new energy production the Japanese — in some cases in cooperation with the Americans — are much more advanced in comparison to the Europeans; therefore the Europeans must try hard to catch up. He also maintains that such countries which do not share the R&D for new key technologies like semi-conductors etc. will not belong to the leading industrial countries in the future.

In this respect as well Japan is suspected of being a 'closed shop' to outsiders, at least in the past. But now Japan is opening up here as well. The famous Japanese Ministry for International Trade and Industry (MITI) has started to invite foreign companies to take part in its think-tanks about new technologies like the flat TV-screen. And a new idea for Integrated Manufacturing Systems (IMS) was also opened to Europeans and Americans alike.

One solution to the problem of technological imbalances may be new strategic alliances between Japanese, European and perhaps American companies, who could carry out their research for new technology jointly and even foresee joint production of these goods. Such a perspective seems to have been opened through the cooperation between Daimler-Benz and the Mitsubishi-Group, the aim of which is to develop new technologies together, e.g. in the environmental sector.

Final Remarks

Obviously Japan as well as Europe, and especially Germany, need foreign trade to exist. Hence the maintenance of a global free market system is of paramount importance to both of them. In this context the present GATT or Uruguay-round is of great significance. Only if these negotiations are brought to a positive result it will be possible to maintain this system without major frictions. Although this may be not enough, but it is a minimum in order to secure the functioning of the world market.

Europe, Japan and the USA have huge tasks to tackle. We will have to find ways to support the reforms and reconstruction of the countries in the former COMECON area after the collapse of the communist doctrine. We will be confronted with similar tasks in Indochina and North Korea in the near future. The North-South problems can only be attacked through concerted actions of the industrialized countries under the leadership of the three regions mentioned. Moreover the global environmental damages, which increase every day, urgently need to be addressed by all states, but here again the three areas will have to take the initiatives and start concrete action.

In this situation a breaking down of the world economy into regional blocks facing economic and technological dominance could easily lead to economic warfare. We must therefore concentrate all our efforts and energies on the search for new ways of cooperation and division of labor for the benefit of the whole.

EC 1992 and Japan

Wolfgang Hager
Professor of Economics & Euro-consultant
Brussels

"1992" is one of the most radical systemic revolutions ever undertaken in a Western economy. While outsiders tend to concentrate on details of the external trade regime which emerges from this largely domestic reform, for the future of EC-Japan relations three questions matter in the medium term:

Will Europe regain competitiveness, and hence face the "Japanese challenge" with equanimity? Will Europe gain/retain a collective strategic capacity? Will Europe be strong enough to be able to shift its attention from yesterday's techno-mercantilist agenda to the real issues of economic welfare and security?

If the answer to these questions is positive, elements of partnership will dominate. Not long ago, the following view of "1992" was prevalent abroad: After 1992, Europe will "turn on itself and become a sprawling sluggish entity about as relevant to the outside world as the Austro-Hungarian Empire — a decadent pleasure resort."

This is a summary, dated 1988[1], of the U.S. perception showing a profound misunderstanding of the aims of "1992". The internal market program, as conceived in the first half of the 1980s, was a child of two partially conflicting currents of policy thinking: supply side thinking stressing markets; and strategic thinking stressing technology. Both approaches had the overriding objective to regain economic dynamism and international competitiveness. "Turning inward" is not the issue — at least not in the terms usually understood.

The relationship with Japan thus turns about two sorts of competition promoted by "1992": competition in the liberal sense, which provides opportunities for Japanese exports and direct investments; and competition in the strategic sense, which is about outcomes: power, security, and the ability to pursue domestic priorities within a global context.

The thesis of this paper is as follows: For a number of reasons, Europe is now less willing or able to play the neo-mercantilist strategic game

---

[1] Anthony Harris, Financial Times, August 30, 1988

than it was in 1985. On the other hand, Europe's economic agenda is slowly shifting back to the core of the European model, which is about real prosperity, not numbers. In that competition it is still winning hands down against the competition. Moreover, this is largely a friendly competition, where positive sum aspects dominate and cooperation is highly rewarded.

The Changing Nature of "1992"

"1992" was a response to two glaring failures: (1) macro-economic stagnation (stagflation), diagnosed as resulting from rigidities in factor and goods markets, including services; and (2) declining shares of high-tech exports centered around lagging competence in micro-electronics.

It would be wrong to "assign" the two main policy remedies — supply-side competition and R&D cooperation exclusively to one or the other symptoms of what was then called Euro-sclerosis. Indeed, the prospect of competition and deregulation, by stimulating defensive or adaptive investment, did more to accelerate the take-up of IT technologies in the European economy than all Community and EUREKA programs put together — by a wide margin. On the other hand, R&D cooperation centered heavily on standards, themselves a precondition for creating competition in a larger market. Moreover, macro-economic success was seen as linked to technological success: only by maintaining a presence in high-growth sectors could overall growth be assured.

Nevertheless, the original "1992" design was a balance between a German interest in free trade; a British and Dutch interest in freeing services; and a French transfer of its post-war model — voluntarist public leadership in technology development and application — to the European level. The balance between supply-side liberalization and a more voluntarist commitment to technological excellence was backed by a broad coalition of industrialists for whom the larger "home market" meant both market and shelter.

The Technology Community

Apart from nuclear research in central laboratories, European R&D schemes on a significant scale are a very recent phenomenon. ESPRIT[2] was adopted in 1984, RACE[3] in 1987. These programs, and their more recent cousins BRITE (production technologies), EURAM (materials) DRIVE (intelligent road/car systems), and ECLAIR (agro-biotech) are all based on the "shared-cost" principle, with industry and other participating institutions putting up 50%.[4]

Properly called strategic (i.e., based on a lengthy analysis of long-term needs, both social and commercial), these programs are "top-down" as regards priority-setting and project selection. In keeping with the EC's older rules, they are also "pre-competitive": commercial products are meant to be developed separately. By contrast, EUREKA — outside the EC but with the EC as an important "member state" — is an international framework agreement without central funding and a bottom-up approach: groups of firms and research institutions propose projects which may get the "EUREKA label" and hence priority national funding where available. They are "closer to the market", although later versions of ESPRIT etc. also moved in this direction.

While some of these programs reflect purely internal priorities (e.g., distance learning), others are linked to improved competitiveness. MITI, with its cooperative approach, has inspired these programs at least as much as France.[5]

At their simplest, they are intended as import substituting (ESPRIT, JESSI) and export promoting policies. As such, they are classical "industrial policies", albeit with a difference. The subsidy element is almost wholly devoted to off-setting the extra cost of transnational cooperation. In other words, it is the cooperation itself — with all its problems of management time, language, risks to proprietory technology, etc. — which is subsidized, rather than technology development itself. (Cooperation is also induced by a blackmail effect — companies staying out risk being faced with information deficits about their rivals, if not outright cabals against them.)

---

[2]European Strategic Program in Research and Development in Information Technologies

[3]Research and Development in Advanced Communications Technologies in Europe.

[4]Smaller share cost programs are DELTA (learning technologies), AIM (IT in health care), FLAIR (agro-food), MAST (marine S&T), EUROTRA (machine translation), BCR (metrology). Further additions to the EC alphabet soup are straight grants to research institutions, e.g. STEP (environment), EPOCH (climate), etc.

[5]See Wolfgang Hager, Competitive Modernization:Industrial Policy as a Key Area of EC Development, CEPS Working Documents (Economic) No. 14, Brussels, 1985

On a more strategic level, ESPRIT, RACE and many EUREKA projects as well develop technical standards through which to exercise world market power against the proprietary and national standards developed by U.S. and Japanese firms as part of their world market strategies. On their own — and this is borne out by all technologies developed before 1985 — European IT firms have only the choice between joining one or the other U.S. and Japanese consortia.

Lastly, there is a gray area combining industrial and trade policy. It involves standard setting in the form of collective product differentiation strategies combined with concerted and preferential procurement. Projects such as ISDN/RACE (telecom infrastructure), Prometheus/Drive (intelligent road systems), high speed trains, and HDTV belong in this category. The aim of accelerated introduction within a competitive context and with clear planning horizons for supplier industries is to be met by concerted public investment programs, notably broad band and HDTV and a new high speed train network for Europe. The more recent EURETRA extends this concept to logistics in general; and ENS (the European Nervous System) to high-quality EDI.

Many of these initiatives predate the adoption of the 1992 project (1985). However, they are linked to the project in the sense that they add a concrete political commitment, underwritten by private enterprise, to a Europe which is not just a market but a voluntarist actor in the world economy. Without such a commitment (which, incidentally, is least shared by official and private Britain), the outlook for 1992 would have been considerably less promising. France would have tolerated German-style external liberalism only if some of its subtle mercantilist instrumentarium was transferred to Europe (which, as the French realized, provided its only chance to practice world-market relevant industrial policy at all). Similarly, large corporations living in traditional symbiosis with government — and this applies to all member states — were more inclined to cooperate in the dismantling of national privileges if something else was put in their place. The Sunday speeches of enthusiastic support for free markets should not be allowed to disguise this fact.

While these programs go on, their relative weight in the overall "1992" design is diminishing. One piece of evidence for this is a power shift within the EC Commission. In November 1990, to the great disappointment of the industrial policy directorates (III, and its IT offshoot, XIII), the liberal (and Liberal) forces in the Commission managed to get a policy document adopted which rejected sectoral industrial policies in favour of free markets, competition, and firm regulation.

There are several reasons to expect a relative slackening of the Community's commitment to a neo-mercantilist agenda.

First, the balance of power in Europe is shifting away from France and towards Germany, which is aided, at least under the present conservative government, by Britain, and likely to gain new recruits for a more liberal stance from new member states in Scandinavia.

Secondly, one of the main targets for neo-mercantilist competition was the United States, which was then expected to become a sui generis technological superpower under the impact of SDI. The United States is now written off as a serious competitor for at least a decade. It still produces first class technology, but lacks the social and institutional requisites to draw national (as opposed to global corporate) advantages from it. Poor human capital at the technician level and an industrial culture and capital market which reward cost-cutting over asset creation are key elements in this assessment (which extends, however, to Great Britain). Another group of competitors, the NIEs, have also lost some of their terror, as they are constrained by limits to technology acquisition[6].

Thirdly, the keystone of European R&D policy, ESPRIT, has suffered grave damage from the weakness of two of its principal sponsors, Philips and Thomson, while Siemens now feels it can go it alone.

A Japanese Challenge?

The systemic challenge posed by Japan has been brilliantly analyzed by Wolferen[7]. The image of a headless juggernaut, programmed in a militaristic past to subordinate economic welfare to the power of a self-perpetuating nomenclature which is safe from internal retribution or outside pressure precisely because it is headless, is as chilling as it is persuasive. For Europe of the early 1980s, the growing evidence of Japanese success represented black ships which called for a Meiji revolution. "1992" was one response. Like Japan a century ago, the European revolution includes elements of borrowing and learning from Japan. But Europe's bottom line, as it was for Japan, is defence of "cultural" essentials.

---

[6]OECD, Technology and Global Competition. The Challenge for Newly Industrializing Economies. Paris, Dec. 1989

[7]Karel van Wolferen, The Enigma of Japanese Power, Macmillan, London, 1989

Yet with widely publicized exceptions, such as the remarks by Mme. Cresson or the writings of Germany's Konrad Seitz[8], Europeans now face Japan with relative equanimity. Unlike the U.S., which feels betrayed, intellectually puzzled[9], helpless and demoted as the number one economy, Europeans have not yet felt the full brunt of the Japanese challenge and feel more confident of meeting it. That confidence rests less on outstanding excellence in any field than in a more balanced technological and human capital across the whole range of economic activity.

While most European elites do not share the emotional rancor against Japan evidenced in the United States, it can be argued that Japan is now seen as the EEC's chief competitive adversary. This is not a political choice with deeper and perhaps sinister significance, but results from the perceived weakness of the two other candidates for competitive rivalry — the United States and the NIEs — leaving Japan "as the one to beat" by default.

Such rancor, and associated bellicose language, as exists comes from the representatives of two industries — automobiles and electronics — and the governments which champion them. Both sectors are strategic, if for different reasons. Autos are a general locomotive for demand, both in macro-economic and in dynamic industrial terms. The value of production of motor vehicles and spare parts in the Community is around ECU 220 billion, with employment at around 1.8 million. The car industry supports a large variety of engineering and other manufacturing industries — many of which risk technological stagnation if Japanese competition makes for stagnant markets and slashed profits in the automobile market itself. If autos are at the top of a large pyramid of input industries, the second strategic industry — micro-electronics — forms the base of an inverted pyramid, no less universal, of value-added for industry and services.

Services: Logistics, Banking, Insurance
Process Technology Communications Consumer Electronics

CHIP
AUTOMOBILES

Textiles, Plastics, Metals, Engineering
Electronics, Tires, Glass, Paints, CAM

---

[8]Konrad Seitz, Westpolitik 2000, Das Amerikanische Zeitalter als neue Gefahr für Europa,. Bonn 1991

[9]For an exception, see Robert Kuttner, Managed Trade and Economic Sovereignty, Economic Policy Institute, Washington 1989

Michael Porter[10] has convincingly argued the creation and defence of world-class technology depends on the beneficial interactions between high quality demand and supply, and that both these elements need to be domestic first. Only a domestic context — the trust, easy communication and long-term commitment which it uniquely provides — can create a see-saw of mutual inspiration, innovation, quality and commercial success which feeds back into private and public investment in human and physical capital and builds lasting competitive advantage. Value for money, not low cost as such, become the basis for success.

Japanese excellence in both the broad, bread-and-butter technology promoter — automobiles — and the cutting edge "technology enabler" — micro-electronics — thus provides a real challenge to Europe's long-term prosperity.

This point is not universally accepted, even in Europe. For the continental policy-maker — technocrat or politician — the possible future fate of Europe can be studied in contemporary Britain: an offshore semi-skilled labor reserve which must compete on cost to stay in the market. Moreover, the horrifying collapse of U.S. pre-eminence in little more than a decade is an even more effective barrier against complacency.

The problem for Europe — and Japan's opportunity — is that no one quite seems to know how to "meet the Japanese challenge".

Some options can be discussed in the terms of Porter's analysis. For European strategy, perhaps the most troubling condition for excellence is the need for the right factor and demand conditions being available "domestically". Since 1985, Europe has sought salvation from threatened decline by redefining and enlarging the term "domestic" to mean the "internal market" (European Community) and the Western European economic space (EC + EFTA). But Porter's valued-added creating networks function because of things like easy communication (language, culture), national research laboratories linked to poles of industrial excellence, etc. None of these seems likely to arise in Europe within a useful time scale. Hence — see below — the EC Commission's efforts to stimulate trans-border links by "promotion".

The picture is less bleak in other dimensions. First, demand — which, to follow Porter, must be "demanding" as regards quality, differentiated and, at the same time, anticipatory of world demand and allow early economies of scale and scope.

As regards the two strategic sectors, Europe has a few crumbs of comfort. Demand for autos is highly differentiated, both as regards driving

---

[10]The Competitive Advantage of Nations, Macmillan, London 1990

conditions, national tastes, and customer profiles. Innovation continues to be rewarded by market share. The world increasingly builds "European" cars, not the other way around. On the other hand, Japan's short development cycles and flexible assembly chains risk targeting European tastes earlier than the home team.

Competition, another of Porter's ingredients for success, is scheduled to rise under "1992" conditions — hopefully slowly enough not to break the profit/investment motor of adjustment. Eastern Europe, like Spain before it, offers both a dynamic market and low-cost production within a geographically useful radius.

Moreover, for some years now "collective" Europe — in the shape of all car makers, electronics components suppliers, and software houses — has laid the groundwork for differentiating the product "auto" by making it part of a broader system of logistics for persons and goods. The R&D programs DRIVE (EC) and Prometheus (EUREKA), as well as EURET (EC) are developing continent-wide electronics systems which allow cars to interact with each other as well as urban and long-distance guidance and freight logistics systems. Electronics as such are, of course, Japan's strong suit. But the particular conditions of Europe, its relative strength in ASICS, and the powerful combination of interests potentially behind the scheme and, last but not least, the need for participation by public authorities at every level are likely to produce a market tailored to home needs in which Japanese firms must participate on terms set by the locals.

That scheme can begin to bring some relief by the year 2000. In the meantime, overcapacity, poor management, Japanese exports, implants, and export from Japanese plants in the United States, are all threatening to push the automobile industry to the sort of slow death which has finished off so many U.S. and UK industries. It is against this background that the recent EC-Japan agreement must be seen.

The August 1991 Compromise

After two years of negotiations, MITI and Trade Commissioner Andriessen struck the following agreement. Between 1993 and 1999 Japan's direct exports to the Community can increase from the present 11% to 16%. In addition, another 16% may be supplied from "implants" (mostly in Britain). In addition — and in contravention of the logic of 1992 — MITI promised to enforce what amounts to national export quotas into the high restriction countries — with export gradually, not suddenly, increasing to maximum 150,000 units in France, 138,000 in Italy, 79,000 in Spain, and 23,000 in Portugal.

None of these assurances is legally binding. They are little more than agreed forecasts. The blend of percentages and absolute numbers alone leaves plenty of leeway for "misunderstandings". The 2x16% figure is predicated on a 1999 demand of 15 million cars, hence 2x1.2 million Japanese. Yet the British government is predicting an EC "implants" production of 2 million — half of it in Britain. Associations with Eastern Europe and new member states from the present EFTA will further complicate the issue. Last but not least, direct imports from Japanese plants in the United States have not been covered at all — a perfect loophole which may leave EC producers with at best 60% of the market. In short, nothing is settled.

This sort of outcome is almost inevitable in the context of EC-Japan relations. Two weak agencies — MITI with no formal powers, and the Commission, internally divided on doctrinal grounds and with a divided membership to contend with — with the United States (and the GATT) looking over their shoulders, cannot expect to produce a legally binding blueprint of the kind sought by the French and Italians.

Electronics

Like the U.S. electronics industry, Europe has been hopelessly battered in "brown goods": imports account for 47% of color TVs, 80% of video recorders, 90% of camcorder cameras and 100% of portable radios. As Philips keeps pointing out, this sharply reduces the market for commodity chips and mass-produced processors.

Like the auto industry, but earlier, the electronics industry has discovered the virtues of public infrastructure-led systems for developing and preserving market share. EC and EUREKA R&D schemes mentioned previously provide the initial focus, to be taken up by concerted investment policies by public authorities. The related initiatives RACE (broad band communication) and HDTV stand out. Mobile telephony — to which similar efforts at European standard setting have been devoted — provides an example of deregulation chiefly benefitting non-Community suppliers, although not to the extent of the fax revolution.

HDTV, France and the Future of Europe

The European approach to high definition television most clearly reflects the transposition of the (rather successful) post-war French model of development to Europe. Public authorities were willing to finance not only R&D — for decades if necessary — but also lead investment in infrastructure with at best medium-term payoff. The Minitel videotext system, the massive overinvestment in telephone lines and, to a lesser extent, nuclear energy, the high speed train (profitable), and Airbus and Ariane (competitive but not profitable), are examples in point. (Japanese industry, it has been argued, takes much the same route — cheap capital, loss-making overcapacity tolerated in the medium term, pursuit of strategic goals — although the means differ.)

The development of a distinctly European HDTV technology is the result of an industrial alliance between Thomson and Philips, later given European stature as a EUREKA project. For some years now, HDTV also has benefitted from substantial EC support, both diplomatic, financial, and regulatory. The latter turns around the attempt to make the European HDTV standard, D2-Mac, developed by Thomson and Philips, compulsory for satellite broadcasters. A directive in this sense, proposed in June 1991, faces stiff opposition from German and British TV interests. While technical shortcomings are cited, the initial high costs are at least as important. More generally, HDTV throws up the conflict between the two forms of single market creation: the voluntarist one (via a unitary system) and the laissez faire one which relies exclusively on free competition.

Yet against the whole of the public and private TV interests of the country, the German government stands firm in supporting the "forced" road to HDTV, via a Council-imposed directive. They are right to do so: HDTV is the San Andreas fault of EC geopolitics.

For while abandoning the (compulsory) standard would strike a devastating blow to the electronics industry, it has much wider implications. The hope of the European electronics industry was that a purely European standard would offer a measure of protection for the most lucrative market — color TV — and, a major bonus, provide a huge market for dedicated semiconductors. This in turn would finally propel European chip makers into mass market production, with Japan-type learning curves and all the rest.

More generally, and as already stated, the original "internal market" project involved a Franco-German deal, marrying liberalization with a commitment to a joint European technological future. ESPRIT and RACE were the expressions of that commitment, and HDTV is to some extent the child of both. In April 1990, President Mitterand obtained Chancellor Kohl's solemn commitment to stick with the European standard. Hence the firm attitude of the German government today.

The full impact of abandoning a European commitment to HDTV can only be judged in the context of other developments whose common element is that France loses out. This risks destabilizing the whole of the European enterprise and a halt to the progress of 1992 through re-nationalization.

The most enthusiastic supporter of "1992" has doubtlessly been France. The reason, put simply, is that the country has transferred virtually the whole of its post-war strategy of technology-based modernization and search for autonomy to Europe. This move was forced upon it by the scale and cost of relevant technologies, and by the need to contain Germany in a tight political embrace.

1991 has kicked most of the props from that strategy. One of its key-stones, monetary union, will not happen any time soon: Germany needs room for manoeuvre to solve the horrendous problems of re-unification. A second major prop, joint space development (Hermes, Ariane 5) is likely to be reduced as Germany's budget is strained to the breaking point. As to electronics R&D, Thomson has been rebuffed in its attempt to woo Siemens for a joint semiconductor development, with Siemens linking up with IBM instead. EC enlargement to formerly EFTA countries Sweden, Norway and Austria is a forgone conclusion, strengthening the feared "Northern" element in the Community and weakening the commitment to political unification.

On the trade front, France must make further sacrifices of its agricultural interests to save the GATT round; while the EC-Japan auto compromise means the death of an independent French auto industry.

To cap it all, France's nuclear deterrent — a major element in the political balance with Germany — has not only become irrelevant, but now threatens only Bavaria and Havel's Czechoslovakia.

Although it seems to lead far from the the theme of EC-Japan relations, it is very much to the point. If France is defeated, much of the EC's strategic mission risks being lost to sight. But equally: without French support, the unfinished pieces of the liberal agenda of "1992" may remain just that; while bargains already settled may become unravelled. For Japan, this means a European Community which is easier to deal with in substance, but more difficult in style. Economic diplomacy will be uncertain and fractious; but Japan will impose its preferences in the end.

JESSI — Germany Draws the Line

JESSI — Joint European Silicon Structures — is the up-stream cousin of HDTV. Both programs involve chips: HDTV mass-produced processors and memory chips, JESSI primarily custom-made ASICs. One is French-inspired and oriented towards the consumer market; the other dominated by Germany and primarily related to production technology. Yet both (EUREKA) programs share the goal of drawing the line against Japanese domination in semiconductors.

The purpose of JESSI is similar to the embattled U.S. Sematech, although on a larger scale: to regain technological competence over the whole range of industrial technology, from silicon production to wafer cutting, from optics to clean room technology and embodied software. Analysts tend to judge the chances of this enterprise in terms of success in competing with Japan on semiconductors. That would be a bonus, but it is not essential. The real stakes of JESSI lie elsewhere.

Germany's prosperity rests uniquely on its machine tool and industrial plant production. These not only form the core of direct exports, but domestic use of advanced production technology is essential for exports of manufacture in general. Three years ago, German industry realized that the medium in which its (production) systems know-how was expressed was the micro-chip. Relying on outside suppliers not only compromised commercial secrets, but allowed outsiders to control if and when the most advanced products were available.

In this perspective, a minimal state-of-the-art capacity at any price becomes a necessity. In the United States, such a demand is always justified on military grounds. For Germany, the stakes are very much higher — its economic future. ("1992" only comes into the equation as a potential obstacle, posed by the EC's competition Directorate, to the huge subsidies involved. Hence the need for a EUREKA label — a formal endorsement by Europe's governments of the joint political interest of the venture.)

Yet even JESSI is in trouble. Like its U.S. cousin, Sematech, it must rely on the cooperation of a wide variety of industrial players in different if related sectors and involving small and medium-sized companies rightly suspicious of the likes of Siemens. Siemen's "defection" to IBM for chip development signals a weakened commitment not only to Europe, but to creating a national technology infrastructure of the kind advocated by Michael Porter. By U.S. standards, European still exhibits remnants of what

Japanese would call wet rice behavior, but grains seem to be drying out at the top of the bowl.

Liberalizing Trade and Investment

Having set the analysis in the terms which really matter for EC-Japan relations — the strategic issues — we can now turn to the more familiar agenda — that of trade and investment.

As has been stated, Fortress Europe is not the issue. What is at issue is to what extent the mobilization of hitherto badly used "domestic" resources through increased domestic competition — which is the supply-side agenda of 1992 — requires a further net increase in external openness, in addition to the easier access to outsiders which results from internal liberalization. Hence, the foreign trade regime is one of the elements of the future economic "model" which, under the impact of "1992", Europe must define with much greater precision than in the past.

However, the extension of the international negotiating agenda to include such diverse items as special impediments, direct foreign investment, subsidies or intellectual property rights suggests that, increasingly, the management of economic relationships involves interactions between the whole "system" of economic management and even private social relationships. Trade behavior as such, which continues to be of interest to the ayatollahs of Geneva, obscures the deeper roots of what the Japanese so accurately call "misunderstandings".

Discriminatory Liberalization?

The economic "model" of "1992" is supply-side thinking grafted on the old Monnet idea of the "large continental market" as a condition — as it then seemed — of equality with the United States. While formally the EC's writ only runs to cross-border competition, in practice vast areas of strictly national regulation or monopoly have to be liberalized if cross-border competition is to have real meaning. The "1992" tail is thus wagging a much larger dog: the totality of member states' economies.

The crucial point is that the breakdown of the remaining areas of national (intra-EC) protection automatically eases access for all foreign suppliers, whether from the Community or elsewhere. The question is only whether some former national tools of protection — NTBs, subsidies, procurement preference — are to be partially re-created at the Community level. Even if this were fully feasible, it would merely maintain the status quo, not involve turning inward. In fact, the very nature of most "1992" liberalization — deregulation involving an absolute decline of public power in the economy — makes the notion of re-creating the (sum of national) status quo ante at the Community level irrelevant.

Three examples may serve to illustrate the fact that "1992" provides a "free ride" to outside competitors. The first comes from telecommunications, traditionally a sector dominated by public monopolies. It would have been very difficult to harmonize conditions of access to the various national terminals markets as long as the selling or licensing of fax machines or PBXs remained a public monopoly. By decreeing that the PTTs' reach had to stop at the plug, the Commission not only liberalized the internal market, but opened it up for outside suppliers — including those from the United States and Southeast Asia.

The second example concerns mutual recognition of product standards, provided certain broad (EC-wide) performance standards are met. This means that, say, a Taiwanese exporter of a machine tool need have that machine certified for safety in only one member state to have access to the other eleven — a major saving in time, effort and uncertainty.

The same transfer of benefits to outsiders occurs in the area of public subsidies. To the extent that subsidies are controlled more tightly — as they are — to provide a "level playing field" in the Community, "financial protectionism" towards foreign trade competitors is also necessarily dismantled.

This opening to outsiders, however, constitutes a potential obstacle to the realization of "1992." The French view of the dilemma can be stated as follows: yes, we are willing to lower the remaining NTBs towards partners with whom we do half our trade. If you force us to extend this liberalization to the other half, however, you are not merely doubling the potential competitive and adjustment burden; you are exposing us to trading partners over whose basic macro-economic and micro-economic trade strategies we have no control whatsoever. The risk is thus much larger.

Some opportunities for intervention arise from the very nature of the liberal core of the "1992" exercise. Often misunderstood as trade liberalization, "1992" is in essence the integration of the regulated sectors of member states' economies, and/or those aspects of economic activities (safety, etc.)

whose regulation has thus far been the legitimate preserve of national sovereignty.

The regulated sectors and markets are overwhelmingly in services — transport, finance, and telecommunications. But they also include a horizontal item — public procurement. Both services and procurement liberalization are linked to (manufacturing) technology — and hence provide opportunities for intervention of a neo-mercantilist kind.

Public procurement means, among other things, big ticket items: airport signalling equipment, airplanes, high speed trains, telecom exchanges, water treatment plants and incinerators, electric power stations and communications satellites. For an American, many of these examples may not belong to the public procurement market at all. But in most member states the sectors mentioned happen to be public, or publicly regulated, monopolies. Liberalization of (trans-border) services requires, as a precondition, the erosion of the public monopolies, e.g. by allowing private competitors on equal terms; or by reducing the monopoly to the core public network (telecom, railways, electricity grid). Thus, only the two strands of "1992" together — liberalization of services *and* procurement — open up Europe's high technology markets.

"Integration" of these markets is achieved by three means: deregulation, re-regulation, and Euro-systems creation.

Deregulation involves member states abandoning areas of traditional government control — not to Brussels, but to the market. Twenty years earlier, the attempt might have been made to integrate public monopolies into a single European entity — a copy of national practice on a larger scale. But supply-side thinking (privatization, competition) and the virtual impossibility to mesh widely divergent national legal and administrative traditions favour the market route to integration.

One problem with this approach is that it destroys a powerful instrument of national industrial policy and, more practically, risks opening competition not to other Europeans, but primarily to U.S. and Japanese firms. The unpalatable truth is that EC national champions are often less well equipped than their OECD competitors (including, occasionally, Scandinavian or Swiss firms) to capture the larger market. The handicap — or so the pessimists believe — lies in (1) the established world market orientation of the competitors, while Europeans have been practically encouraged to work within a national context of protection and regulation, which all but destroys their ability to sell to any one else; and (2) the scale and scope economies these firms have today, and which European firms will reach only after the "1992" logic, notably a cross-border rationalization process, has been at work for some time.

Alacatel and Siemens (or, to take another area touched by deregulation, French water management multinationals) prove that speedy adjustment to the larger market is possible for EC companies. Philips has long been European. Thompson is still trying to become so. But in rapid growth areas in electronics, notably terminal equipment and VANS, the Japanese (and Koreans) are capturing part of the hardware market, while the United States is strong in telecom software, notably the management of mobile telephony. Only central switches remain a strong area of European competitiveness.

The second route to market integration is partial re-regulation at Community level. This is simply the consequence of the fact that not all reasons for the previous national regulation are foolish or outdated: prudential regulation of financial markets and insurance; public safety and environmental concerns for road and air transport; and, last but not least, technical standards which reflect these concerns and — crucially — allow "plug compatibility" of networks which remain public in purpose, if no longer in ownership.

As already stated, this approach blends into the most voluntarist instrument of market integration for the regulated sectors: the creation of common European infrastructure systems. Here again, we find the issue of standards. But within the context of systems creation, standards do more than regulate the market. They are the basis for joint planning which of necessity involves public authorities in an active role. Planning future European systems in turn involves a double target: a "common market" target involving commonality and the easing of mutual exchange; and a technology target, involving the promotion of technological advance.

Dumping

These potential long-term defences of the home market are, in the views of both the Commission and industry, useless if there are no longer strong industries to take up these opportunities. Once again, a British example — ICL — provides a glimpse of the future to avoid. Given the constraints of the international trading system, notably its non-discrimination rule, anti-dumping actions at the fringe of GATT legality have taken up much of the burden of trade protection.

Anti-dumping is a form of trade war reminiscent of the limited ritualized warfare of the 18th century. Once in a while blood is drawn, after which the generals salute each other and continue diplomacy by other means. Inevitably, there is an arms race which may destabilize the tolerable status quo.

The first and essential function of dumping powers is to persuade potential disrupters to agree, informally, to cool things down. Most trade disputes with the NIEs and Japan are settled, informally, by EC officials and representatives of the offending industry. The latter are persuaded to raise prices, reduce the rate of penetration, or else. The "else" is almost as burdensome for the Commission as for the trader, since it involves a costly anti-dumping investigation and, usually, an informal agreement among member states. The actual threat of dumping sets in motion a lobbying effort in Brussels and selected member states (e.g. those without production in the offending item and a pending direct investment offer from Japan) — a pattern not unfamiliar from the United States. Even once dumping duties are imposed, recourse to the European Court may lead to cancellation.

Like the U.S., the EC bureaucracy (and their souffleurs in industry) has come up with innovative methods for calculating dumping. One response of Japanese exporters has been local European assembly operations — the so-called screwdriver plants. When governments such as France challenged these on rules-of-origin grounds — effectively requiring high local content — Japanese firms presented accounts, including marketing costs, which allowed even the simplest metal-bashing operation to surmount the 65% barrier. At this point, the old-fashioned trade argument based on jobs and balance-of-payments consideration was abandoned. What mattered was not local content expressed in value, but the component representing the strategic technology.

This view of the matter was promptly condemned by a GATT panel in 1990. But even when anti-dumping duties are imposed — and stick — the attackers are not without recourse. Thus, when the EC imposed anti-dumping duties of between 8 and 32%, Japanese and Korean suppliers dropped their prices by as much as 40% to maintain market share, claiming that their production costs had (since) fallen by that amount.

In the normal way, another lengthy anti-dumping investigation would now have been necessary. Whatever the outcome, the affected EC producers — Philips/Grundig, Bang & Olufsen — would be out of business (like scores of U.S. electronics, with plenty of pyrrhic victories under their belt, before them). The Commission's new weapon for the occasion is the strangely named "anti-absorption" procedure, which allows an accelerated anti-dumping investigation after duties have been imposed previously. The procedure is being described in Brussels as an "after sales service" for injured (and cured?) manufacturers.

Direct Foreign Investment

Ultimately, however, direct foreign investment in the EC is the almost unbluntable weapon in any strategic battle Japan chooses to fight. Even if local content approaches 100% and the most "sensitive" (strategically significant) bit of hardware is manufactured in Europe, the autonomous capacity to develop the technology or product in question may be lost — with (European) customers served at the pleasure of headquarters in Tokyo.

Does it matter? Will Japanese firms not become like IBM or Ford and GM, for whom the European operations are a crucial source of corporate revenue and, increasingly, technology? A sceptic would argue that a) in the long run we are all dead; and b) Japanese wet rice behavior — the strategic favouring of domestic over foreign suppliers or customers — is too ingrained to allow U.S.-type multinationals with European subsidiaries genuinely run by Europeans.

The table below seems to correlate inward investment inversely with economic success. Japan, and to a lesser extent Germany, seem to be "unattractive", while Britain sweeps the table.

Inward Investment Flow
(Large Industrial Countries)

	1980-84	1987	1988	1989	1990
U.S.	18.6	46.9	58.4	72.2	25.7
JAPAN	0.3	1.2	-0.5	-1.1	1.8
EC	13.3	34.0	49.5	69.8	72.2
— France	2.2	4.7	7.2	9.7	8.1
— Germany	0.8	1.9	1.0	6.8	1.5
— UK	5.3	14.1	148.3	28.8	31.6
Total	34.2	92.0	120.5	155	114.9

While the main arguments for direct investment — the creation of jobs — does not hold on static considerations[11] the positive structural effect of Japanese investment on the "affected" sectors may be considerable. The most dramatic example is the UK motor industry which, from seeming terminal decline, has rebounded as a viable industry. Japanese quality, flexibility and reliability were transferred to both supplier industries and unions, while technology transfers to Rover revitalized the last formally British producer. Similar upgrading has occurred for subcontractors to Japanese firms in France.

As the tortuous debate over direct foreign investment goes on, Japanese strategists have a card up their sleeve: the U.S. implants and their exports to Europe. While the Commission may stand up against Japan and the NIEs, it would be overwhelmed by the combined power of the United States protecting "its" jobs by assuring access to Japanese controlled output. This is a clear possibility as regards motor cars.

The Real Challenge

Just as the end of the cold war showed the protagonists — victors and vanquished — enfeebled by decades of investment in rather sterile output, so the neo-mercantilist competition between the three large Western powers has too long diverted attention from the real challenge: that of creating prosperity. Japan, in this respect, is a failure — but with the strength to become a success. Translating the world's highest per capita GNP into a real consumption at Spanish levels, and with a quality of life well below that of Spain, is becoming the scandal, in Japan, that it deserves to be. Women, schoolchildren, workers outside the large corporations, and the salarymen inside it are all victims of the system.

The U.S. system has produced failure of equal proportions. Two decades of growth have raised median incomes by a few promille; in spite of all the blessings of highly productive technology, the young are worse off

---

[11]Net job creation from Japanese investment in sectors suffering from overcapacity is negative, when it leads to closure of older European firms hampered by trade unions, etc. Of course any greenfield investment has that effect; but Europeans will not jeopardize their existing plants by adding new ones.

than their parents at the same age; the poor are an expensive burden; and the rich are richer in terms which are meaningless in other than paper terms.

It is time to return to basics. Economics is not about statistical rankings but about creating a better life. Starting from a more balanced base than the other two powers, Europe is turning its attention to issues which matter at home and which, unlike the world-market driven issues stressing cost cutting and investment in tradeable, require public intervention and investment in social assets. Education and the creation of "human capital", the environment, and infrastructure increasingly dominate the agenda of the rest of the decade and beyond.

Properly understood in a long-term and strategic perspective, none of these priorities is in conflict with international competitiveness. But all require a willingness for individuals and corporations to be taxed and regulated. Industrial cultures like the United States and Britain, which stress cost-cutting over asset creation and the short term over the long term, will therefore act as a brake from within or without [12] the European Community. Japan may become a valued partner for some of this agenda.

A new concern over education is not unique to Europe. If anything, the debate has a higher profile in the United States, and the Japanese are beginning to question the non-creative rote learning common at high-school level. In most countries, moreover, concern over education, especially at mid- and low level, is very much part of the mercantilist, competitive agenda, although human capital creation cannot be targeted at exportables, and the real pay-off is more, and more equal, wealth creation domestically.

Infrastructure, too, is on the agenda in all three regions. In Japan, the debate of the early 1970s about inadequate social infrastructure, interrupted by the oil crisis, has been revived and the then-mooted Plan for the Archipelago is being implemented. Present budgetary constraints, entirely due to inadequate taxation, will be lifted when protectionist limits on exports or slow world growth force Japan to tap domestic markets for growth. This will then be presented as a concession to U.S. demands in this sense. The United States, much more profoundly constrained by an almost visceral aversion to taxes, will nevertheless have to tackle its physical infrastructure, crumbling from decades of neglect.

In today's Europe, infrastructure is in fashion. Starting from lowly water and sewage pipe systems and treatment plants, which need investments in the $100 billion range, to roads, bridges, and tunnels to "implement" the new economic space on the ground, to the renaissance of the railway —

---

[12] U.S. influence ranges from Chambers of Commerce to institutions like OECD.

notably dual-use freight and high speed trains, and ending with energy and communications, industry, the public sector, and the public increasingly share a consensus to improve and modernize these essentials for economic efficiency and the quality of life. Eastern Germany and the Europe beyond provide further huge markets. A new consensus to allow private financing, matched by deregulation of traditionally publicly owned infrastructure services, helps to alleviate financial constraints while improving efficiency.

Parts of the infrastructure agenda overlap with perhaps the most significant shift in Europe's priorities: the environment. Here the mental divide with the erstwhile leader, the United States, is widest, at least at the federal level, while Japan has much in common in practice, if not in its underlying attitude, with the advanced countries in Europe (the Alpine republics, Germany and the Netherlands, and Scandinavia). "1992", directly and indirectly, is pushing the rest of Europe to adopt best practice. Highly interventionist laws on water quality, air emissions, packaging and waste disposal and, on the horizon, an energy tax are part of a concerted attack on needlessly harmful industrialization.

Politically, the growing concern over the environment reinforces a trend back to legitimacy for setting economic priorities collectively, ending two decades of celebration of individual choice as the only basis for civilized society. Technically, the massive adjustment required liberates forces of innovation, not least in process technology, which can only be compared to those formerly ascribed to war as the mother of invention.

As regards EC-Japan relations, European concern over infrastructure and the environment together amount to taking one's marbles and going home. The trade-carried rivalry which threatened to align the priorities of societies separated by half the globe was and is as insane as the cold war. This new agenda opens opportunities for the exchange of technology — not least with Japan, which domestically applies some of the highest environmental standards in the world while also developing high-tech solutions to public infrastructure problems.

In the context of the international environmental agenda, Japan opposes stringent measures on greenhouse gases and ozone depletion. On other matters, such as the exploitation of sea and forests outside Japan — the country is viewed with suspicion by many Europeans. Perhaps these issues provide a more profound test of "inward-looking" behavior than "1992" and all that.

Competing and Cooperating with Japanese Firms

Hellmut Schütte
INSEAD, Fontainebleau

In today's world, we can no longer deny Japan her place among the leading industrial nations. In the four decades following the immediate postwar years, Japan consistently achieved the highest growth rates among the developed countries. Not surprisingly, Japan's per capita income has surged ahead of that of the United States, Germany and all other OECD member countries, with the exception of Switzerland. There is no obvious reason why Japan should not achieve the highest growth rates again in the 1990s.

The success of postwar Japan is best demonstrated by the international competitiveness of her best firms. Within an extremely short time, Japanese firms have transformed themselves from inward-looking, government-supported companies which relied on their exploitation of cheap labor into large, technology-driven corporations with multinational operations. The global expansion of these firms now threatens the survival of established Western competitors in key industries, such as automobiles and computers; their innovative capabilities challenge the technological leadership of the United States and Europe; and their financial strength allows them to acquire their foreign competitors and collaborators alike.

It is difficult to find examples of Japanese firms which have gone abroad and failed, but it is easy to find examples of Western firms which, when attacked by Japanese competitors, either retreated or gave up.

Conventional Western wisdom dismisses the success of Japan with the following two observations: protectionist Japanese government policies prevented foreigners from competing on a `level playing field' and Japanese management , which is based on a 'unique' Japanese culture, rates the success of the nation or the group higher than the well-being of the individual.

Although there is some truth to both statements, they are somewhat simplistic and outdated. Even assuming that government support to industry would be absolutely equal in Japan and in the West, would the competitiveness of the Japanese firms facing Western competitors be seriously affected? Would GM, Ford, or Chrysler regain lost market share? Would

Bull, Unisys and Philips reemerge as strong, healthy competitors? Would Japanese machine tool manufacturers, pharmaceutical companies or department stores close their first outposts abroad and return home? Would Peugeot sell more cars to Japanese customers, or Cray more supercomputers?

Let us look at the increasing investment abroad and employment of local staff at all levels by Japanese firms. So far, the results of managing outside the cultural boundaries of Japan are good, even during the first years of operation.[1] In the UK, for example, there is talk of a `revival' of certain industries which are being run by the Japanese. Output in these industries, both in terms of quantity and quality, is frequently reported to be higher in Japanese-run plants than in those run by domestic firms.

In light of these developments, Japan-bashing based on political/cultural differences is counter-productive More importantly, it distracts the Western businessman from facing reality: Not countries, but firms compete, and they compete increasingly on a global basis.

Japan's Domestic Environment

Although the competitiveness of Japanese firms in their specific markets at home and abroad is purely individual, their strengths and weaknesses, and the way they behave, are influenced to a certain degree by their domestic environment. This applies particularly to Japanese firms as they have typically developed within the domestic context prior to overseas expansion. The formative influence of the home environment justifies discussing `the Japanese firm' as such, with the qualification that individual firms differ substantially.

In his new theory of the `competitive advantage of nations,' Porter identifies four interdependent characteristics of the domestic environment which influence the ability of the firm to compete in international markets.[2] The four determinants are: factor conditions, demand conditions, related and supporting industries and a set of variables called firm strategy, structure and rivalry. The following analysis will apply Porter's framework to the

---

1. K. Ohmae, "Japan's Role in the World Economy: A New Appraisal", in: California Management Review, Spring 1987, pp. 42-58
2. M.E. Porter, "The Competitive Advantage of Nations", The Four Determinants Form the 'National Diamond'. Free Press, New York 1990

Japanese situation in order to explain what has made some Japanese firms so successful and why others have, as yet, failed to expand abroad. We shall, however, deal separately with the variables which Porter considers to be the fourth determinant under the headings `structure' and `rivalry'. Departing from Porter's logic, we shall consider `strategy' as the result of the thinking of firm owners and managers rather than as a determinant itself.

Factor Conditions

Japan is not endowed with any of the resources which classical economic theory defines as the original comparative advantage of nations. It has no natural resources to speak of, a severe shortage of land, energy and — up to the 1970s — of capital. Labor, which once came cheaply and in abundance, is today expensive and in short supply. However, Japanese firms can access raw materials and cheap labor through global sourcing or off-shore production, or alternatively, they can overcome shortages through technological innovation. What matters more in today's knowledge-intensive industries is human skill and a solid foundation in R&D. Japan's firms have at their disposal the most highly educated, hardworking, and disciplined workforce in the world, one that is particularly strong in terms of engineering skills. This achievement is the result of sustained investment in knowledge development by the individual, their families, the firms themselves and the government.

Demand Conditions

The Japanese market is the second largest in the world and has been the fastest growing among the industrial countries over the last 40 years. Consumers are ethnically and culturally homogeneous and the vast majority perceive themselves to be members of the middle-class. Information on the fashionableness or obsolescence of products and services is widely accessible, a situation which has allowed firms to achieve rapid market penetration, particularly for new models of durables. Perfect quality is taken for granted, as is a superb service before, during and after the sale. As consumption and ownership determines one's status in Japanese society, the purchase of an upgraded or differentiated service or product is preferred to buying the purchase of the same product at a lower price. (For the Japanese customer, a lower price often classifies the product as one of lower quality.)

Firms respond to this consumer behavior by catering to minuscule segments with a large variety of products and rapid model changes. Industrial buyers, faced with strong competition in their markets, are equally anxious not to be left behind. As they normally do not compete on price, but on innovation, product differentiation and service, they are themselves as buyers not price sensitive.

Related and Supporting Industries

Very rarely do firms succeed in a given industry as stand-alone enterprises. In most countries, firms succeed because they are surrounded by other companies in related and supporting industries with which they can interact as either suppliers or buyers. This allows them to specialize without losing their grip on fields which will be further developed by other, equally specialized firms in the `industry cluster'. Nowhere in the world is the relationship between the various members of the cluster as close, or the cooperation between them so refined as in Japan.

First of all, firms have diversified themselves into new, but mostly related fields in order to redeploy people and facilities. This applies mainly to companies which operate in mature markets and are looking for growth opportunities, but also to firms in need of separating different business cultures (e.g., hardware and software development in the computer industry) without spinning them off entirely. The second type of cluster of related and supporting firms concerns the keiretsu, i.e., groups of companies often (though not necessarily) linked through minority shareholdings, and by a vaguely defined `common spirit'.

The vertical *keiretsu,* i.e., the assembly of a large number of small- and medium-sized firms under the umbrella of a major company, is the most effective among them. Total exchange of information, joint product developments, and simplified delivery procedures among these firms reduce transaction costs and time to a minimum and therefore contribute to the competitiveness of the entire group. (This applies particularly to those in automobile manufacturing.) In contrast, the horizontal *keiretsu,* such as the Mitsubishi, Sumitomo or the DKB group, are much bigger, but less internally related in terms of business activity. When considered as a whole, they do not represent a cluster. The group members do, however, consult each other, provide each other with captive business opportunities, and exchange information on general matters. Operationally, only the banks and, more importantly, the large trading houses, contribute to the overall competitiveness of the individual firms in the group.

Structure

The way the management system in a given firm is set up is strongly influenced by the composition of its stakeholders. In Japanese firms, the stakeholders are not only the shareholders, who are arguably the least important part of the organization. As the Japanese firm can be defined as an association of people pursuing the common goal of serving customers, the primary stakeholders are: the employees (both workers and management); the bankers, who provide long-term funds; the local and national governments, which provide the infrastructure; and, in the broadest sense, the firm's loyal customers and suppliers.

The Japanese firm, in trading lifetime employment and protection against the lifetime commitment and loyalty of its individual employees, creates a system in which serious controversy between employees and management is counter-productive and where long-term investment in human resources pays off.[3] The discouragement of individual achievement and a fast career track mentality fosters both internal communication and organizational learning. Shareholders in Japanese firms are often institutions, representing either other members of the keiretsu group or financial institutions, such as banks and insurance companies. Like the employees, the shareholders have a sustained commitment to the firm and expect long-term capital appreciation and other benefits which result from an ongoing business relationship instead of quarterly dividends.

Rivalry

If there is one determinant in the domestic Japanese economy which contributes more to the overall competitiveness of the firm than any other factor, it is rivalry among the various competitors. To succeed, it is not enough to exploit the home country advantage (comparative advantage), because its competitors can do the same. The firm has to perform better than its competitors in terms of cutting costs, improving quality and foster-

---

3. Lifetime employment exists only for 30% of Japan's work force, but it is the rule in the leading firms with which we are concerned in this article.

ing innovation. Domestic rivalry, therefore, tends to be more intense, more emotive and more personal, than competition with foreign competitors.

In addition to the concentration of rivals in individual industries, competition for Japanese firms operating in Japan is intensified by the fact that a stable oligopoly with one dominant leader and several smaller followers is rare. More often than not, leading Japanese firms are of equal size and are all committed to taking over a leadership position which they know they can only retain through the greatest effort. Finally, the existence of a well-informed and demanding customer base adds another level of pressure on the Japanese firm.

Not Everyone is Favored

While Japan's environment has fostered the competitiveness of some industrial sectors, others have suffered from the lack of supporting and related industries or from rivalry, for example.

This inconsistency explains the existence of two radically different types of Japanese industries: world class contenders with outstanding products and technologies, such as in electronics and automobiles; and backward, inefficient producers, such as those in agriculture and commodity chemicals. Not all Japanese industries are successful or bound to succeed in the future, and not all firms within a given industry succeed.

The close long-standing relationship between firms, their banks, and their affiliated companies has historically enabled them to raise long-term capital without too much pressure to produce short-term results. In cases where such close co-operation does not exist, however, raising money becomes a critical bottle-neck. As a result, new Japanese ventures often have difficulties taking off in Japan. Similarly, the emphasis on group work and group responsibility enables Japanese employees to concentrate on solving problems rather than on fostering their career prospects. Nevertheless, the system appears to discourage outstanding individuals from `thinking the unthinkable,' which makes it difficult for firms to succeed in industries in which creativity is required.

The slow development of the Japanese pharmaceutical firms can be linked to weak related and supporting industries. The Japanese chemical industry is fragmented and inefficient and the Japanese health care system is severely outdated, with doctors not only prescribing, but also selling their products. Competitiveness also suffers in situations where rivalry is weak and business allocated among members of cartels, as is the case in the construction industry, and where prices and fees are fixed, as was the case in the financial industry.

The government has also played a part in influencing the above-listed five determinants — factor and demand conditions, related and supporting industries, the structure of firms and the rivalry among them. These determinants in turn are also influencing government policy. On the whole, the Japanese government has actively pursued pro-business policies over the last few decades. Big business has reciprocated by funding the ruling political party, and as such indirectly the government. However, as the above-mentioned arguments illustrate, the government's supportive role has not always been successful.

The Strategies of Japanese Firms

Japanese firms do well in industries in which a competitive advantage can only be gained by sustained investment over long periods of time. As global competition intensifies, pressure on technological achievements increases, and international marketing operations become more complex to manage, more and more industries may require such 'long termism' in their thinking.

Two major developments allow Japanese firms to pursue long-term goals: the advent of the lifetime employment system and the access to long-term capital through a web of interlocking shareholdings with friendly companies.[4]

Lifetime employment opportunities provide employees with job security; they also reduce lateral job mobility for them. As a result, the employee's future is closely tied to the well-being of his firm. This gives employees a strong incentive to look after the interests of their firm, reduces potential conflict between employees and other stakeholders, and brings a certain amount of harmony into the firm. Japanese managers have been able to convert this group spirit into a strong commitment to the objectives of the firm and a devotion of the employees to the ultimate task, i.e., of winning in the market. This ambitious 'strategic intent,' which is often out of all proportion to existing resources and capabilities, is pursued at all levels of the organization and is now recognized to be one of the most important

---

4. K. Matsumoto, "The Rise of the Japanese Corporate System". Kegan Paul Intern., London and New York. 1991

features of globally successful firms.[5] Creating `strategic intent' requires open organizational communication, both vertically and horizontally within the firm, and the commitment by the stakeholders to the continual improvement of `everything by everyone'.[6] Lifetime employment and lifetime loyalty have other consequences: additional labor cannot be recruited when new skills are needed and surplus labor cannot be shed when circumstances make them superfluous. The Japanese firm is, therefore, continually forced to train its employees and look for possibilities for diversification in fields which roughly match existing skills and make immediate and efficient use of transferred staff. Heavy investment in learning and skill development is worthwhile, not only because better-trained employees produce better results in knowledge-intensive industries, but because employees rarely leave the firm and allow other companies — in the worst cases, direct competitors — to benefit from their superior knowledge. Postsecondary education and training in Japan takes place mainly in large firms and is geared to the specific needs of the industry and of the firm. Combined with a willingness to share information and a strong `strategic intent,' this investment in education leads to the development of an overall competence in the work force. This competence can be used in different applications, combined in new configurations, and exploited in a wide variety of markets. Honda's competence in engines and power trains, for example, has been exploited in a wide variety of markets; it is based on the firm's long-term commitment to engine technology and represents a system of embodied, tacit know-how which is difficult to unbundle and impossible to imitate.[7]

When the `zaibatsu' or the powerful Japanese industrial combines were broken-up by the American occupation authorities after World War II, Japanese firms which were financially independent, but historically still linked looked to each other for financial support. They formed a system of cross-shareholdings which now includes the former members of the `zaibatsu' (now referred to as *keiretsu* or literally, `links'), new affiliates such as suppliers or customers, and financial institutions. The system protects the new *keiretsu* firms from hostile takeovers or unfriendly shareholders. *Keiretsu* members now account for a very high percentage of the Tokyo stockmarket capitalization. Shares are held for the very long-term, if

---

5. G. Hamel and C.K. Prahalad,"Strategic Intent", in: Harvard Business Review, May/June 1989, pp. 63-76
6. M. Imai, "Kaizen: The Key to Japan's Competitive Success". Random House, New York, 1987
7. Hamel and Prahalad describe this as 'core competence'. See footnote 5.

not forever, and few shares are left to trade.[8] Consequently, Japanese firms do not have to worry much about dividends, share prices or the recommendations of security analysts. Instead, they can concentrate on developing new products and new markets. Freed internally from the `tyranny of accountants,' they are able to pursue strategies which either have a very long time frame or are very risky.[9]

Traditionally, shareholders expect business rather than dividends as the pay-off for their long-term commitment. Such business may come in the form of purchasing orders for manufacturing firms, agency representation for trading houses, loans for banks or insurance contracts for insurance companies. As the firms in which the *keiretsu* have invested are often shareholders in their own companies, mutual respect for management autonomy is maintained. Mutual support is expected, in good times as in bad, and a common interest exists in growth on which future business with each other depends.

Growth as Dogma

The expectations of both the employees and the shareholders force Japanese firms to adopt growth as their overall strategy. Growth is needed in an environment full of competitors. Survival and victory, however, are only ensured when a `winner's competitive cycle' has been established and can be maintained. This cycle requires faster growth than that of the competitors through higher investment on a continuous basis.[10] The investment can go into the build-up of additional capacities or the development of new markets and products. The above-mentioned `strategic intent' leads firms to ambitious undertakings and to a focus on competitive rather than on financial risk.[11] From time to time, this can result in tremendous overcapacities.

As a logical consequence of this system, financial indicators such as return on investment are seldom used to measure the success of the firm. The final judgement can only be derived from the markets in which the firm

8. M. Anchordoguy, "A Brief History of Japan's Keiretsu", in: Harvard Business Review, July/August 1990, pp.58-59.

9. D.B. Montgomery, "Understanding the Japanese as Customers, Competitors, and Collaborators", in: Japan and the World Economy, March 1991, pp. 61-91

10. P. Kotler, L. Fahey and S. Jatusripitak, "The New Competition". Prentice-Hall, Englewood Cliffs, N.J., 1985

11. J.C. Abbeglen and G. Stalk, "Kaisha: The Japanese Corporation", Basic Books, New York., 1985

operates, both in terms of sales (as an absolute measure) and market share (as a relative measure). The emphasis on sales and market share is driving firms to pay extraordinary attention to virtually every new move their competitors make. Individual competitors can be targeted and the effort of all employees channelled to beat a specific firm in the market. Honda's battle with Yamaha over leadership in motorcycles made headlines in the early 1980s. Komatsu's fight against Caterpillar is another example of such targeting. At one stage, Komatsu even posted an employee to live in the town in which Caterpillar was headquartered in order that he report on its activities. In terms of rallying support and group spirit, company-wide sales and market share achievements and objectives are obviously easier to communicate than profit ratios mainly of interest to shareholders.

In very hotly contested markets, such as in consumer electronics, the strong focus on competitors has led to `product churning' and `product covering', or the constant outpouring of new models at breakneck speed and at any cost in order to stop others from taking over the lead, even in the most minuscule market segment. Should a firm miss out on an opportunity to introduce a new product variant, it will very quickly cover its risk of losing market share by launching an product equivalent to that of its competitor. In such an environment, time-consuming market research and rigorous analyses are discarded in favour of market experimentation, and inevitable failures are considered learning opportunities for the future.[12]

Japanese cost accounting practices allow firms to conduct fast forays and counter-attacks against competitors. By neglecting standard costs, applying target-costing techniques and assessing the profitability of product portfolios rather than individual products, firms can concentrate on achieving growth. This attitude is reinforced by a deeply held belief that high growth will lead to higher market share, which will in turn reduce overall costs per unit relative to those of one's competitors. A high market share can be seen as a vote of confidence by customers, who will then be disinclined to switch to other suppliers as long as the products and services offered by `their' company can compare to the most advanced ones on the market. This customer franchise offers opportunities for price increases without losing significant sales volume. Lower costs combined with higher prices will ultimately lead to higher profits.

---

12. K. Jones and T. Ohbora, "Managing the 'Heretical' Company", in: The McKinsey Quarterly, March 1990, pp. 20-45

Economics of Scale, Scope and Speed

After World War II, cheap labor was just about all Japanese firms had to offer the world. By the 1960s, however, labor costs had increased to such a level that they caused the Japanese to lose out in major industries. (Textiles, Japan's largest industry at the time, is just one example.) In order to boost labor productivity, investments in large and capital-intensive facilities were made and output increased substantially. This lead to enormous economies of scale, i.e., a lowering of unit costs by a certain percentage each time production volume doubled. Competitiveness was in this way restored and even sharpened. In the 1970s, Japanese firms made major inroads into international markets by combining scale effects with a concentration on a very limited number of standardized products, often at the lower end of the product range. Less-focused Western competitors found it difficult to muster an adequate response.

Towards the end of the decade, Japanese firms realized that their focused approach both limited their growth potential and was unable to satisfy increasingly sophisticated and differentiated demand. Reorganizing their factories with the help of flexible manufacturing systems and a network of related and supporting industries, they moved towards economies of scope, i.e., increasing the variety of a firm's products without losing the benefits of mass production. This process is partly achieved by artificially extending product ranges — simply offering a large number of variations of the same base model. Increasingly, however, a broad spectrum of very different segments is covered with entirely different products. Western competitors are therefore seeing Japanese firms introducing new products, not only at the bottom end of the market, but everywhere. Shiseido, for example, has entered Western markets exclusively from the top end.

At the end of the 1980s, Japanese firms added yet another level to their competitiveness by trying to respond to customer demands faster. The result was the creation of economies of speed, i.e., benefits from shorter development and production cycles, closer relationships with customers and an increasing dependence of them on the firm as supplier. In the 1990s, providing a large variety of products for the lowest cost in the least amount of time is considered the new pattern for success. Productivity increases, prices can be raised, and risks resulting from difficult forecasts due to long lead times are reduced.[13] By being speedier one can also exploit transitory windows of opportunity, take over the market

---

13. G. Stalk and T.H. Hout, "Competing Against Time", The Free Press, New York, 1990

initiative, drive the market and seek first-mover advantages, such as setting new technical standards or monopolizing scarce resources. Japanese firms are well positioned to exploit this new phenomenon in competition: just-in-time systems have been in place for years, and both employees and the network of suppliers can easily be rallied around new campaigns. Sharing of information within the organization, the emphasis on action rather than analytical problem-solving, and a high degree of competence at all levels of the firm — all of these characteristics make the Japanese firm highly responsive to competing on time. It also prepares the ground for the next level.

International Expansion

Following the classical pattern of internationalization, Japanese firms start to enter foreign markets through exports. In some industries this happened shortly after World War II, while in others, such as elevators, this move has taken place only recently. The Japanese insurance industry, on the other hand, has yet to enter foreign markets. In general, international activities are launched by firms operating in mass markets at a time when growth in demand slows down or declines. Exports are then needed to compensate for lost growth opportunities at home. The large trading houses, the 'sogo shosha', were initially instrumental in supporting foreign market entry, though their role has changed over the years. As the trading companies originally operated abroad mainly as importers and whole-salers, the subsequent appointment of local distributors was needed.

Actual market entry by Japanese firms is preceded by a time-consuming and exhaustive information-gathering period. Data collected include not only information on the respective product markets, but also on political, social and cultural issues. By carefully observing potential competitors and market trends, the firm tries to identify a small, currently ignored or poorly served market niche. In Japan, this is likened to a `sukima' strategy, which refers to the small opening which remains when a sliding door does not quite fit its frame.[14] In major markets this observation period can take up to three years and entail the foreign posting of a senior executive, who is instructed to first immerse himself in the local environment in order to fully understand it.

---

14. J.K. Johansson and I. Nonaka, "Japanese Export Marketing: Structures, Strategies, Counterstrategies", in: International Marketing Review, Winter 1983, pp. 13-25

As entry costs are considered to be investments, no pressure is exerted to achieve quick profits. Prices below initial costs are acceptable in anticipation of costs falling with volume. Increasing sales and a growing need for closer interaction with customers leads to the establishment of company-owned sales offices, either with or without local partners. At the same time, the firm starts to broaden the product range and begins to introduce products better adapted to the local market. Local assembly follows, initially relying heavily on parts and components imported from Japan, then gradually moving to increase local content. The factories are preferably newly built or acquired; a green field plant makes it easier to transfer techniques and procedures directly from Japan to the location abroad. Where politics suggest, joint ventures are concluded with local partners, a sogo shosha acting as project promoter and as a small minority shareholder.

Although developing countries offer the possibility of cheap labor, better access to raw materials, and closer links between production and marketing, the main reason Japan firms move their production abroad is to circumvent protectionism. In this respect, Japanese firms are only reluctant multinationals.

Today, leading Japanese firms like Sony and NEC are converting themselves from export-oriented companies, with a large number of centrally controlled sales offices and factories, into truly global firms. Centralized control has, in the past, made it possible to retain core competences in Japan and to channel economies of scale to factories at home; it has also facilitated cross-subsidisation from firms in one country to those in another. The move towards globalization requires a finer balancing of the need for global co-ordination with the need for responsiveness towards national markets and local operations. There is an urgent need for the internationalization of senior management and for key functions such as R&D and the introduction of regional headquarters. Japanese firms find this process of change a difficult one.[15]

Geographically, Japanese firms started their internationalization drive by exporting steel, cars, consumer electronics, watches, cameras and other goods to their `front garden', i.e., Southeast Asia. These countries provided both high growth and opportunities for technological upgrading. The industrial countries were targeted at a later stage. More sophisticated products coming out of Japan in the late 1970s were immediately launched in the major Western markets, particularly in the United States. Australia is the other advanced country in which Japanese firms are exploring new

---

15. H. DeNero, "Creating the 'Hyphenated' Corporation", in: The McKinsey Quarterly, April 1990, pp. 153-174

market opportunities as is the United Kingdom in Europe. In Asia, Hong Kong and Singapore serve as foreign `test markets' for consumer electronics. Major investments in assembly plants by Japanese manufacturers in the United States pulled along a large number of Japanese suppliers. This resulted in a wholesale transfer of Japanese networks and a build-up of `mini-Japans' in the country. Japanese firms are unlikely to be able to repeat such a pattern in Europe, where suppliers are stronger and local integration will be required for political reasons.[16]

The strategies of Japanese firms are often said to have been inspired by the military strategies advocated by Japanese thinkers like Miyamoto Musashi, who in the 17th century encouraged singlemindedness, nowadays called `strategic intent' and advised the protagonist to know the enemy's mindset, take the initiative and `injure the corners' first.[17] Although no proof of causality exists, the Japanese approach to expansion is even more frequently compared to strategies proposed by the Chinese thinker Sun Tzu, who lived around 400 - 320 B.C. and wrote the classic "Art of War," a book which has recently re-appeared in Asia in best-seller form. Sun Tzu argued that although the terrain is fixed, the battleground within this terrain can be chosen. The choice should be made after thorough familiarization with the battleground and should concentrate on areas where one has distinct advantages and the enemy is weak due to ignorance.[18] The major thrust of his advice is the avoidance of direct confrontation and a preference for flanking attacks and pincer movements.

Direct, frontal attacks in which both enemies use all of their available resources are, in fact, seldom launched by Japanese firms. They prefer encirclement attacks, OEM contracts for parts and components, for example, and flanking attacks which hit the competitor where he is weakest in terms of products, segments or geographical markets. A by-pass attack basically leaves the competitor `stunned' and is made possible by switching to entirely new technologies or changing established rules of the game.

---

16. D. Turcq, "New Managerial Patterns Emerging from the International Japanese Presence". Paper presented at EAMSA conference, 17.-19.Oct. 1991, Fontainebleau
17. M. Musashi, "The Book of Five Rings", 1645, referred to by Kotler et al, see footnote 11.
18. T. Sun,T., "Art of War", 4 th century B.C., referred to by Wee,C.H., "Battlegrounds and Business Situations: Lessons from Sun Tzu", in: Singapore Business Review, January 1990, pp. 24-43

Counterstrategies of Western Firms

For many years Western firms have ignored their competitors from Japan. Today, nobody will deny that Japanese firms have made significant progress in a number of industries. Politicians, academics and the media give a lot of attention to the 'Japanese phenomenon'. Despite all evidence of continued Japanese expansionism, Western businessmen remain surprisingly unconvinced of the threat which Japanese firms represent to them.

Two arguments prevail: The first one acknowledges the Japanese inroads into certain markets, but reasons that the industry in which the specific businessmen are working are not and will not be affected. Although it is true that Japanese firms in certain industries are not competitive, it is dangerous to assume that this will not change. As we will argue further on, the liberalization of the Japanese market may force formerly backward industries to wake up and become competitive. The label of "being behind the West," often used by Japanese businessmen to spur themselves on, should not be taken at face value.

The second argument is more complex, explaining the 'Japanese phenomenon' as a temporary one due to the need of the Japanese to work hard and catch up with the West in the aftermath of World War II. It argues further that with the emergence of an increasingly leisure-oriented younger generation, employees will soon no longer be prepared to put in long hours and to commit their life to the economic success of the firm. A corollary is that customers in Japan, who are now more and more knowledgeable about life outside Japan, will no longer accept the high domestic market price levels Japanese firms rely on to achieve high margins at home. This argument also posits that Japanese firms have benefited from government support and low capital costs, but that the current integration of Japan into the world economy reduces or nullifies these advantages. Finally, one observes the late change forced upon Japanese firms from export-oriented companies to multinational and global firms, confronting them only now with problems which their Western competitors learned to manage many years ago.

Most of the above arguments could be described as wishful thinking. And even if it is historically true that nations rise and fall, there is no indication as to how long Japan's period of prosperity will last. In recent years, Japan has out-invested all the other industrial countries on a per capita basis by a wide margin. Assuming that these investments have been feasible, economic logic would suggest that the Japanese will continue their expansion for quite a while. One may in fact suggest that what we are seeing today is only the tip of the iceberg, particularly as Japanese firms are really only just beginning to internationalize. There is no doubt that the younger Japanese consider their private life more important and increasingly resist lengthy working hours. This is only a relative change, however; it is the gap between the Japanese and their Western competitors which is important, not the reduction of hours in Japan per se. While Japanese firms are only just moving to the 40-hour week and the abolition of work on Saturdays, German workers look forward to a reduction to 35 hours per week and a two-and-a-half day weekend. In any case, it is questionable whether Japanese firms, which have already pushed automation to great lengths, need long working hours or rather a more flexible work schedule. In shifting the emphasis from mass production to innovation, Japanese firms will in fact benefit from more well-travelled, more playful and more creative employees, who should, at least theoretically, be more in demand in the future than their workaholic predecessors.

By increasing the percentage of business done outside Japan, Japanese firms have reduced their dependence on the high margins they used to rely on in their domestic market. Even a possible and sudden reduction in prices would not affect them very seriously. With their healthier balance sheets and lower debt exposures, Japanese firms are also much less vulnerable to higher interest rates. Today, many Japanese firms are cash-rich and higher interest rates have a positive effect on their profitability. The argument that less government support would handicap or slow down Japanese firms assumes that all government support has a positive effect on their competitiveness. As experience everywhere — including in Japan — shows, protectionism and subsidies may do just the opposite and prevent firms from succeeding in international markets. Less support, therefore, does not necessarily mean that firms are less competitive. Finally, the relatively late attempt by Japanese firms to establish foreign operations affords them plenty of opportunities to learn from those who expanded abroad earlier. This is especially true of Japanese firms, which are known to study others very carefully. The fact that Japanese firms come from a country with a rather homogeneous society combined with their acute consciousness of being different from the rest of the world may make integration into culturally complex and heterogeneous countries difficult. On the other hand, Japan's sense of its own cultural uniqueness may make it easier for her firms to accept cultural diversity and to develop a high degree of sensitivity towards different-minded governments, workers and their communities. This could enable Japanese firms to avoid many of the pit-falls encountered by Western firms operating multinationally.

In summary, most of the commonly used arguments do not stand up to critical examination. They are either questionable or simply unfounded. The Japanese firms will not stop competing; in fact, all available evidence points to an increase in their activity and a heightening of their competitiveness. Western businessmen who continue to underestimate the strength and determination of Japanese firms would be well-advised to stop dreaming.

Fright and Flight

Mixed with the dangerous assumptions and wishful thinking of Western business people, we can detect a heavy dose of fright. This is often reflected in the expression of hopelessness among businessmen who feel that they can no longer compete with the Japanese because their own home environment does not measure up. Western weakness is ex-cused and attributed to the unfair advantages (protected home market, fa-vorable labor laws, subsidies, etc.) which their Japanese competitors ap-parently obtain from a generally supportive government. It is worth noting that these accusations are made by industries long pampered by their own governments, such as the French automobile producers or the American high-tech companies, many of whom depend on defense contracts to sur-vive. Bowing to public pressure and eager to identify scapegoats, some Western governments are now demanding changes from Japan in order to establish a `level playing field'.

Arguments which favour putting pressure on the Japanese govern-ment are as flawed as the demand for further protection at home is ques-tionable. There is no doubt that the Japanese market was, in the past, heavily rigged in favour of domestic producers. But that is the past. Today, the Japanese market is open, even though the society may remain closed. As the experience in the negotiations under the Strategic Impediment Initiative have shown, it is difficult for Westerners to even articulate credible demands for further market-opening measures. Where progress is achieved, it generally leads to a dismantling of structural barriers in the market and to greater efficiency in the Japanese economy. Foreign firms will have easier access, but no guarantee of their success. Domestic firms, on the other hand, will be forced to improve efficiency in order to survive. Western demands could eventually be counter-productive in the sense that

Japanese firms will adjust to changed rules and greater rivalry at home. They may even become more competitive, eventually venturing abroad to challenge precisely those Western firms which `disturbed' them at home. Japanese retailers are already undergoing major changes in light of American pressure to shake up the existing antiquated `Mom-and-Pop Shop' system and to allow the establishment of larger outlets such as Toys "R" Us. Concessions made by the Japanese government in the form of preferential purchasing of foreign car parts and components may be considered a political success, but they smack of favoritism, artificially distort the market and are certainly counter to the spirit of GATT.

Just how continued protectionism in the automobile industry, both in the United States and in Europe, will improve its competitiveness in the future remains to be seen. Over more than a decade of imposing quotas on Japanese imports, Western competitors lost considerable ground against them. The detailed and comprehensive MIT study on the world automobile industry shows Western firms trailing their Japanese competitors in almost every aspect.[19] Similarly, publicly funded research in the semiconductor industry has neither led to a turnabout nor a revival of the firms concerned. Although government intervention may, in the best cases, be supportive to firms, it cannot generate a competitive advantage they are unable to establish for themselves. Successful competition is the responsibility of the firm and the firm alone.

For Western firms, any complaint of `unfair' behavior on the part of their Japanese competitors and consequent calls for government intervention can create serious communication problems. Blaming others for one's own shortcomings and at the same time demanding more support, and even sacrifices, from one's own work force in order to strengthen competitiveness, is an approach that lacks credibility. In keeping competitors outside one's own market, employees have become complacent and are blinded to external challenges. The result is reflected in substandard products sold for higher prices in the domestic market than they are abroad. At this stage, protectionism becomes politically almost impossible to dismantle. Firms who should have taken action earlier of their own accord are gradually reduced to inefficient domestic producers dependent on the state.

Flight is another option open to Western firms which feel they are losing out to their Japanese competitors. This either takes the form of a withdrawal from mass markets and a subsequent concentration on upmar-

---

19. J.P. Womack et al, "The Machine which Changed the World". Rawson Associates, New York, 1990

ket niches with higher margins, or a withdrawal from manufacturing and a shift towards marketing and services — the `soft' side of business. The flight option, though possibly beneficial in the short-term, can be suicidal over longer periods.

Traditionally, Japanese firms enter foreign markets at the low end and only later move into high-volume segments. By going for market share rather than profit, and applying predatory pricing strategies, Japanese firms render these segments unattractive to Western firms, which begin to shift their attention upmarket. Benefiting from their economies of scale, Japanese firms reduce their costs, while their Western competitors move towards costly product differentiation without necessarily increasing their volume. As a result, the cost gap between Western firms and their Japanese competitors widens. This is irrelevant as long as customers are prepared to pay a substantially higher price for upmarket products, and as long as the volume of this segment remains large enough to cover over-heads and development costs. Japanese firms less constrained by financial demands from their shareholders and in a more competitive cost position, will be able to make considerable expenditures for the upgrading of their own products. Typically, they will also attack the most interesting up-market segments, either with low priced, dressed-up variants of standard-ized products, or entirely new upmarket products. In the mind of the customer, no clearly defined categories of standardized versus differentiated products exist; the product range now presents itself as a continuum. This makes `fleeing' Western firms extremely vulnerable, as companies in the motorcycle, consumer electronics, and (more recently) automobile indus-tries have experienced. Admittedly, Harley Davidson still exists, as does Bang & Olufson from Denmark. Until recently, Mercedes-Benz and BMW seriously argued that the only real mass-produced luxury cars come and will continue to come from Germany. The situation has changed very quickly and one wonders how long all these firms will be able to fund sus-tained investments in R&D to ensure that their products remain technically advanced and hence justifiably higher-priced. Product images play an im-portant role in these markets, but are in danger when `milked' over time, i.e., when they are no longer supported by product performance. Newcomers with sufficient funds and technological back-up can also build reputations fairly quickly. Rolls Royce cars are still produced and may con-tinue to be sold for decades to come; the number of customers, however, who are prepared to pay very high prices for outdated products solely for the name is too limited to represent a solid base for most Western firms un-der attack in mass markets.

The move out of manufacturing and into marketing and services is most apparent in the computer industry. Recognizing the Japanese strength in production technology, Western firms increasingly buy their hardware from Japan, add their own software and consulting services, and sell the whole package to their customers under their name. The general shift towards software makes this a viable shift, at least for the time being. Western firms that have a better understanding of their customers' problems create value by offering tailor-made solutions. This can be a profitable, but vulnerable business. The borders between hardware and software are fluid and production processes and competences to master them can change. Today, certain software programs have already been transferred onto chips and become parts of the hardware. Also, the first tentative attempts are being made to transform the production of software from the creative work of an individual into a systematic assembly of prefabricated building blocs. Systems integrators, software developers and equipment distributors with in-depth knowledge of local needs are not exclusively the large Western multinationals, but are often smaller national firms. These firms and their expertise may well be acquired by Japanese competitors. To cite just one example: Xerox felt untouchable in the photocopier business due to its ability to offer service to their customers almost everywhere in the world. This proved to be a fallacy when the Japanese launched small photocopiers which hardly needed any service.

Fight

Western firms are actively responding to the challenge from Japanese competitors. Obviously, this applies to those whose very survival is already at stake (the computer and automobile industries), but equally to those firms who sense that competition may be slowly evolving from Japan (the cosmetics industry or retailing, for example). Others who feel free from any threat, have nevertheless started to analyze what is going on in the Japanese market in their industry. Those firms which neglect this type of research may live to regret their complacency.

Cost-cutting campaigns, benchmarking, reorganizations, reduction of product development times, productivity increases and many more activities are undertaken to make Western firms leaner and more responsive. This is expected of firms which are in competition with others, whether of Japanese origin or not. Should they confront Japanese competitors or expect to confront them, then those operational measures may not be sufficient. Since the publication of the devastating MIT report on the world automobile industry, Western firms have made great progress in boosting productivity and reducing defect rates. The problem is that the Japanese competitors have not stood still, but have advanced even further. This does not imply that incremental improvements are futile; they are, in fact, a necessity and a system inducing them should be introduced in every organization. But to meet Japanese firms successfully in undistorted markets, more fundamental changes are required to match their strengths.

'Long-termism' has been described as one of the key factors of success of Japanese firms. It is based on life-time employment practices leading to employee commitment and to a lack of shareholder interest in short-term financial returns. There is nothing typically Japanese in this kind of 'long-termism'; any firm which possesses both a committed work force and patient capital has a significant advantage over those which do not. The reality, for whatever reason, is that most Japanese firms are long-term oriented, while many Western firms are not. Continental European firms — German and Swiss firms in particular — fall somewhere between the two prototypes.

In line with economists' preference for free factor markets and due to managers' complaints about complacent workers, lifetime employment as a concept in the West has been widely discredited. It has been argued that although the system provides employees with social security, it does not assure the firm lifetime loyalty or commitment. According to the argument, individualism in the West would not lead employees to a full identification with the firm. Instead, conflicts between owners/managers of the firm and their workers are systemic, leading each party to adopt a confrontational negotiating stance, or to seek a narrowly selfish advantage from the other. These arguments are influenced by ideology and belied by the example of many organizations outside Japan. Lifetime employment exists in many Western firms (though it may not be referred to as such) and is not strictly implemented. The term is used here, not in its narrow legalistic meaning, but in the broader sense of the company caring for its work force, recognizing the contribution of the individual, and therefore treating him with respect. It also follows that the firm will protect him from hardship in return for his own efforts as long as the firm can afford it. Very successful companies, such as Unilever, Shell, IBM, Xerox, Bayer and Nestle practice such 'moral agreement on mutual support' and have work forces committed to the cause of the firm. This commitment, however, does not come automatically. It depends more on the ability of the management to motivate their workers and to instil in the organization a feeling of 'everybody sitting in the same boat to win' than on the work force itself. Those firms which pursue the objective of 'increasing shareholder value' will obviously have difficulties creating such a spirit or in retaining devoted workers. Equally, firms with very large disparities in pay and other benefits between the top and bottom layer of the organization will not find it easy to communicate a team spirit within the work force. Last, but not least, the manager who cannot instill a fighting spirit or the desire to win, runs the risk of turning his firm into an aimless, self-serving vehicle. A common vision, committed shareholders, attentive management, and a degree of external pressure, can all lead to a mutual loyalty between the firm and its work force. Creating this often elusive spirit is the first condition for success in competing against Japanese firms.

As outlined above, most Japanese firms are linked with each other through an elaborate system of cross-shareholdings and interlocking directorates. This relieves the firms of the pressure to deliver high returns to the shareholders and separates the 'real' world of industry and markets from the 'artificial' world of share price fluctuations and price/earnings ratios. It allows companies to focus on long-term investments and customer concerns. In many respects, this corporate system is exemplified by many German firms.

The American firm, on the other hand, operates with a structure which is entirely different. Roughly half of the companies traded on the New York Stock Exchange are owned by financial institutions (mutual and pension funds, but not banks) which by law are not allowed to take an active role in shaping the future of the firms they own. Driven themselves by short-term profit considerations, these financial traders buy and sell shares based on quarterly results.[20] Managers of firms have to deliver high dividends in order to stabilize or boost the share price. Sacrificing short-term results in order to invest in the future will drive away the financial institutions, depress share prices and destroy shareholder value. In taking a long-term view, top managers often risk their re-appointment by the shareholders and may forego lucrative stock options which are part of their compensation schemes.

The emphasis on short-term profitability makes it impossible to compete with Japanese firms pursuing market share goals. Western firms feverishly 'massaging' quarterly results have no chance to succeed against Japanese competitors who measure their results over a period of decades and not necessarily in financial terms. To succeed, Western firms

---

20. L. Thurow, "Let's Learn from the Japanese", in: Fortune, November 18, 1991, pp. 87-89

need committed and patient capital. Commitment must come from important shareholders and providers of loans, whether private individuals, companies, financial institutions, banks or the government, taking an active interest in and accepting responsibility for the well-being of the firm they are financing. They have to sit on the boards of these firms and play a role in decision-making. As providers of patient capital they must be prepared to forego short-term losses in the expectation of long-term gains for the firm and themselves. They should, as Lester Thurow argues, be converted into 'capitalist builders' and not be allowed to succeed financially without ensuring the success of their firms as well.[21]

The change towards long-term capital is the second condition for succeeding against Japanese firms. The need has long been recognized, but no action has followed. The American anti-trust legislation has become obsolete and is out of synch with current thinking in the rest of the world. Any attempt to impose it on the Japanese is again wishful thinking. Why should they accept a system which so obviously does not work? Cross-shareholdings will have to come to the West, as banks in the United States should be permitted to own shares of manufacturing companies. Perhaps Western or American keiretsu should be created, not only in the sense of supporting each other through a stable financial structure, but also in the shared development of core technologies in the pre-competitive stage of research.[22] Striking a balance between the extremes of complacent collusion and ruthless competition will be needed to make such a system work. This system operates very well in Japan and to some extent in Germany, and there is no obvious reason why it cannot work in other parts of the world.

Firms do not have to wait for the framework under which they operate to change. Managers have to clearly understand their disadvantageous structure and convince their shareholders that 'short-termism' when dealing with Japanese competitors is equivalent to digging one's own grave. Any work force is likely to accept this thinking, being more interested in long-term survival than short-term gains for shareholders. Shares could be offered to long serving employees with multiple voting rights and minimum board representation. Internally, systems have to be designed to reward efforts directed towards the future rather than past performance. As such, a sense of 'long-termism' can be introduced into Western firms even if they operate under a system not conducive to it.

---

21. ibid
22. C.H. Ferguson, "Computers and the Coming of the U.S. Keiretsu", in: Harvard Business Review, July/August 1990, pp. 55-70

Western pharmaceutical firms dominate the world and have made significant inroads into the Japanese market. It is an industry in which shareholders, managers and workers alike know that success is mainly based on commitments in effort and capital over very long periods. This strength is not imposed from the outside but is inherent in the nature of the business.

Customer Orientation without Marketing

'Long-termism' alone does not create a competitive advantage, which can only be the result of efforts to serve the customer better, either by offering him superior products or better value for his money. Firms must constantly improve to create and maintain the edge over their competitors. To do so, they must understand the present and future needs of the market and carry out market research. This requirement is the same for Japanese and Western firms, though in certain, selected markets Japanese firms have started to actively drive the market instead of following trends discovered through research.

Driving the market is indicative of the hands-on Japanese approach to the customer. Not only salespeople, but various kinds of office and factory workers, managers and engineers are encouraged to seek direct contact with buyers and users. Company-owned `antenna' shops have been installed in Japan in which staff can, without any filter whatsoever, directly experience the reaction of customers to new products. Most Western firms are concentrating the information about products and markets in marketing departments. In these departments, co-ordination of all activities related to specific products, markets or segments is carried out by ambitious and highly educated brand managers. Strategies are formulated and changes proposed after thorough analysis, and internal battles between the departments invariably follow. The marketing people have the ideas and the data, the salespeople the feeling for what will work. Meanwhile, the Japanese competitors test the first product in the market, perfectly aware that it is not yet the perfect one, but getting the first real feedback.

Losing time is not the only argument against such a structure and process. In pretending to know the market and the customer, marketing managers discourage others in the firm from getting any real feedback. In the worst case, the task of getting to know the customer is limited to the marketing department. Any responsiveness then has to come from the marketing department and no one else pays even the slightest attention to customer needs. The result, at best, is a slow and costly process and, at worst, an insufficient customer focus. Parallels to factory operations come to mind. Why should workers along the assembly line bother about quality as long as a quality controller sits at the end of the line? Correspondingly, why should the rest of the organization bother about customer needs as long as there is an all-knowing marketing department? Many Japanese firms do not even have such a coordinating department. As the firm's objective is to satisfy customers better than competitors do, it is the task of every employee to be concerned with marketing.

Western firms often consider their first task to be the defense of their home territory - basically at any price. In military terms, this is called a position defense. No compromise can be accepted; any encroachment through flanking and encirclement attacks must be responded to quickly. If the home turf cannot be protected, defeat world-wide is not far off. Position defense by itself is not enough, however, since it often makes the existing business a sitting target for the competition.[23] It must be combined with other defense, maintenance and attack strategies abroad. For most Western firms, industrial markets apart from their home market are the most important and receive the most attention. Holding onto a position is equally important in order to remain truly international contenders. Should Japanese firms become too strong, a retreat becomes inevitable — as some of the European automobile manufacturers have seen. But bold moves in territories not yet occupied by the Japanese can compensate for those losses. These territories can be other industrial countries or newly emerging markets such as in Eastern and Central Europe. The desire of the Japanese firms to thoroughly explore new countries before taking any entry decision gives time to courageous Western firms to move first, make vital investments and acquisitions, and bloc entry channels for latecomers. In the more promising, fast growing countries of the Asia Pacific region, such strategies should have been undertaken 30 years ago. Today, Japanese firms represent in all countries in the region the largest number of investors and the most successful importers. They have also built up significant holdings in distribution channels and retailing. As a result, European consumer goods are increasingly sold through Japanese department store chains in Asia. Nevertheless, selected action must be taken to stop Japanese competitors from reaping too many benefits from the high growth of certain sectors. In this context, Volkswagen's expansion plans into both Czechoslovakia and China have to be seen as not only

---

23. Kotler et al, pp. 151-172, see footnote 11

market-driven. They are clearly designed to prevent the entry of Japanese car manufacturers in Central Europe and to impede the unrestricted flow of cars from Japan into the potentially interesting market of China.

For Western firms, the market more important than all other markets except the home territory — but much more difficult — is the Japanese market. Apart from being the second largest market, often boasting the highest margins in the world, Japan is the environment which has made Japanese competitors strong. Whatever can be learnt in this market should strengthen the global competitiveness of the Western firm, provided that this knowledge is transferred back to the home country and used appropriately. Any Western firm which aspires to be a global competitor has no choice but to overcome entry barriers and fight for survival. As Japanese rivals will protect their home turf at any cost, frontal attacks are out of question. Therefore, flanking attacks are called for, although even the most indirect one will not go undetected. Listening posts in Japan are the minimum presence that Western firms have to establish. To really understand the competition, however, listening is not enough; sales offices, research centers and manufacturing plants must be considered, depending of course on the industry and the technology concerned. Although it is often difficult to make profits, even over extended periods of time, any substantial operation by a Western competitor will reduce the growth and profit potential of his Japanese rival. Failures may serve to make managers at headquarters aware that there are Japanese competitors which have to be taken seriously. As Procter & Gamble experienced, surviving and winning in Japan meant challenging many aspects of their business as world leader. The experience, by all reports, has made their company leaner and more responsive. It also made Procter & Gamble more competitive against other Western firms which have not had to do battle in Japan. These benefits do not show up in the cost/benefit analyses, but are probably more important than the actual results achieved in Japan.

Competitive Collaboration

Today, even very large firms find it difficult to market their products equally well in all countries, to conduct state-of-the-art research in all technologies relevant to their industries, and to remain fully competitive in every part of the value-added chain. As a consequence, they increasingly enter into cooperative ventures with other firms, or become members of ever changing networks of relationships with various firms in different parts

64

of the world. Western firms have actively sought partnerships with Japanese firms, sometimes following the old Asian saying: "If you can't beat them, join them." The experience has not always been good.[24]

On the surface, cooperative ventures between Western and Japanese firms look attractive. Due to their different geographical origins, strengths and weaknesses, partners should ideally complement each other. Implementing such collaboration, however, requires a degree of knowledge sharing which is difficult, especially if the partner is a competitor or a potential competitor. This competitive collaboration is the rule rather than the exception and demands an ability to simultaneously share and protect knowledge.

There appear to be three dominant types of agreements between Western and Japanese firms.[25] In the first kind of agreement, the Japanese firm obtains the technology from the Western partner and then manufactures and markets the product in Japan. The Western firm cooperates either because it has problems developing the technology into a product, or because it considers the Japanese market negligible or too difficult to penetrate. Such agreements have dominated the pharmaceutical industry in the past and are now increasingly used in areas such as new materials and biotechnology. Using the technology acquired from the Western partner, the Japanese firm is able to make up for the lack of either efforts or success in research. Over time, the strength of the Japanese firm in developing a given technology further, improving and altering it, and applying it to a larger product range than originally conceived for it, lessens its dependence on the licensee. The incremental approach of the Japanese firm, by improving existing products, is crucial to the success of this process. More often than not, the Western firm finds itself competing with products marketed by their own partner, based on their original technology, but superior in quality, performance or at a lower price.

The second type of agreement exploits the manufacturing strength of the Japanese partner who allows the Western firm to market its products outside Japan but under the Western firm's name (OEM agreements). Such agreements cover large parts of the international trade in computers and peripherals, office equipment and consumer electronics. The Western partner is interested in sourcing from Japan mainly for cost reasons. The

24. R.B. Reich and D.D. Mankin, "Joint Ventures with Japan Give Away Our Future", in: Harvard Business Review, March/April 1986, pp. 78-83.
25. H. Schütte, "Euro-Japanese Cooperation in Information Technology", in: "International Business and the Management of Change", by Trevor,M. (editor) Aldershot, (1991) pp. 22-48 and "Strategische Allianzen mit japanischen Firmen", in: "Der asiatisch-pazifische Raum", by Schneidewind, D. and Töpfer, A.(editors), Verl. Moderne Industrie, Landsberg, 1991, pp. 251-275

Japanese partner can increase its volume and, as a result, reduce its costs. Along with the orders come opportunities for improving production capabilities and facilities in general, not only in terms of lines sold to the Western partner, but also in terms of products against which the Western partner may be directly competing. In effect, what appear to be attractive outsourcing opportunities boost the Japanese partner's competitiveness while at the same time endangering the long-term viability of manufacturing in the Western firm.

Marketing agreements represent the third type of cooperative ventures. Western firms let their Japanese partners take care of their products in the Japanese market, while the Japanese partners ask the Western firm to do the marketing of their products in the West or some Western markets. Both sides expect to benefit from offering a broader product range in their own market and from serving additional customers abroad. The more successful the firms are in selling their partner's products, the more the latter will wish to be directly involved. This is characteristic for all international marketing agreements.. While Japanese firms are taking over the distribution themselves in many markets, the Western partner of a Japanese firm may find it difficult, if not impossible to apply the same strategy in Japan. Sales in Japan are primarily based on the relationship between buyer and seller and, as such, are hard to replace or substitute. Kenichi Ohmae's recommendation to Western firms that they join forces with Japanese partners in Japan in order to be represented in all "triad" markets and, therefore, be truly global has to be seen in this light.[26]

Although these are the three most common types of agreements between Western and Japanese firms, they do not necessarily lead to the consequences described above. Much depends on the commitment of the partners to making the venture a success. Success, however, has to be carefully defined in this context. For the Western firm it is normally the explicit outcome of the joint undertaking in the form of a certain profit margin, cost-saving, market share or research results. The Japanese partner will also be keen to see a concrete, positive result for the venture. In most cases the firm will be equally keen, if not more so, to learn from the partner's contribution to the venture and from the way in which activities are jointly carried out. The know-how absorbed by Japanese firms will then be transferred to other parts of the organization in order to strengthen its competences and sharpen its competitiveness. This process of leveraging may

---

26. K. Ohmae, "Triad Power", Free Press, New York, 1985

well provide the Japanese partner with greater benefits than the explicit outcome.[27]

The problem with this transfer of know-how is not so much that it seems to be an automatic process taking place on the Japanese side, but that in many cases the Western side is either less interested, or unable to organize the same flow of information towards its own firm. The hemorrhaging of know-how can be minimized and certain information declared off-limits to the Japanese partner. Learning from each other, however, cannot be regulated in contracts and has nothing to do with the percentage of one's equity share in a joint venture. It depends on the intellectual curiosity of the people involved and the briefing they receive from their headquarters. It can only function if these people are given sufficient time to learn and are rewarded for sharing their knowledge with others. The internal diffusion of information needs to be organized and feedback encouraged from the parts of the Western firm that actually make use of the know-how. Only this will ensure systematic intelligence gathering and organizational learning.

Both short-term and long-term competitive collaboration with Japanese firms can be very fruitful. Collaboration, however, provides no easy, short-cut solutions to problems which Western firms have been unable to solve on their own. Opportunistic approaches, combined with weak commitment and a meager allocation of human resources to the cooperation are bound to end in competence-milking and the overall strengthening of the Japanese partner. But this is not inevitable.

Conclusion

In this paper we have argued that the success of Japanese firms is mainly due to better structures, better strategies and better processes within the firms themselves. But not all Japanese firms are successful and not everything works well. Many firms exist in Japan which manufacture products of low quality, neglect the environment, and fail to offer lifetime employment. Small subcontractors are ruthlessly exploited by large firms, contracts are not necessarily awarded to the most efficient suppliers, and consumers pay artificially high prices. Although these realities may offer solace to Westerners, they are irrelevant for those competing with Japan's well-known international firms, especially those which represent the country's industrial power. These firms are now well-managed, financially

---

27. G. Hamel, Y. Doz, C.K.Prahalad, "Collaborate with Your Competitor", in: Harvard Business Review, January/February 1989, pp. 133-139

sound, and technology-driven; they are also in pursuit of expansion and leadership in world markets. To be 'No. 1' still has value in Japan, for the nation, as well as for the firm and the individual.

There is no fundamental reason why Western firms cannot match the performance of their Japanese competitors. Dubious cultural explanations of Japanese success stories are misleading and will only lull Western managers into a false sense of complacency. Accusations of "unfair" government support are mostly out-of-date. Why should government intervention in Japan be conducive to business when the West considers that it is precisely such action which has created distortions and inefficiencies in the system?

The Western firms which will be able to stand up against Japanese competitors are those who will define themselves as associations of people, not as aggregations of assets to be documented in any balance sheet. Their executives will see their main task to be the management of people, not assets. They will concentrate on creating a common vision for everybody, a commitment to achieving certain targets, a willingness to succeed and, above all, to win. Consequently, their objective will not be the achievement of a certain profit or increase in shareholder value, but the achievement of a satisfactory added value. This added value, defined as total sales minus total expenses paid to outside suppliers, needs to be distributed to all stakeholders of the firm: first of all to the employees, in form of salaries; then to the providers of long-term capital and assets, in form of interest and rents; to the government in the form of taxes; and, finally, to the shareholders in the form of dividends. Chief executives of those firms will not be influenced in their decisions by the performance of the shares of the company on the stock market, but will balance the interests of all groups of stakeholders in order to ensure the long-term survival and growth of the firm.

The much-discussed victory of "committed firms" over "paper capitalists," is now exemplified by the success of Japanese firms over American firms, which have been driven by an obsessive focus on financial targets such as return on assets. This victory represents a fundamental challenge to the Western corporate system, the Anglo-American one in particular. This system, which puts shareholders' value before employees' commitment and pays financial wizards on Wall Street multiple salaries compared to those of factory managers in Ohio, is coming to an end. The West must wake up to the reality that price/earning ratios have as much to do with the ability of the firm to service its customers as socialists' talk about egalitarian principles had with guaranteeing the general welfare of 'the people.'

Business schools and their excessively narrow emphasis on financial analysis, functional expertise and individual performance, have failed to provide Western firms with new ideas on how to counter Japanese competitors. Their "hard skill" approach, by shaping generations of MBA graduates, may in fact have contributed to the relative decline of at least those American firms on which the sheer number of MBA-graduates at all levels in the hierarchy must have an impact on management thinking. In the rest of the world, business schools play only a limited role. Interestingly enough, they hardly exist either in Japan or in Germany, and neither country has undertaken serious efforts to start them.

In Japan and in Germany, management-training basically takes place on the job or through in-house programs. This combines the transfer of relevant, company-specific know-how with the infusion of a strong group spirit. MBAs are eyed with suspicion and their studies are considered to be more of a broadening exercise than of use for the employing firm.

In the United States, the more enlightened business schools are trying to adapt to an environment which demands more attention to "soft skills," such as human resource management and organizational learning, the strengthening of cross-functional capabilities and team building, cross-cultural negotiations and the globalization of business. Catching up with reality will not come easily for academics whose research in some fields according to Harvard's Kaplan "has yielded little or no fundamental knowledge relevant for managing contemporary or future business organizations" over the last 20-25 years.[28] Courses on quality, communication, ethics or culture therefore remain exceptions in the world of business schools. Best-selling text books on marketing still make only sketchy reference to customer service, and operations management is still widely viewed as a technical area instead of an integral part of organizational behavior.

Most appalling is the lack of knowledge and understanding of Japan and of the challenge which Japan's corporate system poses to the West — an ignorance which persists despite all the publicity surrounding the success of Japanese firms. Masses of Japanese students, tourists, and businessmen study Western countries, but few Westerners make the effort to familiarize themselves with Japan. A serious imbalance of information flow and understanding is the result. This has to change. The West cannot expect to compete successfully with Japan as long as the Japanese know more about the West than Westerners do about Japan.

---

28. as cited by A. Deutschmann. in "The Trouble with MBAs", in: Fortune,July 29, 1991, pp.119-127

A European Industrial Perspective

Dieter Schneidewind
President
Wella AG

Highly developed civilizations have always spread in human history their cultural influence to other peoples and nations. This applies particularly — but not at all exclusively — to technological aspects. Technology tends to be borderless. Even in prehistorical times new technologies have been widely distributed over vast areas, as the use of bow and arrow or the potter's wheel do suggest. Countless are the engravings of old cultures on our European life: Indians and Hethitians, Greeks and Romans, Arabs and Turks have all contributed to our philosophy, sciences, conveniences and necessities of daily life. Even noodles, oranges and silk from China or potatoes, tobacco and maize from South America have entered the life of our ancestors centuries ago.

Japan herself has adopted strong cultural features from India, China, Korea, Portugal, the Netherlands and in more recent times Germany, France, England and the United States of America.

Looking out of an office-window in Tokyo suggests, that almost everything outside is imported or adopted from the so-called "West": concrete, asphalt, rails, wires, motorcars, raincoats, fountain pens and what have you. However, Japanese people are hardly inclined to recognize all these things as "Western"; they are entirely used to them as parts of their life since generations. They consider them if need be as "modan" (from modern). So are we Europeans wearing jeans or using personal computers from the USA.

In the following we exercise our phantasy to arrive at an imagination of which influences from Japan might enter our daily lifes in forthcoming years.

We do know of course that our households are full of things made in Japan, though they might have been developed in Europe originally: cameras, audiovisual equipments, microwave ovens, mountain bikes, pianos, watches etc. But there are also things marketed first by Japanese entrepreneurs. We think of the walkman, handy private video cameras, electric pencil sharpeners, a variety of electronic toys for children, CD-casettes etc.

There are already six Japanese restaurants in Frankfurt alone and many more in London. Because Japanese food is recognized as light, poor in calories and fat but rich in proteins it is increasingly enjoyed as health-food. Many a housewife in Europe is using Japanese seasonings like Mirin sauce, shoyu or Ajinomoto glutamate. She is even starting to try to prepare dishes like tempura, sukiyaki or seaweed-soup. This trend will continue further. A variety of Japanese snacks might be offered in future open-air at kiosks; like udon (thick noodles), *o-soba* (spicy thin noodles), *yakimeshi* (fried rice), *tonkatsu* (a special soya-sauce schnitzel), *takoyaki* (small crispy cereals with octopus) or *tomorokoshi* (roasted Indian corn).

Until entering school Japanese society is very friendly to young children. A variety of games, songs, tales, toys and handicrafts are provided for them. One could foresee that those might be much appreciated once they are actively promoted by the interested industry. In TV there appeared already the very Swiss story of the girl Heidi in a Japanese version. Origami — cutting figures out of special papers — is increasingly popular in kindergarten and nurseries. Many more card-plays, puzzles and rigging-up models could be introduced with enthusiastic responses by the young generation.

Things Japanese are also penetrating increasingly European houses and gardens. The influences start right with the architecture. During the Twenties the Bauhaus introduced already modules in construction, which were very close to the traditional Japanese modules like "*tatami*" or "*tsubo*". Many windows linked house and garden. Today windows are popularly provided with freckles, though their coverage with the shoji-ricepaper is still rare, but known. Inside the houses sliding doors, screens as room-dividers and decorative objects can be spotted in various dwellings.

Flowers in vases are less evenly cut but arranged in a fashion derived from the traditional Japanese art of flower arrangement (*ikebana*). Also not a small number of persons engage in the technics of trimming shrubs and trees to dwarfed sizes, known in Japan as bonsai. Plenty of professional gardeners are engaged in this business. Gardens themselves are occasionally styled in Japanese manner; public gardens and private gardens alike. Stone wells and stone lanterns appear. The whole mode goes away from symmetrical arrangements in favor of those with more natural and asymmetrical set-ups. Pebbles in large quantities can be seen in gardens and a variety of Japanese flowers, bushes and trees. Whole boulevards are seened in spring with Japanese cherry blossoms. In many public and private ponds Japanese ornamental carps *(koi)* are bred.

Many European housewifes have delightfully adopted the Japanese custom to take off shoes when entering a house. During leisure time — especially in summer — family members might wear the light Japanese summer kimono made from cotton (*yukata*).

The Japanese sports of judo are already firmly established in international sport-events, including the Olympic Games. Others like *sumo* (a special kind of wrestling) or *kendo* (fencing with wooden bars) might follow.

There are already European associations for the Japanese variation of chess (*shogi*) and *go* (a very Japanese game played on a board). Many families arrange with friends and neighbors mahjong-parties, playing either the Chinese or the Japanese version. Of course almost all children have already played with sticks *(mikado)*.

The latest advertisements promise the European consumer the Japanese fun of *karaoke*, when buying the intriguing equipment developed for this national sports in Japan. *Karaoke* means literally "without orchestra". After the stress and frustrations of a hard working-day, people produce themselves as singers. They use a special microphone which is connected with a machine, that adjusts to almost all mistakes the soloist performer might run into. In front of him appear on a screen the next notes to be sung, the text and also some video-films that correspond with the mood of any particular song.

One can envisage that countless more Japanese customs and products will enter the European style of life, without being rejected as strange, on the contrary welcomed as something new and instigating. Modern Japanese fashion designers have made inroads not only into the difficult scene of Paris but all around the world of fashionable places and contributed with great creativity to international fashion.

Cultural Aspects

Wichmann[1] has proven once more in his wonderful volume of plates "Japonismus: Ostasien-Westeuropa" once more proven, that European art has been greatly influenced by Japanese arts since the times of the late Baroque.

The world exhibitions in London (1862) and in Paris (1876, 1878 and 1879) contributed very much to the diffusion of Japanese arts and handicrafts throughout Europe. Dozens of famous European artists have

---

[1] S.Wichmann; Japonismus;Ostasien-Westeuropa, Begegnung in der Kunst des 19. und 20 Jahrhunderts, Herrsching 1980

been greatly influenced by the Japanese style and artistic perception; the painters Henri Toulouse-Lautrec and Vincent van Gogh might be named as outstanding examples. The whole movement of Art Nouveau and Jugendstil was originated from those Far Eastern sources. Apart from the famous Japanese woodblock-prints, also lacquerware, porcelains, ceramics, silk paintings, botanical plates and and above all the textile arts served as inspiration for the somewhat rigid formalization of European arts at that time.

Free-flowing and natural movements, a new view of colors as well as the technique of *ishizuri* (white compositions on a black background), sketches with strokes and points, lively gestures, portrayals of flowers, trees and animals, waves as ornaments, the introduction of high format, asymmetric as derived from the Japanese sword flake *(tsuba)*, black and white graphics, textile patterns (as widely used by Gustav Klimt), the diagonal arrangement of pictures, the technique of the picture as frame in the picture, the grid in painting, cross-cutting of objects, the division of pictures by a post, the introduction of the silhouette, ghostly themes and the abstraction of landscapes are major introductions into the art of painting. Calligraphy and interior design are further areas which have influenced European art.

Besides that also Japanese literature had its impact on the cultural scene in Europe, though only one Nobel-Price for literature has yet been awarded to Nippon's writers. This is probably because only a few books have been translated into "Western" languages; and these translations cannot really transmit the real beauty of Japanese literature written with kanji, the Chinese characters.

Zen, a Buddhist school of meditation, exercised an enormous influence on Japanese culture. It found also considerable interest in Europe, particularly its aesthetic principles have been adopted by European scholars and laymen alike.

Thousands of books have been meanwhile written by European authors on matters Japanese, dealing with a wide variety of subjects. Whether positive or negative in their tendency, in any case they have introduced many facets of Japanese life and thoughts into European civilization. There are many reasons to believe, that this processes will be further enhanced.

Whereas the Japanese society is rigidly enforcing groupism and deriving its strength out of it, one can observe distinctive individualism in the field of arts. This is not regarded as an antagonism in Japan but as a fruitful polarization. From this a powerful strength can be derived. "The perceptual in Japanese tradition largely underlies Japan's rise as a modern society and economy. It enabled the Japanese to grasp the essence, the fundamental configuration of things foreign and Western, whether an institution or a product, and then to redesign. The most important thing that can be said about Japan as viewed through its arts may well be that Japan is perceptual "[2].

Japanese Capital Partners

It is widely recognized that culture and thus the spirit and attitude of citizens in a given country form the base for developing or adapting technologies . Technologies in turn are the basis for successful economic development. Natural resources, land and capital are also important, however, they are only secondary.

Winston Churchill is quoted to have exclaimed, that empires of the future would be empires of the mind. Because of the well known abilities of Japanese managers and staffs one can conclude that they will successfully settle in European countries, once they have decided to do so. Because of recent power shifts it looks very much like Japanese companies will cover increasingly European grounds in the future.

Doubtless North America, Western Europe and East Asia (with Japan in the leading position) constitute the cornerstones of global economic power. After Japan has gained considerable positions in the markets and industries of the USA they will shift now their strategical interests to Europe.

Japan participated in the European Bank for Reconstruction and Development; her ranking in the International Monetary Fund is second only to the USA. She has disclosed her desire to be represented in the Conference on Security and Cooperation in Europe. Among the top twenty in the Eurobond business we do find no less than five Japanese companies, with Nomura Securities at the top. When Japan opened the Tokyo International Financial Futures Exchange on June 30, 1989, it turned out that the EuroYen trading outpaced the other contracts after a few months. It is estimated that annually half of all new capital in the world is channeled through Japanese financial institutions. And another guess again is that 2/3 of this finds it ways to Europe.

---

[2] P. Drucker; Toward the Next Economies; New York 1981

Financial Aspects

In 1989, all eight of the world's largest banks by assets[3] were Japanese:

	Assets in Bio US $	PbT in Bio US $
Daiichi Kangyo Bank	390.0	2.9
Mitsui Taiyo Kobe Bank *	383.0	2.2
Sumitomo Bank	379.0	3.1
Fuji Bank	367.0	2.9
Mitsubishi Bank	354.0	2.6
Sanwa Bank	351.0	2.5
Industrial Bank of Japan	270.0	1.5
Norinchukin Bank	244.0	0.5

* The merger of the Taiyo Kobe Bank and the Mitsui Bank became legal in 1990.

No.9 and No.10 are occupied by two French banks (Credit Agricole and Banque Nationale de Paris).

All this suggests, that Japanese companies can engage in European economic activities just to their liking, provided they command a foothold in the EEC. This foothold they are about to obtain in Great Britain, where they are investing heavily. It appears that the Thatcher administration tried to fend off a German-French hegemony in Europe by associating with Japanese capital. It has to be seen, how this short term goal would comply with long term Japanese strategies.

Generally it is certainly better to invite prospective Japanese partners to participate in a European company or new venture, rather than to face at a later date Japanese efforts in unfriendly takeovers. So far the latter procedure is not favoured by Japanese investors and runs counter to their management philosophy. Nevertheless a big pack of organizations and individuals engaged in Europe in the dealing with mergers and acquisitions might persuade Japanese investors into respective undertakings and do the business for them.

Japanese organizations have in some instances spent spectacular amounts of dollars to acquire a few really big companies. But they do usually not spend their money lightheartedly; on the contrary, a large layer of bureaucratic staffs screen every project rigidly and use to delay pending

---

[3] The Consulting Group Ltd.; Ranking the World's Largest Banks; "Institutional Investor"; New York London Tokyo, June 1990

decisions. Funds are not at all spent carelessly. Where Japanese corporations act quickly and are occasionally supposed to have been overcharged in acquiring a new organization, there do we find either an organization run by a strong-man or a privately owned enterprise.

Because it is quite customary in the Japanese industry that companies hold cross participations in each other, it might be advisable for the European counterpart — in the case of equity or minority share — to have a matching stake in the Japanese organization.

There exist partnerships between German and Japanese enterprises where each side holds a 20% stake in its partner. Additionally they operate joint ventures all over the world; some with German and some with Japanese majority, and a few even at a 50/50 ratio.

In most instances a Japanese investor might want to acquire a hundred percent controlled company which fits his overall interests. His aim is more to compete than to coordinate. This competition is usually healthy for the concerned national economy and should thus be welcomed. The EEC authorities are however well advised, to permit investments freely only if the same rights are granted in Nippon in a reciprocal manner.

The international financial movements are borderless indeed. Also the emergence of truly transnational companies becomes evident; they challenge the national authorities and might develop new global patterns in addition to national states. Ultimately also strategic alliances of all sorts and kinds do evolve on a global scale, because single organizations — even very large ones — can not afford huge R&D costs, giant and sophisticated production facilities and above all a simultaneous penetration of the major world-markets.

All this makes it inevitable to welcome capital investments of a leading financial, technological and industrial power like Japan to the European scene. It is in the common interest of the world that Japan will not run into the incalculable situation to remain as an outsider of the international society.

It also cannot be in the best interest of Europe if the nations of the so called Pacific Rim (including North America) would find it difficult to deal with a "Fortress Europe" and concentrated entirely on transpacific ties. Though all of Europe looks quite big in terms of population and development opportunities, by including the former Communist Bloc, the reality remains that these Eastern European countries will impose a burden rather than a benefit on Western Europe — for decades to come. The USA, Canada, Japan, Korea and others should be heartily invited to participate in building-up the economies of Eastern Europe.

At the moment Japanese companies seem to be quite reluctant in setting up enterprises other than for sales or coordination in Eastern Europe. In this case they should be assisted and guided in doing bold investments there.

Implications for Entrepreneurs and Managers

In the case of a capital partnership, the situation looks quite different according to the type of the Japanese partner:

(1) a keiretsu like Mitsubishi, Sumitomo; in this case most likely the general trading house of a keiretsu will be the partner,

(2) an important member company of a keiretsu, usually of its own choice,

(3) a smaller member company of a keiretsu; usually with the consent of the keiretsu-leadership — always the leading bank, on most cases also the general house, sometimes an enterprise from the heavy industries' sector,

(4) a strong, but still independent company (like SONY),

(5) a medium-sized independent company,

(6) a privately owned small company.

In case (1) the partnership will be blessed with the backing of tremendous resources like financial standing, technological expertise, abundance of able staffs, access to various kinds of R&D capacities, supply sources, a dense worldwide network for information, market development, sales or worldwide communication services. The price for that could be a considerable bureaucracy. For better or for worse the European partner would be subjected to the principle strategies of the whole group. Most likely he would be fairly and politely treated, because those giant keiretsu have a long tradition, they are internationally minded and they care much for their good reputation and image.

In case (2) most likely there will be no direct contact with the leading core (bank, trading house) of the keiretsu. This means though the same privileges as in case (1) could be enjoyed, in reality the partner would depend on the goodwill and be at the mercy of his direct Japanese counterpart. Probably the company's European president might stay in office in order to deal with internal and external communications. He might serve as a British or French (as the case maybe) symbol for the company, while

Japanese managers make the decisions. The Japanese partner's objectives and disciplines might be rigidly enforced — if possible.

In respect of case (3), all options are open. Once the keiretsu leadership has given its nod to the venture, the Japanese partner is relatively free to do what suits him. The European partner would be well advised to seek and maintain a good relationship with middle managers in the bank and/or trading house. They usually become acquainted with them during the joint-venture negotiations. This can assure access to know-how and other backing, perhaps even versus the partner. The relationship can be fruitful, friendly and long lasting, particularly when the two partners are of about the same size and strength.

Regarding case (4) the partnership shall be considered thoroughly before the final decision. In many instances it might be seen by the Japanese side as a mere first step to acquire a fully owned subsidiary in a given country. A grace-period would be given only to learn the processes and gain the necessary know-how. However, when both partners have the same stature and their business is of a complementary nature then a reasonable division of labor can be agreed upon. If the matters are clearly defined — which is usually not an easy task — and ultimately agreed upon, then the partnership might turn out to be a long lasting one. Dishonesty on the Japanese side is most unlikely, as long as good human relations are maintained. It goes without saying that in this type of partnership neither partner will interfere with his counterparts management.

Case (5) is most unpredictable. Because there exists a vast variety of good and bad companies in this category in Japan everything is up to a careful screening and selection. Basically this category should provide a lot of interesting potential partners for European companies. Though many middle-sized companies are affiliated with a keiretsu there are still plenty of independent ones. As eager as they are to keep their complete independence at home in Japan as understanding they might be, when it comes to overseas management. Because the management of the better ones can be quite experienced there will never be any harm in taking their advise.

With respect to case (6) it is hard to make any generalizations. But on this level of lesser sophistication it can be observed that shopkeepers, dealers, architects, printers, carpenters or hairdressers have much in common whether they are in Japan or in Europe. It is only the language barrier which poses obstacles to them. The number of individuals setting up shop in Europe will steadily increase in the coming years. For anyone who wants to join their business in Italy or Denmark it is only a matter of screening his or her actual ability. Otherwise they will prove to be uncomplicated partners with common sense .

Likewise, many German, French or Swedish bakers, butchers, restaurant-keepers, dancing teachers, musicians or even doctors of medicine have set up their businesses in Japan in the past and thus contributed to the variety of life in Japan.

The same applies but much more for medium-sized and larger businesses. Thousands of foreign companies work in Japan. The Japanese have learned trade skills, technological know-how and management skills from them. They mainly filled gaps in the industry and market where either Japanese companies have been weak or have simply not existed. There are many reasons to believe that Japanese companies will also serve as an enrichment of the European commercial scene.

The world will continue to see different life-styles. The genuine atmosphere of Ireland, Crete, the Caribbean or Mongolia, different opinions in philosophy or various preferences in religions will, fortunately, continue to exist. But in political structures, social organizations and above all in economical affairs the world will prove increasingly to be borderless indeed.

A proposal, that "in order to ease off a trade confrontation between the three blocks, Asia, Europe and the United States, we should facilitate the emerging Pacific coalition so that it could trade more within itself"[4] seems to point in the wrong direction.

Social Responsibilities

"Social Justice" as an abstract phrase means nothing; but private happiness for individuals and groups is certainly desirable, as proclaimed in "the pursuit of happiness" in the constitution of the USA. So far we could not see that the people in Japan are less happy than elsewhere; to the contrary! Inside Japanese groups there is a lot of laughter and enjoyment, even of small things. With the increasing awareness of Japanese travellers of the high actual living standard in most West European countries this might change in the future; very much propelled by the emergence of a two-class society in Japan: those who own land and those, who do not.

---

[4] B. Hawrylyshyn; Summary; in "European Integration and Global Competitiveness"; 19th International Management Symposium at the University of St. Gallen; St. Gallen 1989

Professor Tamura[5] from the Hosei University at Tokyo reveals his opinion, that Japan in respect of its parks and green space might be trailing up to 200 years behind Paris or London, whereas in the field of adequate housing it could be ranked still behind India or the Philippines. Considering this "it seems quite understandable that workers in other countries do not trust Japanese industrial companies, if the result of their undertakings produces so little in the social standard of their society at home."[6]

Societies in Western Europe shoulder therefore the responsibility for keeping the social standards already achieved. Nevertheless, there are free labor-markets and the employees will only enter into or remain in organizations which are competitive in social achievements. Hundreds of Japanese companies are already working in Western Europe and very little complaints have been expressed hitherto. On the contrary, from Great Britain — and also the USA — it can be heard, that employees in Japanese factories do appreciate the social sense Japanese employers do extend to their workers and the participation they have been granted in organizing their duties on the factory-floors.

General Motors and Toyota established a joint-venture company New United Motor Manufacturing Inc. (NUMMI). Professor Karatsu[7] of Tokai University at Tokyo observed: "Located in Fremont, California, the NUMMI plant was originally constructed by GM. However, its relations with the United Automobile Workers union (UAW) went poorly, with strikes dragging on most of the time, and leading eventually to the plant's closure. When talk of a joint-venture with Toyota surfaced, GM proposed that the Fremont facility be used. The Toyota side said that this would present no problem. However, a demand was made that previously hired UAW members — who had eventually dragged down the plant — be rehired as the labor force Toyota pondered this demand, and came to the conclusion that it, as the only condition involved, could really not be avoided. But the approach adopted by Toyota was special. It brought each of the union members to Japan for six months of thorough training and education, after which it reopened the plant.

---

[5] A. Tamura; Why Money Alone Can't Make the Japanese Affluent; "The Japan Times", January 22, 1987

[6] D. Schneidewind; Bewältigung des Wandels industrieller Strukturen, sowie überseeische Investitionen und Geschäftsführung; W.B.v. Colbe, K. Chmielewicz, E. Gaugler, G. Laßmann (eds) "Betriebswirtschaftslehre in Japan und Deutschland"; Stuttgart 1988

[7] H. Karatsu; The "10000 Visitor Plan" - A Proposal to Revitalize American Industry; Tokyo Business Today; August 1990, Vol. 58

The results have been magnificent. Productivity is twice the U.S. average, while the vehicle quality is on par with Japanese cars. The established theory in America, used to explain the poor quality of U.S. autos and the low productivity of the plants, was the inferior skill of UAW union members. However, the GM-Toyota example proved beyond doubt that this was in error, with the true cause lay in the different management styles.

I am not presenting this story to boast about Japanese accomplishments. Rather, I just want to emphasize that it is possible to build products capable of competing with Japan on American soil, following American laws and utilizing American employees and materials, just as long as the management approach adopted is solid.

Similar observations have been made at Sony or Canon factories in Wales and the USA. It is too early to generalize these experiences. Toyota and Sony are somewhat outsiders in Japan, despite their outstanding achievements. They are considered as newcomers and do not belong to any keiretsu. They have also broken with the Japanese custom of appointing only Japanese managers in their overseas operations. But they do serve as examples for the rest of the Japanese industry, which is keenly observing their successes (or failures).

Apart from companies with superior know-how, it is observed in Japan that those foreign companies succeeded exceptionally, which adopted some Japanese management methods and adhered to the social patterns and customs of their host-market, thus becoming true insiders. Ohmae[8] says, "it is vital for a firm to become an insider in each of the Triad regions" (Triad: USA, Western-Europe, Japan).

Observers of corporate Japan agree that Japanese business conduct and management practices are highly emotional and show a great sensitivity for their employees' needs and desires and dignity. This suggests that Japanese companies deserve a fair chance in Europe and that their contributions might be looked at very favorably in the years to come. Europe will be neither a fortress nor an island; it always has to comply with the future global developments. The bitter experiences of the communist countries substantiate that a detachment from the international experiences and know-how, results in stagnation and loosing ground to the open societies.

On the other hand many Japanese people and organizations do not know and do not care much about the customs and values in other countries. Despite the efforts of many brilliant leaders and scholars in Japan the danger cannot be entirely ruled out that this highly industrialized nation of

---

[8] K. Ohmae; Beyond National Borders; Tokyo New York 1987

123 million inhabitants at the rim of the Western Pacific finds itself isolated and an outsider of the international society some day. In order to avoid this, the EEC should extend a helping and friendly hand to Japan.

The Impact of Japanese Management

Unlike an exact science like mathematics, business administration and entrepreneurial skills are growing differently on the cultural soil of a country. Consequently business philosophies, approaches and objectives are dissimilar in varied societies. Because of the originality and richness of the Japanese culture we can expect also valuable solutions to deal with business matters. Despite the fact that Japanese companies have learned a lot from their competitors overseas, they have integrated that knowledge into their own conduct of management   In the future we can instead expect that some of the art of Japanese management will penetrate the corporate cultures in various other countries.

Also the corporations in the EEC have to face exposure to a partially different management world, when an increasing number of Japanese companies will operate in Europe.

Objectives for Managers and Workers

An American top-manager could point out that his corporation had earned a dividend of 26 cent per share during the last business quarter (on a $5.00 share). A German top-manager would perhaps proudly announce that his company has achieved a real cost-saving of 7.2% versus a cost-saving planning of only 6.8%. A Japanese top-manager is likely to talk about an increase of market share of 9.34% over the previous year, still trailing behind a budgeted 10.25%.

A middle manager in the USA could point out that he performed his job satisfactorily by increasing the earnings of his department by 5% and thus gained himself a fat bonus. A middle manager in Germany would perhaps proudly announce that he has everything in his department "under control". A Japanese middle manager is likely to talk about the useful information which he exchanged with his superior, with his subordinates and with his clients (or suppliers, as the case maybe).

An ordinary employee in the USA could point out that in his present job with Chrysler he gets US $65 a week more than in his former position. An ordinary employee in Germany would perhaps proudly announce that in working with Daimler he had recently performed an excellent job in improving a certain step in the production process. An ordinary employee in Japan is likely to talk about how happy he is to be a Toyota-member and that the company respects him very much so that he in turn will do his utmost, to catch up with every task assigned to him.

To put it in a nutshell — leaving the USA employee aside — the European employee is proud of his own skills and excellent workmanship, whereas the Japanese employee is satisfied to be informed on the objectives of his company, his own — even very small — involvement in planning their execution and his contribution to the smooth success of his team. The European company serves very much as playground for the very personal ambitions and sometimes hobbies of its individuals. The Japanese company serves the national interests of independence and security, the image of the company and as a family for all members to ensure their personal satisfaction and safety.

One cannot foresee what the impact of Japanese corporate objectives on the European management and workers will be. Certainly, hardly anybody will be eager to work for the independence and security of Nippon. But a certain polarization might become established in the long run between European and Japanese corporations. People with individual ambitions will prefer the European type of enterprise. People who like a homely atmosphere and desire to work within a group might prefer the Japanese type of a company.

As long as Japanese companies in Europe make useful contributions to the general industrial scene, they should be welcomed wholeheartedly. If they turned out to dominate certain sectors, invisible but effective barriers for adequate restrictions — which can be studied in the Japanese home environment.— could then be applied, This would be something of a surprise to the Japanese, because they assume that foreigners are not sophisticated enough to invent and implement intricate barriers to outsiders; it hardly crosses their mind that for reasons of fairness or abstract principles — such as free trade — companies in the Netherlands for instance do not resort to hidden protectionism.

But it is rather likely that by living in an international environment, Japanese executives and corporations will assimilate in time various international aspects of business conduct. Only if they are deprived of the opportunities to understand and adopt eventually other countries' management objectives, then they could remain an obstacle for common international beliefs. So far, however, Japanese cause little concern in the international environment, on the contrary they are often praised for genuine new insights into human motivation and organization of labor.

Emphasis on Teamwork

The president of a famous German chemical company pointed out some years ago, that he considered the most important ability of his colleagues in the executive board their capability to work together harmoniously as a team. Indeed the complexity of matrix-organizations has grown so much that their functioning has become highly dependant on the positive collaboration of the numerous personalities concerned.

By their personal character Japanese people seem to be extremely individualistic. Whenever they have a reasonable chance to do so, they build their own house, establish their own company, develop their very personal view of the world and a boundless phantasy in pursuing objects of art. Given the alternative to sing in a chorus or on their own, they prefer usually to perform a song by themselves.

Approximately between 1337 and 1573 Japan was in a state of anarchy and chaos. The imperium was chopped into pieces by old families and new usurpers. Indicatively, this epoch (Muromachi Jidai) was also one of the greatest periods in the history of arts in Japan. The political instability and dispersal of that time continues to be a nightmare for Japanese patriots until today. Unlimited individualism was consequently tamed during the Tokugawa Period by rigid administration systems. Hence the individual had to stand back in favor of the well-being of the community.

Professor Shimizu[9] from Fukushima University describes the idea of collectivism (group-principle), which became the keynote for management in Japanese enterprises after World War II, as "their archetype from the family-system and the village-mentality". He characterizes the mentality of the new corporation communities as "all should be equal, ...everybody's opinions should become standardized, ...severe placing above and placing under, ...conscience of comradeship, and ...not the individual, but the group should shoulder responsibilities".

The absolutely prevailing principle in Japan therefore is group-collectivism above all. As a matter of fact, well guided and well motivated teams, even of individually rather weak persons, do achieve more than

---

[9] T. Shimizu; Japanisches Management; Betriebswirtschaftslehre in Japan und Deutschland; ibid.

mere assemblages of great talents. This phenomenon is well known in the military and in sports

Because a business corporation constitutes a living organism coordination and mutual performance lead to best results. Every part of a chain has to be equally strong. Also the functions of various sections have become so specialized that no single man can control them anymore. The specialists have to collaborate voluntarily. The whole company organism has to be a communication network with informations freely available to anybody who desires it. The old American saying on the shop floors of the "let the people only know what they need to know" has become greatly obsolete.

Japanese organizations have the institution of "chorei," which is a gathering of all employees every Monday for about 40 minutes, where even the scrubwomen are informed that the corporation has achieved certain sales and profits versus the target and the president is about to leave for a business trip to New York. This creates an atmosphere of intimacy with the organization, it renders "big face" to father, when he can disclose to old friends, neighbors and his family how well informed he is.

It has to be seen whether this style of management is attractive to European employees and how European companies will respond in case that this system proves attractive to them. It might well give fresh impulses to the relationship between management and workers.

The ties with one's own group result also in the Japanese attitude to feel obliged to acquaintances and to seek orientation less according to abstract norms. However different the individual groups might be, they all follow but one common target: the maintenance of harmony between the members. The willingness for cooperation, the readiness to come down a peg, and to seek accommodation with the whole, have a greater value than originality and sticking to principles. Europeans appraise intellectual dialogue and the controversial discussion. Whenever Japanese people sit together, statements serve the purpose of creating an atmosphere of contentedness and a feeling of comfort.[10]

Within a group discussion everybody is listened to, even if his arguments are obviously unsuitable for the pursuit of a certain subject. He will not be crudely passed over but can save his face. That makes it easy for him to adjust himself to the prevailing opinion. If he cannot easily be converted and some other participants share his opinion, then the minority is not overruled by the majority, which is an established democratic principle in Europe. Asians call it the terror of a majority. They rather try to involve

---

[10] L.A. Nefiodow; Der fünfte Konradtieff; Wiesbaden 1990

almost all group members in a positive decision, even if that requires compromises.

Sports in Japanese schools follow quite a different pattern than European schools. The winner of an event is not individually acknowledged but can get his medal only, when his team wins as such. He learns very early that any victory is meaningless unless it serves the community. Because ultimately all pupils belong either to the red or blue team and their victory is considered as the main event, at least half of all participants walk away in the evening with a gold medal.

This example elucidates that most Japanese employees do not like to work for foreign enterprises. It could however suggest that a majority of Europeans — at least in northern countries — could find it attractive to give a Japanese employer a try. According to Karl Marx the alienation of the workers from their labor would establish the classes. A Japanese worker is not alone; to the contrary he is integrated into the whole organization and is a member of the winning team. This might explain, why labor disputes in Japan lack the spirit of irreconcilability. Not too bad an achievement of the Japanese company *(kaisha)*.

Self-Autonomous Management

A professionally organized company might run excellently for a certain period of time. But there are two well-known phenomenons:

(1) Technological as well as economical changes will take place and demand changes and adapting to avoid a competitive disadvantage;

(2) it is inherent in natural processes that they permit derailments from time to time. This tendency to chaos, the sister of harmony, generally rules the cosmos.

In the daily pursuit of thousands of smaller and bigger processes continuous deviations from the established programs have to be faced. Adaptions and repairs — usually in minor things — have to be also continually carried out. It is neither possible to establish once and forever a perfect program to cope with all possible events nor is it possible that the supreme management reserves its right to influence decisively all relevant processes.

This requires the establishment of a self-regulating system from the top down to the lowest level and the last employee. In biology we find everywhere cybernetic regulation-systems. Without any instruction from the brain a cancer cell, which invaded the body, will be devoured by killer cells capable to do this job.

In this sense working groups in Japan are self-regulating units. If a machine breaks down, the team members do not sit idle and enjoy the unexpected free time but start to repair the machine by themselves, for which job they are trained and encouraged. Likewise they are authorized and commended for perpetually trying to improve processes. This working philosophy is called "kaizen" and anticipates that nothing is really perfect but everything can be continually improved though by minimal steps. An example of this principle are the Japanese ZD-groups working (Zero Defect).

This explains why time and again the European industry has triumphantly exclaimed that in one or the other field the Japanese competitors had been overcome. That was usually true only for a short period of time. Because of assiduous improvements the Japanese product surpassed its competitors' quality in many cases in the long run. The European champion has a tendency to lean back after a glorious victory and enjoy the fruits of his accomplishment. Differently in Japan after an excellent accomplishment there is only a very brief relaxation and immediately concern is voiced about something else which does not yet work to one's satisfaction.

This whole process reminds one of the selection processes in nature which never cease. A Japanese proverb says: "the way is the goal."

The ever increasing complexity of big modern organizations does not call for simple and autocratic solutions. Rather, it does require engaged teams ready to tackle every task without an instruction by an authority far away.

These actualities demonstrate the importance for European industries to keep in touch with the developments of their Japanese competitors which should preferably be turned into partners. If they are left to their own they might well be able to cause surprises one day to a Euro-centered industry.

The balance-sheets of all companies in the world only show "hard assets". The occasionally more important "soft assets" which ensure the future of an enterprise are for technical reasons not evident:

(1) the potential to create innovations or to deal quickly with innovations which are elsewhere developed;

(2) the image of an enterprise, which for example guarantees the best employees and above-average prices;

(3) the capabilities and the willingness of managers and staffs to adduce efficient results in an enterprise.

Once the general strategic direction is revealed by the top management all layers of an enterprise should be expected to develop initiatives and go ahead in teams of responsibility. This creates the dynamics of a corporation which makes it superior to its competitors.

The time of the big coal mines, rolled-steel mills and textile mills is over; consequently the old American management view is over which looked at workers only as stupid, manipulable and disloyal laborers, which function like mechanical parts.

On the contrary, Japanese team members in process-stages of high-precision technology work mainly autonomous. Their knowledge of the work processes enables them to harmonize their work speed with the departments working before or after them; thus they do not work by abstract instructions but by the rhythm of the actual process. Before any report of a disturbance could reach far-away superiors they have ironed it out in a self-regulating manner. Such procedures are only feasible in a well trained work force, which identifies itself with the company and its general goals.

Such self-organizing capabilities are even more important in the laboratories for research and development. Their team members have to gather informations from various fields like sales and purchase markets on their own. But they have also to consult many research colleagues from different technological fields. If they always have to explain to technologically ignorant superiors why they do this or travel over there, they would lose precious time and end up in frustrations.

But it gives one pause, why the chemical or pharmaceutical industries from overseas have set up their own laboratories in Japan, in the case of Hoffmann La Roche even before they started any other business over there.

Qualitative Aspects

It is deeply ingrained in Japanese people through education to struggle lifelong for excellence. In particular Japanese mothers nourish the dream that their children might become high ranking government officers, win the Nobel Prize for Japan or become at least a company's president. The best and most difficult matters are demanded.

In reality the huge majority of them will end up in positions of tertiary importance. But they may belong to the winning teams of Toyota, Matsushita or Mitsubishi. And these teams chase excellency. Frequently Japanese engineers and artists, too, search for the most difficult performances. Occasionally their courage and naivety will be richly rewarded. Respective decisions in the security of a group, stimulate the gallantry, sometimes too much to be borne by an individual. The group however shows courage and ability to experiment and take on risks. If even a vague chance can be seen, many a Japanese company will establish a small project team that has to tackle nearly impossible tasks. It will grasp even remote developing opportunities, think about bold solutions, experiment with prototypes and present preliminary results only after a few months.

Exactly this report Peters and Waterman[11] about those few American companies to whom they award the title of "excellent company". They complain vehemently that too many big organizations employ too many MBA's, which master well bureaucratic procedures of upper management on one hand, but lack regrettably a feeling for the informal, for the intuitions and the virtually new — in short are not master of the real art of management, on the other hand

The hunt for excellence requires of course not only brilliant fancies but also a simple base, thoughts which can be practically carried out, however non-conventional they might be. Excellent companies in Japan — as elsewhere — favor therefore a corporate culture which takes pride in always commanding the leading position in developments. This does not apply only for new products but also for procedures in purchase, production, logistics, sales and clients' service. In this situation the word *hinshitsu* (quality) acquires an almost sacral character.

Everything important in and around the kaisha has to be first-class. The clerks appear in expensive tailored outfits in the offices, wearing ridiculously sumptuous precision-watches. The most expensive tools and materials are supplied to the factories. Only the very best is qualified to serve the production processes. Equipments and machines have to be state of the art Nevertheless quality is not an end in itself. Excellent quality raises the image of the company; it helps to sell relatively easily and at favorable prices. Quality avoid various costs caused by repairs in the production process and loss of time; but also the costs of recalling goods already delivered and substituted them.

The famous kanban-system expounds the entire production philosophy of Japanese companies. The Japanese factory sees it as its task to provide high quality products and services at relatively low costs at the right time in continuous adaption to the latest developments in technology and consumer preferences. It does not see "production" necessarily in the first

---

[11] T.J. Peters & R.H. Peterman,; In Search of Excellence; Cambridge, 1982

place. Parts and components can be ordered from subcontractors as well, who are familiar, with the working principles of the main company.

The motorcar producer Toyota for instance sees it as a matter of course the desire to win worldwide prestige by excellent products like cars. To arrive at that goal, it is required to have a good research department, a perfect planning system, a high quality standard, low production costs and a lot of flexibility Therefore the company considers the construction on the drawing boards, the disposition of labor, final assembling and self-control as most essential.

On the other side the production of assorted mechanical or electrical parts and components is not considered as one of primary importance. Consequently third parties can be entrusted with their production. Because for reasons of technological sensitiveness and the very high costs involved, there are two exceptions from this rule in respect of big extruding machines and automated production lines for engine blocks.

The mathematical models of cost and manufacturing functions are flanked and coordinated by the very human element, which decides ultimately on a smooth and efficient production process via engagement and motivation. The heading *"kanban"* signals the ultimate vision of a flexible automization, based on a stockfree production process, geared to bring out quality products at the right time just when they are requested by the market. This requires to consider the specific production steps, labor structures and production plans in partnership of management and workshop groups in its entirety.

The resulting quality is consequently a result of an attitude; an attitude which does not neglect any minor aspect in the processes involved. It is ascribed to the catch phrase Total Quality Control (TQC). The claim of TQC is absolute: no faults are permitted. This seems to be in contradiction to the human experience that nothing is perfect. However, experience also tells that nobody is prepared to tolerate mistakes, when the calculation of his own salary is concerned, the functions of his motorcar are explained or he listens to the time-signals of the radio.

TQC recognizes three reasons for faults: carelessness, deficiencies in education and training and inadequate working conditions. And it reasons that all three can be abolished. Certainly nobody can see how an adherence to those principles can hurt the European industry when Japanese companies settle down on EEC grounds.

Technological Advantages and Industrial Norms

The international division of labor in the non-communist countries has advanced very much. Without the direct awareness of their citizens in countries like France and Germany whole industries are shifted from one side to the other. Weak industries rarely survive. Japan holds basically the opinion that it should be autarkic. This does not seem to be a very reasonable attitude for the following reasons:

(1) almost half of the essential supply of food is imported;

2)t he whole industry is based on imported raw materials and fuels, thus they could be cut off in an emergency rather easily;

(3) a large part of Japanese know-how still stems from international patents and licences;

(4) the basic Japanese thinking pattern of *nihonjin* (Japanese) versus *gaijin* (foreigners) is wrong. Japan could never and of course has no need to fight the rest of the world. Japan — like any other nation — needs friends, partners and allies. This, however, requires always to give away a piece of independence. But as the first three points demonstrate already, absolute independence is a fiction at this time. On the contrary the world will further grow together, become borderless and national authorities will lose power.

(5) Japanese companies export already over 15% of the GNP overseas. This is a heavy dependency.

(6) Japanese companies have established big factories and companies overseas and invested otherwise. Apart from the fact that those are precious assets in their balance-sheets, they derive a considerable steady income from them.

(7) Thousands of foreign companies inside Japan do well, employ many people and pay taxes. They spread their technological and management know-how and maintain links to important quarters right back in their countries of origin.

Still many countries suspect that Japan likes to go out but prefers to let nobody into its own territories. However the fact is with patience and perseverance it is very much possible to do good and profitable business in Japan with few exceptions. Regrettably there are various fields in which it has tried to shut out the foreign rivals . Says Ohmae[12]: "In the borderless world, it is harder every day to see where the traditional national interests lie." Nations should not be enemies anymore. However, big and capable

---

[12] K. Ohmae,; The Borderless World; New York 1990

multinational companies are formidable rivals for anyone, regardless of where their head-office is coincidentally located. In this sense bigger and smaller companies with a high technological and managerial level from Japan will be strong competitors for the European industry.

Strategical Assessment

A question raised frequently is: In which fields are Japanese companies particularly strong? There is of course no specific answer — unless one would say they are hard to compete in the field of rice wine (though the Koreans do that successfully) or in the production of Shinto family altars. But because of the basic idea of Japan wishing to be autarkic, its companies are engaged in nearly every type of business, which in turn leads to the situation where there are many old-fashioned and low-level companies in Nippon.

Two basic industrial skills in Japan can be seen in manual dexterity, particularly where tiny items are concerned *and* in coordination. One theory therefore has it that Japanese manufacturers are ahead the more parts go into one product: motorcars, video cameras, pianos, robots. Indeed they are relatively weak in the chemical industry, where not much manual skill is required and only a few dozen components go into the product.

Japanese companies are also strong in the field of project management. Tenders for a huge suspension bridge at Istanbul, a petrochemical complex in Chile or the development of a gold mine in Papua New Guinea will all see Japanese competitors in the forefront. The giant keiretsu provide not only technology and specialists, but also engineering offices, financing, insurance and transportation. They invite also foreign partners in certain instances. But because of the language problem they have a tendency to stay among themselves.

The middle management in a typical big Japanese enterprise might be composed of 65% experts with an engineering or natural science degree, 15% in business administration or cost accounting, and only the remaining 20% have degrees in law, sociology, psychology and others fields. This creates a fruitful atmosphere for technical projects and technological developments. On the executive board level the percentage is still over 35%, compared to just 10% in the USA.[13]

In the following areas Japanese enterprises occupy top positions in the world market: banking, securities, motorcars, ships, steel, camera, au-

---

[13] M. Moritani; Japanese Technology; Tokyo, 1982, pp. 74-79

dio-visual equipments, watches, office-automation, chips, robots, computers, fiber optics, copying machines and passenger bridges at airports.

The basic industrial idea of the Japanese is described by O. Y. Lee[14] in his "Smaller is Better" as follows: "Just as it happened with the fan in the past, the Japanese took something and made it smaller, then turned around and reexported it, gaining control of the market in the process. In the early 1980s, the Japanese developed an even smaller umbrella, one that folds three ways and is the world's shortest, measuring eighteen centimeters. Now the umbrella, just like the fan, can fit in your pocket. Then there is the transistor, which after the war helped Japan break into the international marketplace. This, too, was made possible by the Japanese belief that in order to make something more manageable, more compact, and more functional, one has to make it smaller."

In addition to this, production is regarded highly in Japan and it attracts the attention of the best. Most graduates from universities are first sent to the factory floor to gain some months of experience over there. "In Japan, production runs take off with a bang, quickly reaching yearly outputs of a million units or more. American and European companies are amazed by this. Cautious in their expansion of production, often contenting themselves with simply doubling yearly output over three or four years, these companies are incredulous of the Japanese pace. The principal element in this rapid expansion is active investment in plant and equipment, but what makes this technologically feasible is the unification of development, design and production," says Moritani.[15]

Fuzzy Logic

All technology so far is based on Euclidian geometry and Aristotelian logic and rationalism. Logical and rational thinking is based only on the two alternatives of "true" and "false." Also the whole computer-technology so far is based on this dualistic view. This simple world proved to be very useful and enabled the development of the present status of science and technology.

The calculation of a cloud, of a snow-flake or of a coastline, however, could not be done with those tools. In physics there was no explanation why substance behaved like a wave and the wave could behave like sub-

[14] O.Y. Lee; Smaller is Better; Tokyo, New York, 1984
[15] M. Moritani; ibid.

stance. Nefiodow[16] states: "For the exaggerated application of logic and rationalism did the West pay with disadvantages like loss of entirety, harmony, orientation and mind."

Intuitive knowledge prevents the loss of understanding for the essence of a matter and the reciprocal actions between the parts of the entirety. Intuitive knowledge also combines various factors from different fields and permits between "yes" and "no" a variety of grades like "almost," "nearly," "most close to," "less close to" etc. Mathematically nature will be considered in future as one of fractal geometry. It is calculable by mathematical polyonominals like the iterations. This in turn has become only possible through the super computer generation. "Up to now, all of our examples of dynamical systems have been one dimensional. But most phenomena in nature depend upon more than one variable, often many more variables, so it is appropriate to study higher dimensional dynamical systems."[17]

As so often this new thinking resulting in new mathematical approaches, is being developed in the USA, but remains confined to esoteric scientific circles. With great enthusiasm, however, Japanese engineers have caught up with the new non-monotonous logic. The new keyword "fuzzy logic" was coined. Already the very first programs are applied to stock-market developments and the steering of washing machines with various different textiles. We may also remember that over 90% of all Japanese children finish high schools and that the standards of mathematics are exceptionally high in Japan. That means there exists the possibility that a wholly new technological direction could be occupied in future by the Japanese industry with a considerable advantage of time.

Setting the Pace

So far it is widely recognized that Japanese engineers are very capable in catching-up with highly developed technologies, to further improve them and bring them to perfection. What is not fully noticed yet is that their self esteem and confidence have grown in the mean time. More and more new inventions are done in Japan, though very often acknowledged only with an enormous time-lag by all those countries not capable of reading Japanese magazines and books. The high pace of the new developments

---

[16] L.A. Nefiodow; ibid.

[17]. R.F. Voss; Fractals in Nature: From Characterization to Simulation; H.O. Peitgen, D. Saupe (eds) "The Science of Fractal Images"; Heidelberg, New York, 1988

is particularly amazing. This comes from the total immersion of Japanese scientist into their research projects, where working time is literally unlimited. There are of course no secrecies in Japan's technological and economical success; but one thing is clear, they do barely work harder, but they work longer than other industrial societies; these longer working hours serve the purpose of information and general communication.

Additionally there is the great advantage in getting information on new scientific or technological developments from anywhere in the world in a very short time in a readable language like English or already in Japanese translation. This is because the great trading-houses (sogo shosha) have their information intelligence spread out in all places interesting for industry and trade.

If Japan can maintain its cultural values, then it might be inevitable that it grabs a technological lead for a while and takes on leadership, though the 21st century will not actually become a "Japanese century" as Herman Kahn[18] exclaimed.

The whole Japanese industry is geared to comply with its client's desire to get any deliveries quickly. Especially smaller companies specialize in serving those clients demanding fast services. This requires a high grade of flexibility in those companies and employees not minding to work overtime or on public holidays. In fact, even all department stores are open on Sundays to allow family-shopping. The failures of European companies to succeed in Japan very often derive from the very fact that their executives stick to rather regular working hours to the discomfort of their Japanese business-partners.

Complimentary Cooperation

It should be reiterated that a head on clash between the Japanese and the European industry does not necessarily benefit Europe, despite the revitalizing elements of healthy competition. Rather cooperation can be considered in many fields.

At present Japan is rather strong in the following fields: materials, (high-tension steel, amorphous ceramics, amorphous alloys, new glasses, polymer separation membranes), parts, (charge coupled devices, semiconductor laser, semiconductor memories, liquid crystal display, screws for ultra-precision machine tools, microprocessors), software, (computer operating systems), products/systems, (video casette recorders, copiers, solar

---

[18] H. Kahn; Bald werden sie die Ersten sein; Wien München Zürich, 1970

cells for electricity, magnetic levitation trains, assembling robots, accelerators), biotechnology (bacteria manipulation).

It makes certainly much sense if European companies tie up in these fields with Japanese counterparts. Very interesting in this context is the general intent of collaboration between the Mitsubishi Group and the newly-welded technology concern of Mercedes Benz, who reconfirmed their interests in October 1990 in Tokyo to screen promising areas of cooperation.

At present Japan is rather weak in the following fields: software (databases, CAD, CAM), and products/systems (aircraft engines, magnetic resonance imaging).

The Science and Technology Agency of the Japanese government predicts that Japan will make considerable progress in or even succeed — among others — the following projects by the year 2000[19]:

Large optical disc memories,
Use of CAD for large scale integrated circuits (LSI),
Room temperature superconducting materials cooled by liquid nitrogen,
Optical heterodyne methods (coherent optical communication),
Word processors with handwritten input,
Use of synchroton orbital radiation for LSI production,
Use of cell fusion to develop fast growing trees,
Use of amorphous silicon solar cells capable of converting 20% solar energy into power,
Inner city car traffic control,
Recycling of radioactive waste,
Use of low noise railways and wheels,
Use of light in telecommunications without converting light into electrical signals.

In order to achieve these goals almost all major companies in Japan will increase their R&D budgets. It can be expected that many of the ambitious targets will fall short in their schedules because of difficulties not anticipated. Here it would be advisable to seek mutual cooperation and assistance between European and Japanese companies. To prepare for this, European industry has to track all developments in the Japanese industry. The American industry has realized this necessity already. The Ministry of Trade of the USA has recently issued in a "Japan Technology Program"

---

[19]Toyo Keizai Inc.; The Year 2000: Wonderland Around the Corner; Tokyo Business Today, August 1990, Vol 58

three handbooks and one bulletin on developments of technology research in Japan.

The bulletin contains technical studies, product developments, excerpts from articles of technological interest and newsletters of Japanese companies. The handbooks are titled as follows: Directory of Japanese Databases, Directory of Japanese Technical Reports, Directory of Japanese Technical Resources. They can be ordered from the National Technical Information Service of the Ministry of Trade under the chiffre NTIS PB 90- 163072. [20]

Cooperations between European and Japanese corporations can also be enhanced in geographical areas and there in specific technical fields. As Japanese companies are welcomed in Europe, Japan should welcome European companies as well in Japan and the neighboring Pacific region. It would be naive to expect that most promising markets would be served to the European industry on a silver plate. One has to find out which segments of which markets could be of interest and then approach prospective Japanese partners accordingly. The know-how in respect to Japanese culture and corporate behavior counts as much as any technical know-how — or in many instances even more.

With the USA, China, Japan and potentially also the Soviet Union, the largest portion of the world population is living in that famous trapezoid Bangkok, Anchorage, Houston and Perth (West-Australia). Whether there will be a Pacific era or not, no corporation of self-respect can dare not to be strongly represented in that vital economic hemisphere.

But also outside this area the opportunities for joint projects are unlimited. Neither can the Europeans develop Eastern Europe on their own nor can Latin America — not to mention Africa in its desolate state of development — nor could the Japanese do it alone. With joint strength also the oil producing Arabic countries could be kept in a reasonable partnership. All this visions might be looked at as far away and located in a fantasy land; but the opportunities *are* realistic. The partners have only have to realize that they could never manage those projects without joining forces, that they have to develop trust in each other and that *one* has to do the first step.

Despite the main concern of an industrial perspective between the EEC and Europe the USA should not be left out of any global industrial order. Only the three triad members together are able to solve the manifold problems and take on the numerous chances in the economic arena of the entire world. Good industrial relations between equal partners like Japan and the EEC are much desired. But their purpose must be the well-being of

---

[20]Blick durch die Wirtschaft; Wo hat Japan seine technischen Stärken?; December 17, 1990

their citizens and they do not benefit from the exclusion of a mighty power house like North America.

Once more: The USA has been the biggest economic power in the world hitherto. Europe has to face the reality that Japan has arrived meanwhile on equal terms and deserves its respective place and role in the world. Japan has to bury the perhaps wishful thinking that Europe is a declining area and consequently there are only two rivals left in the global arena. Europe is very confident at this time that it will come back technologically and economically very strongly in the years to come.

The tradition of technological cooperation between Europe and Japan is very long, starting with the Portuguese and Dutch 450 years ago and reaching over the early Meiji Period into the presence. A huge number of technical assistance agreements, technical cooperations and joint-ventures have successfully been carried out to the mutual benefit of both partners. This tradition has to be carried on.

U.S.-Japan Relations:
Implications for Europe

Andreas van Agt
Ambassador, Delegation of the
Commission of the European Communities

Some time ago, the *New York Times* carried an article on its front page entitled "U.S. ads increasingly attack Japanese and their culture". According to that article, American advertisers are stepping up their attacks on Japan and its people, attempting to thwart sales of Japanese products through commercials that feature ominous references to the late Emperor Hirohito, photographs of Samurai warriors, exaggerated accents and veiled ridicule of the Japanese physique. The newspaper article presents some examples of such advertisements and one cannot feel but disgusted about their racist tone.

These wicked advertisements epitomize the hostile atmosphere towards Japan that is developing in the United States. The public relations experts who drafted the ads apparently felt that they would appeal to the public. Many Americans harbor confused feelings vis-a-vis Japan (as do many Europeans). On the one hand, there is admiration and respect for that country's miraculous achievements; on the other hand, there is *envy and rancor.* Envy always grows with success like weeds in a cornfield. The other day, I read a marvelous book about the Dutch in their Golden Age (the 17th century) and it vividly describes how at the time my ancestors were the target of widely-acclaimed Holland-bashing.

Envy and rancor: from where does the rancor stem? It is multidimensional, I think. Firstly, the Americans have to come to grips with the reallotment of power in our world. They are no longer calling the tune, but have to share power with others — collective management of world affairs. Sometimes, the United States behaves like John McEnroe at Wimbledon, scolding the umpire and the linesmen, instead of just acknowledging that other players have risen to eminence.

Secondly, it is difficult to accept and to digest for the Americans to be overtaken, in some respect by — of all people — the Germans and the Japanese. It is not so much the victor and the vanquished relationship that matters. What generates gripes is that the Americans having contributed generously some decades ago to these defeated countries' recovery, feel badly treated now, a bit like a father who once bought a shop for his son in the same town, and sees himself outrivaled by the newly-installed entrepreneur's competition.

There is even a third dimension. Why is it that there is so much Japan-bashing and *hardly any Germany-bashing?* West Germany's balance of merchandise trade features a higher global surplus than Japan's; why, then, is it that Japan is singled out as the malefactor? For a variety of reasons: West Germany is a market that outsiders consider more open than Japan; West Germany has a much higher propensity to import manufactured goods (though I should add here that Japan's imports of manufactured goods have been growing rapidly over the last years). West Germany's huge trade surplus is spread much more evenly around the world. And, finally, whereas there is a lot of American and other foreign investment in Germany (and elsewhere in Europe), there is little foreign investment in Japan — consequently, Americans are hardly profiting from Japan's economic boom. These facts and figures substantiate the charges against Japan. However, the Japanese perceive a lot of discrimination, cultural prejudices and even traces of racism and they are not totally wrong.

It should not go unmentioned here that over the last four years, Japan's trade surplus with the United States decreased rapidly and substantially. In 1987, that surplus reached a record high (over $56 billion), whereas last year it came down to $41 billion. That is a steep decline indeed. President Bush recalled the other day that Japan buys more goods per capita from the U.S.A. than the U.S.A. does from Japan and that U.S. exports to Japan are now 75% higher than only four years ago.

A much talked about about issue in this context is Japanese direct investment in the U.S. There is talk all around about buying-out, economic colonization — often in a language that hints at warfare. Various bills have been submitted by members of Congress aiming at checking or impeding foreign investment. Their real target is Japan. There is much ado about takeovers and purchases by Japanese companies. Similar transactions by other non-American companies do not ruffle anyone's feathers, in spite of the fact that investments from European Community countries, in particular from the UK, vastly outnumber those from Japan. What annoys the Japanese more is the fact that over thirty American states run offices in Tokyo filled with people whose calling is to entice as many Japanese companies as possible into investing in Kentucky, Ohio, Minnesota or Tennessee, and so on. The more Japanese Companies lend their ear to these seducing calls, the louder the outcry in America against their presence.

In the recent past, Japan has come under heavy criticism in the U.S. Congress and in the media for what was perceived as foot-dragging in taking its share of the Gulf crisis burden. As a matter of fact, though, Japan's contribution towards the costs of the Gulf War was the highest among the industrialized countries ranking third after the countries directly interested, i.e., Saudi Arabia and Kuwait. And many critics ignored that it was the postwar Constitution imposed by MacArthur that prevented Japan from sending military personnel and equipment to the Gulf. The big mistake Japan made was to take too much time before offering its contribution: again a matter of political infighting displaying its endemic paralysis, its systemic inability to make bold and well-timed political decisions.

However, let us not indulge in overstatements and generalizations. Dissenting opinions can be heard as well. Cyrus Vance, Secretary of State in the Carter Administration, for example, raised his voice arguing that Japan's economic prowess, combined with a rapidly-fading Soviet threat, has generated a new sense of rivalry and anxiety. Too many politicians and publicists, he said recently, have exacerbated this situation by playing on popular anxieties, arousing fear and anger. The Japanese have reacted with mounting nationalism and frustration. If the world's two greatest economic powers — Vance says (apparently overlooking the European Community for the moment) — allow this emotional infection to lead to real hostility, both will be the poorer and the less secure.

The U.S. Administration is much closer to Cyrus Vance's view than is Congress. President Bush and his team have conducted talks with persistence and determination, but at the same time have withstood the pressure to incriminate Japan anew as an unfair trading nation under the Omnibus Trade Act. Attempts at hitting Japan by legislative action are, time and again, parried by the U.S. Government.

The stakes are high indeed. The American military presence in Europe and in East Asia is viewed by quite a few countries as reassuring. When, in the event of a rupture with Japan, the latter country were to go it alone closing U.S. bases and ceasing to pay substantial amounts for common defense, then keeping up a forward presence in the Pacific would become problematic for the U.S., while other Asian countries (China in particular) could feel the need to reinforce their military capabilities — hence destabilization in the entire region.

The economic consequences of a divorce between the U.S. and Japan would be equally damaging. Cooperation between these two economic giants is indispensable for the stability and health of the world economy. The United States is Japan's largest export market and Japan ranks second on the list of markets absorbing U.S. products (third when the EC countries are counted together as one market). A huge percentage of America's budget deficit is financed with Japanese money. Japan is shouldering an ever-increasing part of the burden that goes with world affairs management. It is now in absolute terms development aid donor number one; it has joined the efforts undertaken by the G24 on behalf of Eastern Europe and it has been called upon to contribute substantially (together with Western Europe) to the implementation of President Bush's Central America Initiative. Is it not appropriate to mention here that, according to authoritative estimates (*Journal of Commerce,* April 11, 1990) one third of the U.S. trade deficit can be blamed on falling exports to Latin America over the last decade? It follows that the wealthiest country in the world can play a crucial role in rebuilding the economies of that continent and thus in readjusting structural imbalances in the global economy, not in the least to the benefit of the United States.

The Structural Impediments Talks were crowned with a remarkable success, from the U.S. viewpoint. The pledges made by Japan exceeded most observers' expectations. Does that mean that the marriage crisis is over?

Not necessarily. The implementation of the Japanese part of the deal is bound to be a painstaking and time-consuming affair. Results in terms of drastic changes in the balance of trade cannot reasonably be expected in the short run. Americans, for all their manifold virtues, are not renowned for their patience and American congressmen have to face re-election every two years, which is not helpful in that regard. Impatience could spawn frustration and anger and all the hullabaloo of retaliatory and punitive actions could quite conceivably be relaunched before long. In that event, a backlash could easily occur in Japan. That would be a serious regression. The SII success is largely attributable to the emergence of an alliance between American demands and ever-more-loudly expressed wishes from within the Japanese society, a convergence of external and internal pressures that only together were forceful enough to break the dams. Were the shelling from Capitol Hill to be resumed while Japan is in the midst of a laborious process of adjustment, national pride would quite likely dictate a collective response by Japan.

There is one more snake in the grass: the SII pact also contains *American promises,* such as lowering the budget deficit, improving the education system, enhancing the competitiveness of U.S. industries. All these things are needed, for the sake of America's own future. But, are these undertakings really going to be executed, as of now or in due course? There is reason for some concern about this. For a long time, the White House and the political leaders in Congress have been jockeying for a deficit reduction deal. The deal has been struck but the prospected results might be put in jeopardy because of setbacks such as the savings and loans disaster and the need to increase government expenditure for pressing problems as the transport infrastructure and education (in a political climate where tax hikes and higher energy prices are still virtually taboo).

Without structural adjustments on the American side, there is no prospect for a substantial and lasting rebalancing, not even if Japan were to deliver all the homework assigned to it without insisting on reciprocity. Japan's industry invests more in plant and equipment than the U.S. does, even though the U.S. economy is twice as large. Japan spends almost a quarter of its GNP on plants and equipment! Japan's expenditures for non-defense R&D, measured as a percentage of GNP, exceed those of the United States by over fifty percent: 1.9% as compared to 2.9% (1988). Others should take that to heart!

We should indeed call into question whether Japan's stunning success on world markets is just a matter of unfairness on their part, inaccessibility of their domestic market to foreign merchandise and a persistent non-observance of the rules of the game. I do not disclaim these allegations altogether. But the question has to be raised whether it is equitable to wholly blame our Asian trading partners and, furthermore, whether our incessant whining over unfair trade practices and predatory behavior really serves our own interests. Are we not blindfolding ourselves to our own shortcomings and deficiencies? Would it not be more beneficial to our own interests to acknowledge that Japan's successes are, to a large degree, a matter of outstanding quality, sharp prices, reliability of delivery and outperforming after-sales-service?

For quite a while, we have resorted to using excuses such as the assertion that the Japanese were only in the business of copying ideas and inventions made by others. Suffice it to put on record in this context that Hitachi, Toshiba, Cana Kubushiki and Mitsubishi Denki were the top four on the list of companies to obtain patents in the U.S. in 1989 and that last year Japanese companies were the top five.

Observing the bilateral bickering between the U.S. and Japan, Europeans could feel tempted to laugh in their sleeves. That would, however, be narrow-minded. We have *nothing to gain* from an unarmed war between these two. Just like our trading partners should rejoice at the prospect of a prosperous and thriving Europe, so are our interests served best by unarrested economic growth in their countries. An economic decline, or even a considerable slow-down of growth in Japan or the U.S. (or in both of them) brought about by economic warfare, cannot but unsettle the global economy and reduce world trade upon which we Europeans are largely dependent. Such developments would, moreover, feed protectionist tendencies all over the place and the game would end up with only losers. Since our economies are much more strongly intertwined with the U.S. economy than with that of Japan, both in terms of exports/imports and in terms of mutual investment, it is particularly the damage inflicted on our transatlantic partner that would affect U.S. But, in a longer-term perspective the negative impact on our well-being would reach further.

The U.S. has long-standing relationships both with Europe and with Japan. Europe and Japan do not (yet) have similar ties. The third leg of the triangle is no more than a dotted line.

Japan is, however, seeking to intensify its relations with Europe. This reflects, of course, its recognition of Europe's economic clout and market potential. But this attempt at rapprochement is also prompted by the looming uncertainties about the U.S. as a marketplace and as a political ally. Until recently, reactions in Europe to these Japanese advances have been rather lukewarm on the whole, though attitudes differ considerably from country to country with regard both to Japanese direct investment and to exports from Japan. There is no zest for more political cooperation with Japan.

The ice is about to break; has the thaw set in? On July 11, 1991, a Europe-Japan Declaration was signed, much on Japanese insistence, calling for a broadening of cooperation and setting the stage for an institutionalized dialogue. That document puts a strong emphasis on economic and trade relations, but is not limited to these traditionally contentious matters.. It also establishes a mechanism for other, notably political, consultations. Whether the lofty language of the Declaration is translated into a full-fledged relationship with a meaningful political dimension remains to be seen.

I think there is a case for *stronger political ties* between Europe, the Community in particular, and Japan. It is not fully consistent for us to expostulate with Japan incessantly on its international responsibilities and, at the same time, to keep it at bay when it comes to issues vital for world peace such as the proper functioning of the Helsinki process. Japan could be associated with that process. It is the Soviet Union's Eastern neighbor. Furthermore, it has met our request to participate in the rescue operation of Eastern Europe and to take an important share in the European Bank for Reconstruction and Development. Europe, in return, could insist on a closer involvement in the Asia-Pacific cooperation mechanisms that are currently in the making.

And what about a review of our stances in the still unresolved dispute between Japan and the Soviet Union over the four islands occupied by the Red Army after a Declaration of War as late as August 9, 1945? To date, this seemingly futile issue has blocked all progress towards improved relations between these two countries. It is not just in Japan's interest only that this stumbling block be removed. If we genuinely believe that the Soviet Union in transition needs substantial support from the West, albeit under certain conditions still to be agreed upon, then we should subtly deploy our political skills (and clout) to help clear the channels through which Japanese capital and technology could flow in abundance to the ailing giant. The President of the United States, during his latest summit meeting with President Gorbachev, urged the Soviets to remove this stumbling bloc; the Europeans should align themselves with this stance.

I just referred to attempts being made at forging an economic grouping in the East Asia-Pacific region. The Asia Pacific Cooperative Initiative was launched by Australia, not by Japan, for Tokyo is politically disabled in Asia by an unhappy past. The undertaking is still early in its formative phase, but it has the potential of developing into a powerful organization and one in which Japan's role would be pivotal. It should be noted here that the U.S. (and Canada) joined this initiative and do take an active part in the deliberations.

The Australians and their newly-acquired allies acted in response to the creation of economic regions elsewhere in the world: U.S.-Canada, which could be extended shortly to encompass Mexico also, and the EC Single Market 1992, which is to be enlarged so as to also comprise the EFTA countries. By the way, there has been talk (begun prior to the Australian action) about the creation of a U.S.-Japan Free Trade area, but that project looks like being shelved.

Is this proliferation of economic groupings leading to an erosion of multilateralism and the unhampered development of world trade? Or could it help to underpin the free trade systems of GATT? It all depends on whether or not GATT will be consolidated and reinforced in the current *Uruguay Round.*

In conclusion, therefore, I would like to make a couple of observations on that Round. The GATT negotiations are now about to enter into their final stage. It is the most encompassing and most ambitious of all ventures ever undertaken since, shortly after World War II, GATT was put into place. Negotiations are taking place in no less than fifteen groups. Impressive results have already been posted. Attention is nevertheless concentrated now on the areas where negotiations have not yet been able to bridge the yawning gaps separating the various positions: agriculture, textiles market access, to mention the most critical issues. The Americans backed up by quite a few other countries have made agricultural reform the centerpiece of the Round, the key to its success or failure. The Community and its member states reject this overemphasis on agriculture, as opposed to other important subjects and maintain serious objections against what the Americans want to achieve in the agricultural sector.

I am not going to scrutinize here and now the various positions and their merits or flaws. But , as the day of reckoning draws near, we should reflect on the *consequences of a collapse* of the Round. The consequences of such a breakdown would be so serious that I really cannot believe that the main players would allow such a disaster to occur.

First of all, we would not succeed in introducing worldwide accepted rules regarding trade in services, protection of intellectual property and cross-border investment. Such rules are badly needed in order to keep GATT abreast of sweeping developments in international trade.

Secondly, a collapse of the Uruguay Round could — and almost certainly would — trigger an avalanche of protectionist actions and reactions and it would give a strong boost towards bloc-ism, interegional rivalry and unilateralism.

Finally, ending in discord would shake the transatlantic partnership and it would take considerable time to repair the damage. An exchange of recriminations would spoil the atmosphere between America and Europe, differences would prevail for some time and in the United States trends toward isolationism and unilateralism, a let-us-mind-our-own-business attitude could get the upperhand.

Japan may take some pleasure, understandably, in watching this wrestling match between others. But it is bound to suffer seriously from the upsurge of protectionism that might ensue.

An old metaphor says: Every morning a gazelle awakens. She knows that to save her life, she will have to run faster than the fastest lion. Every morning, a lion awakens. He knows that to escape starvation, he will have to be faster than the slowest gazelle. It virtually makes no difference whether you are a gazelle or a lion, when the sun rises, you will have to make sure that you are running.

When the Uruguay Round winds up, who will be the gazelle and who will be the lion?

Hopefully, this question has lost its meaning by then. The negotiations may have yielded a miraculous set of agreements and a psalmatic peace may have descended on the battlefields. Lion and lamb repose brotherly together and with them the Asian dragon. Just a daydream? No, it is confidence that, in the end, statesmanship will prevail.

A Western Critique of
Japan's Development Aid

Manfred Kulessa
University of St. Gall

"Japan's economy is changing, but your complaints don't."

Saburo Okita

This remark, addressed to Americans in 1989, contains some general truth. Contacts and exchanges have increased, but there are still many misunderstandings between Japan and the West. In Europe, for instance, it is generally assumed that Japan's economic successes are being achieved at the expense of Japanese workers' living standards; yet Japan topped the list of countries in the Human Development Reports of 1990 and 1991 which put Japanese quality of life before that of the Swiss or Scandinavians. Likewise, our perception of Japan's Official Development Assistance (ODA) may stand in need of correction.

Japan has been "world champion" of aid since 1989. This may explain why Japanese ODA has become a subject of interest to Western scholars and politicians. But why, then, is it still an item for *gaiatsu* or Japan-bashing? Four reasons offer themselves for a preliminary answer: the general disappointment with aid everywhere, the very fact that Japan is the largest donor nation, the recognition that it is the only OECD country with a potential for expanding ODA, and finally the vague hope that Japan, further assuming a global role as lead donor, may find a way to new qualities of international cooperation.

In May 1991, a Japanese-U.N. sponsored forum in Tokyo presented a vivid demonstration of the last two reasons mentioned. A prominent group of participants, led by Saburo Okita, Robert McNamara, and Helmut Schmidt, argued that Japan could do much better, recommending an ODA level of 1% of GNP. If this goal could be reached by tripling present contributions, Japan would clearly become *the* dominant donor with a share of over 40% of global ODA and obvious consequences for its say in international organizations.

For Okita, the one percent figure has been "a personal target" since long. The Westerners found it convenient to argue that defense and aid spending had to be seen as one contribution to international security, peace, and welfare. Comparing GNP figures allocated for these purposes (United States: 5.5% and 0.15%; leading European economies: 3.5% and 0.4%; Japan: 1% and 0.32%), they saw much room for improving Japan's contribution; and realizing that a major military build-up was out of question in view of fears and suspicions in Asia, stepping up ODA appeared to be the logical conclusion. The meeting, meant to foster support to LDCs, even talked about re-defining aid and about its new quality. If not before, Japanese ODA should now become a major subject of international research and policy dialogue. A closer look at its strength and weakness is indeed warranted, and it would have to take account of the contemporary aid critique.

Western scientific interest in Japan's development policies appears to be a rather recent phenomenon. In 1975, Sukehiro Hasegawa published his book on Japanese foreign aid in New York.[1] About ten years later, the topic had become an issue of some importance to insiders of international cooperation. In 1984, Michael Hofmann of the German Development Institute went to Japan and wrote his report on Japan's development assistance from "a German view."[2] Only towards the end of the 1980s when Japan moved to the top of the donor list, its ODA became a subject of priority interest to researchers in the field of development cooperation policy, soon resulting in a multitude of publications and a good number of international meetings. In Germany, two highly analytical books were then written by Bernhard May,[3] a foreign policy expert, and Franz Nuscheler,[4] prominent scientist in the field of development cooperation policy. The latter, though rather outspoken in his critical assessment of qualitative deficits in Japanese ODA, was recently invited to Japan when his book appeared in a Japanese translation, just about one year after the first German edition. In short, the discussion on Japan's ODA is on, and Japan has created its own institutions, such as FASID, to support it.

---

[1] Sukehiro Hasegawa: Japan's Foreign Aid: Policy and Practice, New York 1975
[2] Michael Hofmann, Japan's Development Assistance: A German View; *IDE* Tokyo 1985 (*DIE* Berlin 1984)
[3] Bernhard May: Japans Neue Entwicklungspolitik; Munchen 1989
[4] Franz Nuscheler, Japans Entwicklungspolitik; Hamburg 1990.

The Donor Position

Japan and Germany, the two main former enemies of the United States, became involved in development assistance rather early, not more than ten years after the war. Both were strongly motivated by pressure from the United States, their post-war donor, political mentor and senior ally, as well as by the pursuit of national interest which was primarily of the economic kind in the case of Japan and somewhat more political in the case of Germany, — a difference easily explained by historical and geopolitical reasons. Over the years, the two countries have become fairly solid and predictable players in the global ODA game. In the meantime, however, value and purposes of the exercise itself have become matters of dispute and doubt all over the world. We notice a certain disillusionment with foreign aid which is being considered as rather ineffective, creating dependency, and showing its limitations as a typical phenomenon of the post-colonial era following World War II. Perhaps, that could explain why ODA has become a rather stagnant business, subjected to vested interests of the aid industry and its bureaucracy on both sides and, consequently, being criticized from left and right, North and South. By now, we know what is good and bad about foreign aid. In fact, ODA may well be something like an outgoing model of international cooperation; and it would already have disappeared if there had been sufficient moral conviction and political determination to create a better and more equitable world order. There is no reason for our Japanese colleagues not to discover such facts of life which contribute to "aid fatigue" in other quarters.

Throughout these years, aid policy had also been a matter of consultations between governments, mostly at the multilateral level through OECD-DAC discussions and reviews, but also bilaterally. When Prime Minister Takeshita visited Germany in May 1988, the joint communiqué about his discussions with Chancellor Kohl contained the following paragraph on ODA:

"We also talked about our common responsibility as big and prosperous industrial nations in our relationship to others, to the poor peoples and countries of the world. We agreed explicitly to consider where we could strengthen and intensify our cooperation, e.g. in the filed of development aid, also to the benefit of the people, whom we would like to assist."

Such basic understanding led to a German-Japanese Forum on Development Policy, held in Berlin in December 1989[5], and to further bilateral consultations. While, in earlier years, the United States and other donor countries had mainly urged Japan to increase its contribution, the discussion has now moved to issues of quality improvement and aid coordination.

When quantitative levels of aid were still the main topic, — as may happen again if the U.S. Congress and the new McNamara should find their advice not being followed — , the argument was usually summed up in terms of "burden-sharing". As I was told, such concept of equal and joint responsibility could be referred to as *yakuwari*. However, the term *katagawari* (shoulder-shifting), applied here, describes a different mode of operation: When a shrine is moved through town in procession, it is carried by people from different neighborhoods within their precinct until it is shoulder-lifted to the next neighborhood team. Thus, *katagawari* could mean that Japan is offering a measure of relief to the United States and other donors when shouldering a heavy load of ODA. Perhaps, this is a more realistic perception: while Japan has doubled its contribution, the total of globally committed ODA has not increased much at all.

Such type of cooperation implies a leadership role. Similarly, the movement of flying geese, often used to describe the pattern of economic development of Pacific Asian nations, requires a lead goose in order to function. Japan, naturally, is assuming this role. It has done so in the process of economic upswing, is now doing so in shouldering the main burden of ODA, and is preparing itself for assuming leadership roles in other fields of regional and global cooperation. However, these are clearly temporary functions, as the zoologist will confirm: during long flights, the clever geese follow the *katagawari* mode, taking turns in assuming the leadership position.

It can be safely assumed that the WIDER (Okita-Jayawardena-Sengupta) study, published in 1987, was instrumental in initiating what its title aimed at: mobilizing international surpluses for world development.[6] It suggested to recycle the amount of $25 billion annually into developing countries through a Japan Trust Fund over a period of five years. It also boldly declared that Japan " is in a position to aim for tripling ODA over the period 1985-90." While the government did not follow these suggestions in total, it certainly took major steps in the indicated direction; and if it contin-

[5]For the report see Publications of the Japanese German Center Berlin, Vol. 2, 1990
[6]Okita, Jayawardena, Sengupta; Mobilizing International Surpluses for World Development: A WIDER Plan for a Japanese Initiative, *WIDER Study Group Series* No. 2, 1987

ues further in line with the 0.7% of GNP target occasionally reconfirmed as a basic guideline, it would surely triple its ODA at least over a ten year period. Right now, Japan ranks somewhere in the lower middle field of the OECD-DAC countries, having spent, in 1989, 0.32 % of GNP or $75 per citizen on ODA.

The Japanese Perspective

Like human beings, nations are rarely motivated by a single consideration; their donor attitude is determined by a bundle of motives which are not all clearly spelled out. On a global scale, some once forceful strains of aid motivation have receded in recent years, e.g. the ideological and strategic competition between East and West and the need to secure access to natural resources as raw materials for industrial production. Others have come to the forefront, such as the concern about the deteriorating global environment. Security threats are no longer seen merely in arms and lethal weapons, but also and perhaps even more so in population pressures and international migration or in narcotic drugs, fundamentalist fanaticism, and hitherto unknown diseases such as AIDS[7]. However, while identifying these problem areas and the resulting motives as issues of global dimension, we cannot overlook the historical and geopolitical angle from which they are being viewed. Often enough, such viewpoints may make a difference.

Saburo Okita, the grand old "Mister Japan International", came to Germany a number of times in recent years and also attended the German-Japanese forum meeting in 1989. When, during informal discussion, he was asked why Japan seemed to be immune against "Gorbi-mania" then prevailing in the West, he patiently explained the different historic perspective. In the war, Germany had invaded the Soviet Union. "What the Soviet Union is to Germany, China is to Japan. Japanese feel guilty about China, not about the Soviet Union[8]. Japanese women, just to illustrate the point, buy little dolls called "Gorbi-teishu" (husband-Gorbi), implying that the Soviet leader, like a typical Japanese husband, is active and popular outside, but less useful and appreciable at home.

---

[7]For a typical example of identifying these new motives see Manfred Wöhlcke; "Risiken aus dem Süden"; *Stiftung Wissenschaft und Politik*, Ebenhausen, 1991

[8]For Okita's account of this conversation, see *International Herald Tribune,* August 8, 1990

War reparations, especially those paid to Burma, can probably be considered the first stage of Japan's development cooperation, although friends of the multilateral efforts could also point at the Colombo Plan contribution starting as early as 1954 when Japan was otherwise still at the receiving end of economic assistance. Comparatively soon, Japan started lending and investment activities in line with its general policy of economic cooperation and, beginning from the mid-1960s, with its foreign policies in Asia. It was more than two decades later that Japan felt ready to shoulder the responsibility of an economic super power in true *katagawari* spirit; and it was only in recent years that, as a major current account surplus country, Japan accepted the necessity of a large scale recycling operation.

It is easy to imagine that the stability of China ranks high on Japan's policy agenda, not only because of the feeling of historical obligations which made Prime Minister Kaifu apologize to the Asian neighbors as late as in 1991, but also in view of security threats that could emanate from a destabilized and chaotic Chinese situation which could land, just to mention one of many shocking scenarios, millions of boat people at Japan's shores. No wonder that Kaifu was also the first G-7 leader to visit China and to ask for normalization of relations in August 1991.

Critique at Home

Against the background of world-wide skepticism about development aid, it cannot surprise that the new emperor in ODA has not much clothes to show, either. Sometimes, however, Western criticism of Japan's assistance reminds us of a boxing match where most punches are thrown at directions from where the partner has just moved away. As in many other fields, the country is changing very fast. Already, we observe Japan becoming as adaptable to insights and fashions in foreign aid as any other donor. In fact, we now recognize a major effort to improve ODA performance, both in its presentation and in its practical implementation. While still being accused of patterns of imitation and of committing mistakes Western donors are claiming to have overcome, Japan's ODA can be expected to find its own style and character soon.[9]

---

[9]See, for instance, Ryokichi Hirono, Japan's Official Development Cooperation; in
Performance, Issues and Prospects in the 1990s, *Publications of the Japanese-German Center Berlin*,
Vol. 4, 1991 pp.143-156

Some of the criticism appears indeed obsolete, having been over-taken by events. Those who complain about a lack of awareness in environmental issues could find themselves confronted with Saburo Okita's guiding essay on "Ecology and Resources" of 1989.[10] Those who had pointed at Japan's heavy concentration on aid to Asian countries must have been surprised to see her new emphasis on providing assistance to Africa as explained by Masao Kawai at the Berlin forum of 1989:

"Africa is remote from Japan. We have had few historical and cultural ties with Africa. Yet we are being urged to give special attention to that continent, and we have been responsive. Since 1977, Japan has increased assistance to sub-saharan African countries ten times over. Japan is the top bilateral donor in four African countries, Kenya, Zambia, Malawi, and Nigeria in 1987. Not only bilaterally, but Japan is the No. 2 contributor to the African Development Bank from outside the region and No. 1 contributor to the African Development Fund."

A good number of authors have mentioned the fact that, like the famous "ugly American," there are "ugly Japanese" as well in the aid business.[11] This is a fact. However, we know from personal experience in Asia that, in spite of the burden of history, Japanese experts are usually well adapted and integrated, respecting culture and tradition of the host country. Perhaps, foreign experts have to be considered as "ugly" by definition. But the Japanese surely do not have to fear the comparison with their Western colleagues.

In this connection, it is important also to listen to critical voices from Japan's scientific community. As far as we could observe, Japanese critics of their country's ODA performance seem to raise more or less the same issues as their Western counterparts. Jun Nishikawa,[12] for instance, complains about the low grant element, insufficient attention being given to Least Development Countries, lack of global orientation, the "Japan Inc." character of ODA, its preference for large infrastructure projects, priority still being given to economic growth while neglecting ecological concerns as well as those of human rights and dignity, and last not least, about the lack of a unified administrative structure. Osamu Muro,[13] a development educationist well known for his leading role in promoting international volunteerism and NGO activities in Japan, points at the limited role of the

---

[10]Saburo Okita; Approaching the 21st Century: Japan's Role, Tokyo, 1990, pp. 194-212

[11] Nuscheler, pp. 106-108

[12] Jun Nishikawa; Japan's Economic Cooperation: New Visions Wanted, *Japan Quarterly* Oct-Dec 1989, pp. 393-403; and *FASID,1990 Symposium Report* , pp. 26-28

[13] Osamo Muro; Perspective on Overseas Aid; *The Japan Times,* October 19, 1983. The remarks mentionned here were presented to the author in December 1989 and in November 1990.

National Diet in shaping foreign aid policies. While sharing the critical assessment of "commercialization", "politicization" under U.S. pressure and insufficient research back-up, he concludes that Japan's ODA as yet remains in its "adolescent" stage, its mental growth lagging behind its physical strength. Bitter insider comments like these — in addition to those of Western observers — may have contributed to the general impression that a clearer definition of aid objectives is needed or, as a magazine headline has put it, of "aid in search of a policy" (FEER. November 9, 1989). According to Koichi Mera[14] of Tokyo International University: "For Japan, ODA is today not much more than the entrance fee to the club of the rich" or, perhaps, indirect export promotion. Even Masao Kawai of JICA expressed concern, at the Berlin forum of 1989, about the "giant without a face" image whose purpose is usually misunderstood. Kawai's main worry was, of course, the lack of qualified manpower available for international work.

Motivation: Commercial and Otherwise

Until about 1980, it was generally assumed among foreign observers that Japan was giving foreign aid without any philosophy beyond economic motives.[15] Since then, we have become aware of the fact that discussions about a philosophic foundation of aid to the Third World has been as active in Japan as elsewhere; and the 1990 White Paper on ODA, released by the Ministry of Foreign Affairs on October 6, 1990, contains all the terms and fashions governments would employ these days in order to seek endorsement and democratic approval at home as well as appreciation and recognition abroad. Goals listed here range from poverty alleviation and tackling global problems such as ecological degradation, population growth and drugs, to supporting structural readjustment, democratization and broad participation in development.

Nevertheless, Japan's ODA is still being seen as mainly commercially motivated. The White Paper tries to refute this perception with the information that, in fiscal 1989, the untied aid ratio for ODA loans was 80.5%, and Japanese corporations accounted for only 38% of the pro-

[14] Koichi Mera; Problems in the Aid Program, *Japan Echo*, Vol. 16 (1) 1989,pp.13-18; also *Neue Zürcher Zeitung*, July 24,1989

[15] Ozawa, Terutomo, Recycling Japan's Surpluses; OECD, Paris 1989

curements funded by these loans. These figures do indeed document a major progress achieved in the effort of untying aid which has also found some recognition within the DAC. However, if one has the chance to listen to Keidanren representatives or MITI officials, they are likely to underline the soundness of approaches which are happily and harmoniously combining aid and business interests, as long as foreign assistance is not clearly misused for other purposes.

Bernhard May[16] reports a historic shift in the foundation of development cooperation from commercial and economic interests to those of foreign policy and strategic considerations. Nuscheler[17] takes a close and critical look at the practical networks of interest in the administration and disbursement of Japanese aid, while Ozawa of OECD sees it also "closely tied to the advance of Japanese industry into Asian markets". He does not find such linkage objectionable as he believes in "commercially motivated, market-mediated aid" creating opportunities for dynamic transactions, a view which correlates with MITI's traditional position on economic cooperation in general and the active role the state has played in economic reconstruction.[18]

In this connection, Japanese officials underline the impact private enterprises will have in development, compared with "pure" government-to-government cooperation. Similarly, it is commonly accepted that "government aid has been connected with private interests which further national interest, and that such an arrangement has functioned very well for Japan in the past."[19] Such statements have to be understood in the context of specific experiences, both in Japan and within the region where the emergence of the "four little tigers" could be observed, now being followed by the successes of some of the ASEAN countries namely Thailand and Malaysia. Perhaps, our theories of development cooperation would also look different if we had similar success stories next door. On the other hand, a critical analyst like Nishikawa is also well aware that Japan's national interest sometimes may collide with global interests.

In reality, it is now fair to acknowledge that Japan's ODA, quite similar to that of other larger donor countries, presents a mix of motives of the altruistic/global concerns type and of a more direct pursuit of national interests, either in the direction of "pax nipponica" or of the "Japan Inc." eco-

---

[16] May, pp. 44-100

[17] Nuscheler, pp.62-64

[18] Ozawa: pp. 97-9

[19] Nishikawa at *FASID 1990 Symposium Report* p.85; for an example, see Hiroya Ishikawa, ibid., pp.64-68

nomic orientation. Against this background, the 1990 White Paper's re-affirmation of Japan's 1980 aid philosophy of "humanitarian considerations and recognition of interdependence" appears a rather decent and sober account; certainly, we should not blame any donor for being less hypocritical than others about the business of aid. For those of us who search for utopian orientation, however, the government of Japan is now pledging "to play an active part in the creation of an international society that is free of poverty, tolerant, open and comfortable for its inhabitants".

Structural Weakness

There is a general consensus among critics that the institutional base of Japan's ODA is too weak and too little unified to carry an increasing load of aid programs. There is also the question of necessary reforms in the inter-ministerial cooperation structure which keeps four or more government ministries involved instead of one as advocated by Keidanren. Whether the creation of an ODA Ministry is considered to be desirable or not, may be debated in light of experiences gained elsewhere. But the present state of affairs is generally seen as needing repair, the machinery being criticized as inefficient and its decision making process as "chaotic" or "non-sensical."[20] Perhaps, this is also an area where Westerners are bound to be fascinated by the "mote in our brother's eye." But no one can deny that the decision structure is complicated and that participating ministerial departments are playing their different roles, a phenomenon familiar from other donor administrations. It is here that the suspicion arises that the updated aid philosophy of MOFA may not find its full expression in aid programs and projects influenced by different views and concerns prevailing at MITI or MOF, though MOFA chairs the respective committees of coordination.

Most observers also view the Japanese institutions of ODA implementation as weak and understaffed. This would explain the tendency towards large scale projects, which is often criticized. Here, a word of caution seems to be warranted. We have learned, of course, that "small is beautiful." We also know that people are the agents of development who have to participate in and decide on its course. But, knowing this, why

---

[20]May, p.175; Nuscheler, p.75

should we discourage a benevolent super donor to adopt a few mega projects such as, e.g., watering the Sahara desert or, closer to the neighborhood concerns, creating "the great green wall" in North China, or donating filter equipment to all fossil fuel plants in developing countries of Pacific Asia? Japan, being rather reluctant to accept foreign refugees, might also be persuaded to fund a major initiative in preventing migratory movements and assisting refugees in need. New venues and big schemes will be discussed at UNCED 1992, when all nations will look for Japan's assistance in tackling the large scale ills of the globe.

ODA and Ecology

"They are blind to environmental factors, obsessed with giant hi-tech projects and up to ten years behind of the rest of the world," reported Fred Pearce in *The Guardian* on March 23, 1990. The environmental dimension of international cooperation is an area where Japan has come under heavy attack. A good deal of Japan-bashing is concentrating here. As in other critical fields, we could observe a fast reaction when, for instance, JICA established an Environmental Affairs Division capable of providing state of the art environmental impact studies as documented in a glossy brochure "JICA and the Environment" of August 1989. At closer look, Japan's foreign cooperation slate may not be all that clean, as Nuscheler rightly points out.[21] On the other hand, we notice some sincere initiatives put forward by Tokyo in international fora recently. Also, we should not forget that the Western donors have a good number of ecological skeletons in their closets as well, including some active scandals such as supporting mining abroad with devastating effects for local environment and peace. One should hope, of course, that the Japanese would also learn to lecture other industrial nations on these issues as we do. Perhaps, we could then expect better and earlier progress on a global scale. In the 1990 White Paper on ODA, Japan offers allegiance to the concept of sustainable development as carved out in the Brundtland Report. While stressing the recipient country's responsibility in this regard, the Government underlines its sincere commitment: "As a donor country, Japan is also doing its utmost to harmonize development with environment." It should be expected that

---

[21] Nuscheler, pp.64-70

Japan's contribution to UNCED 1992 will correspond to such policy declarations.

The NGO Component

It is usually assumed that there is no NGO component in Japanese ODA, a shortcoming in view of the useful contribution such private organization are considered to make in reaching the grass roots and involving people in the development cooperation process. The 1990 White Paper affirms the need to support and to involve NGO's. In fact, funds have been made available for NGO-sponsored development projects from 1989 on through the Ministry of Foreign Affairs. Historically, the Japanese NGO movement has been weak, though it has been strengthened through the experience with refugee work in Thailand and elsewhere. In 1987, a center for the promotion of NGO activities JANIC (*katsudo-suishin-sentaa*) was created in order to facilitate NGO development activities. Most NGOs operate from rather fragile base, and there is little chance for them to receive foundation grants, as there are only few Japanese foundations of international orientation and some of them that have such cosmopolitan outlook, as for instance the Sasakawa Peace Foundation, may be of doubtful reputation ("with the generous cooperation of the motorboat racing community").

Perhaps, the NGO contribution is sometimes overrated in Western countries. Nevertheless, they certainly play an important role in building public awareness and in lobbying on behalf of the Third World. Therefore, it could only be regretted if their Japanese counterparts could not, as Nuscheler[22] seems to conclude, play their part in the ODA game of their country. Correspondingly, the North-South problem does not receive much emphasis in public education, as Hofmann[23] and Nuscheler[24] report. On the other hand, the white paper recommends the strengthening of the links with local communities in Japan in the implementation of ODA, since the government is conscious of the need to broaden the public base for aid cooperation. For the same reason, it supports the Japan Silver Volunteers, a senior expert service whose assignments in China are being funded by

---

[22] Nuscheler, pp.98-101
[23] Nuscheler, p.13
[24] Nuscheler, p.108

JICA. Also, we notice the media stepping up their coverage of ODA activities, albeit often by reporting in the fault finding pattern of project reviews.

A Role in World Leadership

In recent years, about 25-30% of total ODA went to multilateral organizations. This reflects the established pattern and the OECD average. The Bretton Woods institutions are the main beneficiaries. Although the headline of the cover story "Japan takes over IMF" (*Euromoney,* September 1988) contained at least a somewhat premature message, Japan is now definitely assuming a more self-confident posture in these organizations, has tabled its own policy initiatives, e.g. the Miyazawa plan, and is claiming a share in voting power commensurate with its financial strength. The Asian Development Bank being firm in Japanese hands,[25] Japan has also placed large amounts in other regional banks, most prominently the African Development Bank.

In the course of the major ODA increase, Japan has also become a leading donor of the United Nations development system, the most obvious example being UNFPA where it replaced the United States as the top donor when the Americans withdraw their support because of a misunderstanding related to China's population policy. In contrast to its image of an economy-centered donor, Japan has placed citizens as heads of two humanitarian United Nations institutions, WHO and UNHCR. Perhaps, the *katagawari* movements are most obvious in the multilateral field, as shifting of the loads takes place between the United States and Japan, though the Western countries are slow in accepting the political consequences that should go along with it.[26]

Whether or not we believe in the tri-polar model of structuring the world economy in the century, Japan will certainly play her role as a leading power in world affairs. Such a role will require the creation of an international society (*kokusai shakai*). Right now, we experience a process of internationalization (*kokusaika*) as third step of opening to the world after the Meiji restauration and the reconstruction after World War II. Correspondingly, we notice how the government is preparing for a larger

---

[25] For a more differenciating view see May, pp.151-161

[26] see Sadako Ogata, pp. 26-35, and others in "The Role of the United Nations in the 1990s," *Publications of the Japanese-German Center,* Berlin, Vol.4, 1991

role of sharing leadership responsibility. Already, Japan assumes the posture of spokesman for Asia in G-7 meetings and elsewhere; and though its claim to a permanent seat in the Security Council may not be too serious in view of the fact that it would ask to open a Pandora's box of counter-claims, her ambition and selfconfidence in international and global fora is obvious.

The first historic test on the new role in world politics did not impress, however. Apparently, the Government was not well prepared for playing such a role when the Gulf War presented it with a serious challenge. While public opinion in the whole of Asia was clearly anti-war. Prime Minister Kaifu missed the chance for carving out an independent policy which could have taken such sentiment into account. Instead, he tried to oblige the U.S. friends by even committing Japan's Self Defence Forces for their cause. In this, he did not succeed, being blocked by half a year's political battle at home; and when Japan finally paid a large part of the military expenses involved, he had lost in standing both at home and abroad. It can be assumed that the lesson of this experience will be carefully studied in Tokyo. Already, Saburo Okita summed up his advice: "better to spend these billions on aid than on arms."[27] On the other hand, the Prime Minister was widely criticized for his "inaction" when, during the critical days of August 1991, he was reluctant to come forward with commitments of support to the cause of democratic reforms in the Soviet Union. Probably, the time will come when, in spite of all friendship and cooperation, the lead goose function of the United States will not go unquestioned even in issues of peace and security.

Summing up his assessment of Japanese foreign aid, Nuscheler[28] concludes with a piece of advice likely to be subscribed to by most observers:

"Japan must reorganize its system of aid allocation and improve its aid administration, in order to cope with the remarkable increase in the amounts of its ODA. If it is to achieve the aims it pursues as ODA world champion, however, technocratic changes in the system are not enough; it must also reform the aims and methods of its policy".

I do not think we will be too surprised to find out that Japan is indeed ready to tackle the task mentioned here.[29] Perhaps, we shall see a process of streamlining ODA in terms of policy and implementation. Perhaps, the critical reviews submitted by Western observers may contribute to ac-

---

[27] *International Herald Tribune,* April 17, 1991

[28] Nuscheler, p.115

[29] Hirono, pp. 155-156

celerating this process. We may see the champion coming out in style. But we should not forget the basic weakness of the ODA approach itself, being, even in a highly sophisticated form, a product of the post-war and post-colonial era, creating its own mix of vested interests and an ever growing set of conditionalities forced upon the developing countries.

Time has come to look beyond ODA to visions of a global system that could guarantee a minimum of world-wide social and ecological security for all. We are still far from the global governance needed, but we can already imagine how to replace the outgoing model ODA with appropriate instruments designed to create a more just world order. Western observers will find it difficult to expect Japan taking a leading role in such historical change. True, there was no response when European participants hinted at this issue during discussions at the FASID and Berlin symposia in 1990. However, as we have said above, the inventiveness and determination of Japan have been underestimated before.

Abbreviations

DAC	Development Assistance Committee (of OECD)
FASID	Foundation for Advanced Studies on International Development
FEER	Far Easterm Economic Review
JICA	Japan International Cooperation Agency
MITI	Ministry of International Trade and Industry
MOF	Ministry of Finance
MOFA	Ministry of Foreign Affairs
ODA	Official Development Assistance
OECD	Organization for Economic Cooperation and Development
OECF	Overseas Economic Cooperation Fund
UNCED	United Nations Conference on Environment and Development
UNFPA	United Nations Population Fund
UNHCR	United Nations High Commissioner for Refugees
WHO	World Health Organization
WIDER	World Institute of Development Economies Research (of the United Nations University)

Part II

Japanese Perspectives

Multinational Business
as a Partner In Trialogue

Akio Morita
Chairman
SONY Corporation

I am proud to have been a member of the Commission since its creation.[1] As a businessman always facing a set of day-to-day questions, I have learned a great deal from the very distinguished and knowledgeable academics, politicians, and guests from governments who know so much about public policy issues. I find that they help provide those of us in the business community with a broad, and longer-term context that helped us understand the dilemmas that face those in policy-making positions.

So why am I here addressing you tonight? Let me confess a little secret — I have a hard time saying "no". So when David Rockefeller asked me to speak to you tonight, of course, I had to say "yes".

More importantly, I wanted to say "yes" because I believe that we are entering a new era of world history in which those of us in international business must play a more active role in public policy debates.

I came to Washington by way of Eastern Europe. We do not yet know whether the new governments of Eastern Europe will succeed in establishing stable democracies and free market economies, but we do know that the old governments failed and disappeared, and that communism is discredited throughout that region as an economic system or political force. Indeed even the Soviet Union is undertaking steps towards political economic reform.

We also know that the political change in the East has profound global implications. For more than four decades, we have taken for granted the cold war rivalry as an almost permanent feature of international life. In Japan and much of Westerns Europe, we accepted the need to host foreign forces and participate in security alliances. The Americans accepted the need to make broad overseas commitments and support large peacetime forces. Even much of the political rationale for strengthening our economic cooperation had a security base; it was through the economic and political unity of the West that we could overcome threats from the East.

---

[1]Speech delivered at the Trilateral Commission meeting in Washington D.C. on April 21, 1990.

The Cold War in its old form may be over, but in the 1990's we face the perhaps even more difficult challenge of winning the peace. We must convince our publics to support an even greater degree of economic adjustment and cooperation, even though the security argument for such cooperation will be lessened. We have a tremendous task in helping the new democracies of Eastern Europe consolidate their positions and renovate economies that have been distorted by decades of communism. We have the continuing challenges of helping developing countries and dealing with threats to our natural environment.

These challenges of the 1990's and 21st century are more than ever economic in nature. The role of industry will be critical. The role of Japan, as the world's second largest economy, will be critical. The role of technology will be critical. Therefore, as a Japanese industrialist involved in frontier technologies, I cannot be silent. That is why I am before you here tonight.

New Trialogues

The new and favorable political environment does not mean that we trialerists can declare victory and go home. The role of trialogue, among governments and in the private sector, becomes even more important. Indeed, President George Bush has urges for the strengthening of what he called, "the political trialogues among the United States, Japan, and our European allies". His terminology and his previous membership in this Commission cannot have been just a coincidence.

President Bush was thinking of trialogue primarily in geographical terms. He was saying that the reconstruction of Eastern Europe, the economic and social development of the Third World, and the variety of other global challenges are simply beyond the capabilities of any one region or nation to carry forward. Japan must play a fuller role in meeting these tasks. It cannot simply be an Asian power. Western Europe cannot limit itself to a primary role in Eastern Europe or Africa. The United States must continue to be a global power in cooperation with its trilateral partners.

The vision or trilateralism of the early 1970's thus remains even more valid in the world of the 1990's. In my remarks tonight, I want to talk about how the trialogues among our regions, can be reinforced by three other important kinds of "trialogues". The first of these is the trialogue between the business community, politicians, and the government civil servants. The second trialogue is between business, labor and the community. And at the end of my remarks, I want to suggest a third trialogue among politicians, business leaders and technologists.

Turning to the first of these trialogues, I am concerned about what I regard to be fundamental differences in the way in which the leaders of the international business community, the politicians and the bureaucracy view the world. Very powerful economic forces compel leaders of the business community to think globally and act globally. Very powerful electoral pressure force the politicians to think primarily in terms of local constituencies. The government bureaucracies lie in between; they have to ensure that local interests are accommodated within a national policy framework, but they exist primarily to defend what is then defined "the national interest".

The global forces acting on the business community are obvious. Multinational corporations, such as my company Sony, must operate on the basis of a global strategy. Our products are manufactured in more than 70 factories in 16 countries, and sold in 160 countries. Our 100,000 employees are from almost as many countries. Only half of them are Japanese. Our shareholders, who are our ultimate bosses, are also found throughout the globe. Our stock is traded on 23 exchanges worldwide.

Sony and the other multinational companies that are responsible for the tremendous growth of international trade and capital flow are both the agents creating a borderless world economy and also the beneficiaries of such an economy. But we are in a constant tension with politicians and bureaucracies that are trying to reinforce rather than tear down borders. We are also in tension with those in the business in the business community who have not internationalized, and who look to protection or subsidies for survival.

As the international economy has become more integrated, those threatened by internationalism have become more nationalistic. This is shown in increased pressures for managed trade, trade blocs, local content rules, all of which reduce efficiency and growth.

The suppliers, customers, owners, and labor force, or "constituents", if you will, of a multinational company are global, but those of our political leaders and bureaucracies are not. No matter how active a politician may be in international politics, no matter that he or she may be a member of the Trilateral Commission, political survival depends upon the continued favor of voters in the home district. These voters are unlikely to believe in a borderless world economy. They want their politicians to support their local industries and interests.

The challenge for politicians and for bureaucrats, therefore, must be to reconcile the demands of an interdependent world economy with those of the local constituency or nation. This is a process of developing globally-minded constituents. International business has a responsibility to help change the political climate at the local level by fostering what I call "local globalization". Our efforts take place through the next trialogue, that between management, labor and the community.

Global Localization and Local Globalization

International companies must be an active and vital part of the local community. In 1988 I invented the Sony slogan "global localization" to refer to the process by which multinational corporations should develop strategies at the global level, and the allow local operations the autonomy and decision-making power to tailor these strategies to suit unique local requirements. With an understanding of global directions as a base, local management must then make operational decisions that relate meaningfully to the labor forces and the communities on a local level.

Localization requires accommodations with local customs and work habits. It requires a comfortable degree of autonomy for the local factory or office. It means working directly with local businesses and community organizations to be a good corporate citizen in boosting the local economy and enriching social and cultural life. It means involvement with United Way, the PTA, and other citizens group. The challenge of global localization is to make the locality a meaningful and vital part of a global corporate strategy.

Foreign investment plays a vital role in the localization of companies and in the globalization of localities. Too often those of us who speak about the benefits of foreign investment have cast our arguments in purely economic terms. Of course, foreign investments increase economic efficiency, transfer capital and technology, and increase incomes in the host localities. But there is also a very important cultural dimension that should not be overlooked.

Inevitable the investment processed change the outlook of both the corporations making the investments and the host communities. Japanese companies have been behind their European and North American counterparts in multinationalizing their production. Now that they are moving very rapidly in this direction, this is changing the attitudes and corporate cultures in the home offices in Japan in a wide variety of often unforeseen ways ranging from marketing techniques to the treatment of females empoyees.

Foreign investments also help globalize local attitudes by creating an interest in foreign countries. For example, surveys of U.S. states in which significant Japanese investments have taken place have shown that this investment is associated with a rise in interest in Japanese language, culture, and travel to Japan. We should appreciate and encourage these interests. By being actively engaged in support for cultural activities in the localities, a global company can also help to globalization process in those localities.

Globalizing Japan

Thus, foreign investment plays a tremendous role in the process both of global localization and also that of local globalization. This process of international integration is particularly important for Japan at this point in its development. For all its economic importance, Japan is still a relative newcomer to the world of advanced democracies. It is also the only Asian member. Many Japanese are still unsure whether we can really be accepted and are sensitive to any sign of discrimination.

For this reason, for example, we react very strongly to the American so-called"revisionists" who argue that the Japanese economic system is so different it cannot be accommodated within rules the rules of the international system. The emphasis in the international community on economic coordination and cooperation, therefore, provides Japan with a good opportunity to further its integration into the world system.

When the key task of the Western alliance was perceived primarily in military security terms, Japan could only be at the margin of the dialogue. Now that the key tasks, including securities issues, are defined in terms more of economic policy and technology, Japan becomes central. Does Japan, however, have a sufficiently internationalized outlook to become fully a partner with other democratic industrializs countries to meet these expectations?

I believe that Japan has a long way to go before it is truly globalized. Our largest corporations, I have argued, must and are becoming global citizens. But much of our business community is still local in its attitude. Most of our bureaucrats think more in terms of resisting foreign demands than in spontaneously opening Japan to the broader world for the enlightened self-interest of Japan. And most of our politicians, like those of many other countries, think in constituency-oriented terms. All countries, as part of the integrating process, need structural reforms — Japan perhaps most of all.

What is called "Japan bashing", in this situation, is usually not helpful. It reinforces Japanese fears of discrimination and distracts attention away from the merit of policy changes and toward nationalistic issues. What is helpful is for the international community to take advantage of the increasing pluralism within Japanese society and work constructively with those parts of Japan that are already internationalized. That is the route that the Trilateral Commission has been taking and I believe it is a very appropriate and positive one.

In this context, let me return tp my comment at the beginning of this talk about my weakness for saying "yes". I have argued that for Japan to be an effective player in the international community it needs to be able to say "no" as well as "yes". In other words, Japan needs to have a clear sense of its interests as a member of the international community and to conduct its policies accordingly. This is a view that I believe is widely shared among Japanese internationalists.

Japan is a beneficiary of free trade. Therefore we need to say "no" to those in our own society who want trade barriers, and we should say "no" to external interests who argue for various forms of managed trade to promote their interests. Japan and the world benefit from the free flow of technology. We need to say "no" to techno-nationalists who want to restrict technology flow or use technology as a political bargaining chip.

The Role of Technology

I want to emphasize however where we should say "yes". I believe that I have been successful as an entrepreneur and industrialist by saying "yes" even when technologies or commercial opportunities were considered uncertain. I am a techno-optomist. I believe that new technologies basically create their own markets. I believe that the expansion of communications technology was one of the most powerful forces leading to political change in Eastern Europe, and that it may be the ultimate solution to the problem of narrow localism. I believe that many other international problems, particularly the environment problem that will be discussed at length by one of our panels, can be resolved through the application of new technologies.

If our energy situation improved in the 1990's, it was not because we reduced our standard of living, but because we developed new semiconductors, recycling, and other technologies that allowed us to enjoy an even higher quality of living with less use of energy and natural resources. In most of the continent of Asia, with half the world's population there is now little prospect of famine. This is not because population has been reduced, but food production has increased through the application of new technologies.

This leads me to suggest a trialogue among politicians, business people and "technologists". This is not a geographical trialogue, but a trialogue of internationally-minded individuals who are committed to improving the human condition. Technologist is a term that we use at Sony to describe our scientists and engineers who are seeking to develop ways to apply science for the enrichment of human life. I believe such a trialogue is essential to deal with the environmental, resource and development challenges we face in the coming decades.

These are challenges that know no national boundaries and affect us all. The solutions require technological progress, but technology is not simply a matter of discovery; it requires government policies that encourage innovation and business visions and marketing skills. It is only through such a trialogue that we can come up with proposals that are politically realistic, commercially feasible and technologically attainable.

I believe that the Trilateral Commission is a valuable forum for sustaining this and other trialogues. We are trilateral not simply in our geographical representation, but also in our professional backgrounds. In particular, the Trilateral Commission can be the foundation for the new "trialogue" in which technologists join our efforts to solve the multifaceted questions that will be the central issues of the 21st century — how to insure that the 6 billion or more people living on this planet by then can all enjoy high standards of living without ruining our environment or depleting our resource base to the detriment of future generations. We need to pool our efforts and technology at the local, national and international level in order to meet these challenges. Trialogues, in this sense, is not limited to three partners; it is a way of suggesting that dialogue encompasses everyone.

Technology and Japan-U.S. Relations

Yoshitaka Okada
International University of Japan

Trade disputes are not a new phenomenon in Japan-U.S. relations. They started in the 1960s over the Japanese exportation of standardized technology goods such as steel, textiles, and black and white televisions to the United States, and continued in the 1970s over several commodities. Disputes in the 1980s started showing unprecedented characteristics. As Japanese technological sophistication and economic capabilities advanced, negotiations shifted from the exportation of standardized-technology goods to that of high-technology goods (semiconductors) and from the importation of agricultural goods to that of high-technology goods (supercomputers and satellites). Moreover, surprised with Japanese high-technology advancement — but simultaneously frustrated with the Japanese slow increase of U.S.-goods imports and technology transfer — the United States added unprecedented dimensions to negotiations. It concluded agreements with Japan to export military-related high-technology goods to the U.S., to transfer highly advanced technologies from Japan to the United States through cooperative research, and to transform the Japanese institutional structures. The United States efforts to transform institutional structures, called the Structural Impediment Initiatives (SII), focused on such structural issues as over-pricing mechanisms, distribution systems, savings and investments, land policies, keiretsu (corporate groups), and exclusive business practices [15, 22, 44].

Disputes in the 1980s suggest that the United States attributes the basic cause of the Japan-United States trade imbalance to, on one hand, the firm belief in the fair and open market system in the United States , and on the other hand, the impenetrable Japanese commodity and technology markets to foreign corporations. In this point the United States seems to be making a too simple-minded assumption that the market is the most efficient form of institutional arrangement. If so, the Japan-United States perceptual discrepancy clearly exists over the question, "What form of institutional arrangement in the private sector is the most efficient and what form is necessary for the development of future technologies."

It is an undeniable fact that Japan, given its economic power, now has to show strong leadership and to make innovative initiatives in the world. In that sense, its balance-of-trade surplus ($95.0 billion in 1988 and $76.9 billion in 1989) and its imbalance between incoming ($2,860 million) and outgoing ($67,540 million) investments in 1989 show quite a low degree of Japan's international mutual interdependence [19]. Japan has to increase the amount of imports and incoming foreign investments in order to increase interdependence with other parts of the world. At this point, there is a match between the need for transformation in Japan and United States national interests.

Under a banner of fair and open trade, the United States exercises its strategy to open markets and create investment opportunities in Japan in order to realize its national interests. Opening of the beef and citrus markets, forcing the increase of supercomputer and semiconductor imports, and increasing demand by reducing savings and stimulating public investments may increase United States exports and construction projects. Furthermore, simplifying distribution channels, strengthening the application of the anti-trust law to prevent collusive practices, reducing intra-keiretsu transactions, and lowering land prices may also significantly facilitate United States investments as well as exports. These United States pressures are definitely becoming a stimulation to transform Japanese institutional structures. However, the direction of transformation does not necessarily mean significantly increased arms-length market transactions. It is because comparative advantages of newly-formed and highly-efficient Japanese techno-governance structures are based on cooperative relationships, and because any rational corporation is not likely to abandon comparative advantages.

United States perception seems to ignore the importance of techno-governance structures. They identify relations between technology and institutional structures as a factor that significantly contributes to promoting efficiency in production. Japanese techno-governance structures are the merger of highly advanced technologies, process innovations and a cooperative production relationship, not only cultivated within hierarchies, but also extended to outside organizations. The structures are a new system and ideology of production strongly supported by Japanese harmonious and cooperative relationships [8]. The system is often called flexible manufacturing or lean production [47, 57], which came into birth with the accumulation of such process innovations as quality circle activities, just-in-time production, production maintenance programs, process control, total quality circle activities, automation, computer integrated manufacturing, robotization, etc. (For example, by utilizing the flexible manufacturing system, the Kawasaki factory of Toshiba Tungaloy succeeded in reducing the number of machines from 50 to 6, the number of workers from 70 to 16, the failure rate from 5% to 1%, the machine operating rate from 20% to 70% [58].) In external relations, such institutional arrangements as intermarket *keiretsu,* vertical *keiretsu,* technological alliances, and associations constitute techno-governance structures, as well as playing significant roles in developing technologies cooperatively, expanding and intensifying the sphere of cooperation, and disseminating new information regarding technologies quickly and effectively. In short, cooperative techno-governance structures in a competitive environment seem to have generated more efficient production than market-oriented individualistic business behaviors. This new system of production can be considered as revolutionary as the mass production system developed by Ford in the early 1900s [57].

The current basic problem of Japanese institutional structure lies in the intricate mixture of, on one hand, traditional, unhealthy, and closely-linked cooperative relationships, and on the other hand, rational, flexible and dynamic ones. Indeed, Japanese self-generated transformations that will attenuate and transcend unhealthy traditional corporate practices generated from closely-linked cooperative relationships, are becoming a necessary qualification for an effective world leader. Under these complex conditions, simple-minded and excessive emphasis on market opening and the destructive accusations of inter-corporate harmonious relationships may not truly contribute to the development of more globally efficient and effective Japanese production systems, or rather may reduce, or even destroy corporate benefits and efficiencies. They may also aggravate emotional conflicts and stimulate the rise of stronger nationalism. This is because the accusations are based on simple assumptions that the market is the most efficient mechanism to allocate resources, and that any institutional arrangement that lies in between markets and hierarchies always generate unhealthy collusive activities.

Since corporations are not likely to sacrifice efficiency or comparative advantages, they will try to meet international demands and maintain those factors of efficient production. Under the assumptions that achieving the efficiency of production, not in a nationalistic or mercantilistic sense but in a global sense, is the goal of the two nations, and that Japan is trying to change its institutional structures and corporate practices to meet international demands, we can examine the nature and characteristics of current transformations in techno-governance structures. Specifically, are the current Japan-United States relations succeeding in opening up markets or are they instead generating a new form of institutional arrangements that enable Japanese corporations to meet foreign demands, but simultaneously preserve gains derived from an efficient form of techno-governance structures? If we find that the latter is true, then it may suggest problems in the current approach to Japan-United States relations. On-going transformations may give us some hunch for a new direction for negotiations and cooperation.

Now I shall first explain the concept of techno-governance structure and then examine evidence indicative of the development of current Japan-United States interdependence.

The Concept of Techno-Governance Structure

Some social scientists in the past analyzed Japanese society by making rather simplistic dichotomous comparisons with other foreign countries, for example, suggesting such categorization as "the plan rational state vs. the market rational state" [17]. However, the concept of"governance" and "transaction cost economics" developed by Oliver Williamson [55, 56] brought a paradigmatic change in interpreting the complex reality. Instead of conceptualizing hierarchies (organizations) and markets as two dichotomous entities of economic institutions, the focus on transactions enables one to perceive both hierarchies and markets as two extreme forms of institutional arrangements; and in between the two exist such institutional arrangements as joint ventures, cooperatives, associations, subcontracting, alliances, etc. These institutional forms differ in the degree of internalizing transactions within a hierarchy. Thus, the reality can be understood as a complex mixture of different sets of institutional forms, which actors deliberately choose or create to harmonize activities and to perform efficiently under a given contingency. This complex combination of institutional forms is called a governance structure. For example, General Motors (GM) in the past had quite a high rate of internal production of parts. But due to increased international competition among automobile producers, higher labor cost, more frequent labor disputes, increased bureaucratic costs and less competitive quality and productivity, GM decided to procure more parts from markets rather than internal production. It shifted its governance structure from hierarchy-oriented to more market-oriented. This example clearly suggests that institutional structures differ with changes in contingencies, and that diverse types of governance structures exist.

However, Williamson's narrow focus on the concept of"transactions" and consequently on issues directly related to contracts generates some difficulties in applying his theory to the analysis of the Japanese context. By focusing only on transactions and contracts one fails to value the importance of non-transaction-oriented and cooperative relationships in developing future transactions among Japanese corporations. It is the concept of interaction that may well capture the essence of these relationships. In cooperation, an actor perceives that its interactions with a partner toward a goal facilitate each other's goal attainment and bring positive gains on both sides, while in competition the perception is that competitors' movements hinder the actor's own goal attainment [52]. This perceptual difference generates diversity in the nature and characteristics of interactions, and results in a different type of governance structure. Since the Japanese quite strongly emphasize cooperation in daily interactions, its institutional arrangements can be called "cooperative governance structures" It means a patterned combination of such governance mechanisms as markets, hierarchies, and in between forms, which actors interactively and cooperatively choose with other actors in order to facilitate the pursuit of common goals [45].

Cooperative governance does not necessarily explain the dynamics and flexibility of the Japanese economy [6, 46]. Much of the literature on Japan emphasizes that traditional values such as diffuse and personal relations based on trust, obligation and affection are the base of cooperative relationships. Cooperative governance simply based on these values could result in negative consequences such as collusive activities or loss of dynamic movements due to strong reciprocal bonds. In this point, the SII pinpoints the problem of governance structures very well, and the loss compensation of Japanese security firms is quite indicative of this problematic aspect. However, the genuine force of Japanese dynamics and flexibility seems to be in the combination of governance structures and technological factors, which can be termed as a "techno-governance structure." To be more precise, it may be the merger of rational process-innovations, highly-advanced technologies, and cooperative governance structures that have successfully contributed to Japanese economic dynamics. I shall call it "cooperative techno-governance structures."

Several scholars in the West focus on the relationship between economic governance structures and technological factors. One group argues that mass production technology, though it acknowledges the importance of other conditions such as legal structure, political choices and market conditions, tends to require a large scale hierarchy, a complex bureaucratic apparatus, and less subcontracting relationships. In contrast, craft production technology tends to involve a smaller size hierarchy, a simpler bureaucratic apparatus, and more subcontracting relationships [2]. If we follow the logic of this approach, a Japanese production system should still employ craft production technology and maintain subcontracting relations.

Another group argues that stages in a profit cycle, greatly influenced by a product cycle of goods and technologies, differentiate economic governance structures [21]. The initial stage of the profit cycle involves a significant amount of small-firm subcontracting, while the second oligopolistic stage results in a large scale hierarchy and a complex bureaucratic apparatus. Then, the last declining stage results in dismantling hierarchies and resorting back to subcontracting. According to this approach, Japan may be in the first or the last stage of the cycle. Contrary to the predictions of these approaches, Japanese production systems advanced from craft type to mass production even in the pre-World War II period, not to mention the quick return to mass production during the post-war recovery period. However, transformation of the Japanese economy in the 1960s did not weaken the basic structure of subcontracting or intermarket *keiretsu*. Instead, it rather strengthened inter-organizational cooperative interactions and even succeeded in reducing uncertainty in part supplies and qualities and other related transactions. The profit cycle stage theory may argue that Japan has finally reached the beginning of the second stage. However, oligopolistic conditions were already reached in an early period of post-war development, partly owing to industrial policies of the Japanese government. Hence, it is an undeniable fact that cooperative relationships have existed throughout different stages of the profit cycle.

Despite their focus on technologies, the application of these theories to the Japanese context misinterprets the reality. They failed to identify correspondence between, on one hand, the growth of Japanese corporations and, on the other hand, the advancement of rational process innovations, the application of high technologies to production processes, and cooperative governance structures. Namely, these theories failed to identify the development of cooperative techno-governance structures as the persistent characteristics of Japanese institutional arrangements, which succeeded in generating dynamic rather than stagnant behaviors. Such structures are not likely to be found, when a strong anti-trust law prevents the growth of inter-corporate cooperative relationships and governance mechanisms that lie in between markets and hierarchies, and when the environment is highly individualistic and competitive. In this sense, the concept of cooperative techno-governance structure is not likely to play any significant role in the perceptions of Americans and United States trade negotiators.

Then what really is the benefit that a firm can find in cooperative techno-governance structures? In the early post-war period and the 1950s, a need to cope with serious labor-management disputes, an unstable economy, and the uncertainty in operation all compelled Japanese firms to specialize, to remain small in size, and to engage in a significant number of subcontracts and inter-corporate contracts. Such inter-corporate relationships came to formulate cooperation among firms. Consequently, they succeeded in creating the scale of economy in production without bulky bureaucratic costs caused by internal production [25]. Also, the need for securing resources, producing high quality goods with much lower prices, preventing opportunistic behaviors, and sharing risks for investment made it necessary for firms to create the stable cooperative relationship of production and resource and information sharing. Basically, in this period, firms for the sake of survival needed to formulate such relationships, but they also succeeded in cultivating ground for more mutual support and facilitation, positive feedback, accurate communication and information exchange, and trust and generosity. Especially for less competitive companies in vertical *keiretsu*, a powerful company: 1) provided financing with favorable terms, financial guarantee and discounting; 2) transferred more advanced technologies; 3) rented equipment and materials at the initial stage; 4) gave functional training; and 5) shared complementary assets [40]. When the norm of cooperation was well developed, cooperative relationships also functioned as a method of mutual insurance and stability, helping each other in crisis situations through favorable procurement, finance and labor exchange. Even though technological cooperation was certainly one of the most important areas, mutual assistance played a stronger role in formulating cooperative governance structures. Such relationships, though they tended to be a bit closed, were found commonly in vertical *keiretsu* and less commonly in intermarket *keiretsu*.

As Japanese corporations expanded market activities and faced severe domestic and international market competition in the 1960s, technological innovations came to receive much more attention. In the early period there was a bit of a boom for big corporations to establish research centers in order to catch up with new and highly sophisticated technologies developed in the West. Also many firms began to develop stronger and persistent movements within their organizations for implementing such process innovations as reducing-rejection movements, quality circle activities, total quality circle activities, just-in-time production, and process control. What is much more significant in this period was the beginning of extending these innovations beyond their organizational boundaries to other related firms. Through linkages cultivated by cooperative governance structures, process innovations came to be practiced inter-organizationally, especially in vertical keiretsu. Thus, cooperative governance structures nurtured in the 1950s and 1960s provided ground for the development of techno-governance structure that linked corporations by process technologies.

Flexible application of mutual assistance and intensified technological cooperation enabled Japanese firms to survive through the devastating impact of the two oil shocks in the 1970s. Both intermarket and vertical *keiretsu* played a significant role in rescuing ailing companies through favorable financing, special procurement, and temporary displacement of workers from declining industries to prospering ones. Besides, their effective implementation of corporate rationalization further enhanced their flexibility and absorptive capabilities. In the early 1970s the rationalization resulted in increasing the usage of fixed automation lines and specialized machines, and in intensifying the involvement of related companies in such process innovations as just-in-time production, total quality circle activities, and zero-defect activities. So rapid was technological development that already in the latter 1970s the rationalization efforts resulted in a revolutionary development of production systems. The development of flexible manufacturing systems that combined numerical control machines, industrial robots, and process innovations, enabled corporations to shift from the mass production of a few products to the medium amount production of diverse products in one line [3]. To fully benefit from this new technology, corporations further intensified inter-firm technological cooperation through just-in-time production and total quality activities, especially in vertical *keiretsu*. Though the crisis situation during the oil shocks uncovered the persistent existence of some mutual-assistance interactions among corporations, instituting new systems of production and strengthening cooperative techno-governance structures basically ensured their survival.

In the 1980s the growth of Japanese corporations made mutual assistance among corporations in financing, managerial exchanges and procurement less significant or even unnecessary. Furthermore, industrial restructuring speeded up by the internationalization of Japanese corporate activities and needs for technological innovations brought following turbulence in cooperative governance structures: (1) the use of computers intensified the integration of cooperative techno-governance structures, especially in vertical *keiretsu*; (2) techno-governance structures promoted coordination even in some areas of decision-making and exchanges in information; (3) some unsophisticated subcontractors faced the severance of formerly-believed unseverable ties with assemblers; (4) corporations extended cooperative techno-governance structures to new companies, even to former competitors; and (5) some of the intermarket *keiretsu* corporations that formerly complemented each other in specialization turned into competitors due to the diversification of products. I shall explain each turbulence briefly.

Since the middle 1980s, some corporations advanced flexible manufacturing into computer integrated manufacturing (CIM) with the use of extended networks of computers, intelligent robots, and numerical control machines. Computers and local area networks (LAN) in a company integrated design, production preparations, plant operations, production control, quality control, and sales. Naturally, this integration further intensified the involvement of related companies in design and production coordination, simultaneous engineering (simultaneous development and designing of new parts by sharing the same computer) [48], and just-in-time parts deliveries to customers through order-production computer linkages [3].

When production comes to be coordinated or integrated among corporations, decision-making coordination is an unavoidable extension of cooperative interaction. Coordinated production involves intensive discussions over product development, necessary investments, production scheduling, and even strategic coordination in marketing [18, 49].

The need for quick access to accurate market and technological information also forces firms to maintain a system of primary information networks such as intermarket *keiretsu*, producers' associations, subcontractors' associations, venture networks, etc. These also function as interest mediators, industry coordination promoters, or R&D initiators.

Such intensification of integration is creating some drop outs from governance structure in vertical *keiretsu* relationships. Inefficient and technologically unsophisticated corporations are expelled from primary information networks, and face the termination of relationships that are formerly believed to be unseverable. Subcontractors are also often urged by big corporations to diversify their operations and become more independent and high-technology oriented.

The need for quick acquisition of new and developing technologies is promoting diverse cooperative relationships, in many cases without being confined to traditional expectations and ties. Japanese competitors are working at sharing vital information together in government-sponsored research cooperatives and consortiums in which foreign competitors have recently been included. Foreign and Japanese competitors also formulate alliances through cross-licensing of highly advanced technologies and R&D cooperation. A significant number of complementary technological alliances also exist among Japanese firms as well as with foreign firms (e.g. Hitachi and Nikon jointly develop semiconductor processing machines). Alliances with foreign competitors are now considered inevitable in order to act efficiently in the international scene.

In contrast, former cooperators turned into competitors or became more independent. Industrial restructuring in the 1980s promoted the diversification of corporate productions and brought competition among former intermarket *keiretsu* members (e.g. Kobe Steel now produces the semiconductor and competes against Hitachi and Sharp in a limited area within the Sanwa *Keiretsu*; Kawasaki Steel and Kobe Steel also compete against Hitachi and Fujitsu in Daiichi Kangyou *Keiretsu*) [9].

Complex as reality always is, competitors become cooperators in government-sponsored cooperatives and in international alliances, and former cooperators become competitors or face termination of relationships that formerly seemed strong. Hence, the past cooperative governance structure nurtured the development of cooperative techno-governance structure, but the latter's recent development shows two contradictory directions of more tightly-linked production integration and flexible and widely-open technological alliances. This means that cooperative techno-governance structures are becoming much more important than and independent from those that are non techno-governance, and are functioning to select partners and refine the nature of cooperative interactions. Such highly technology-oriented cooperative interactions among corporations generate inter-organizational synergy effects by creating dynamics in innovation, information transmission, resource cost minimizing, decision-making coordination, and collective interest articulation. It is this effect that may generate stronger comparative advantages over non-cooperative interactions such as those found in markets.

The possible danger of Japan-United States negotiations, in an effort to reduce negative effects attributable to static aspects of cooperative governance structures, lies in the erosion of these highly efficient techno-governance structures. Too much emphasis on market opening coupled with the disregard for cooperative governance structures may result in a complete denial of even highly efficient and effective techno-governance structures. Naturally, corporations are not likely to abandon efficient and effective mechanisms of production. Facing international political pressure as well as a turbulent international business environment, they may try to accommodate the pressures as well as maintain cooperative techno-governance structures. Hence, it is quite important to know, under the political pressure of trade disputes, what type of institutional arrangements between Japanese and United States corporations has been developing in the recent period.

Recent Developments of Japan-United States Interdependence

Japan-United States trade disputes in the past focused primarily on export restrictions to United States markets; but around the end of the 1970s United States emphasis on reciprocity in import activities led to the liberalization of Japanese beef and citrus markets. Decade long negotiations, which started with the expansion of import quotas for beef and citrus in 1977, finally resulted in the complete liberalization of these markets from spring 1991, as well as the juice import market from spring 1992. Meanwhile, ten out of twelve agricultural products earmarked by the General Agreement on Tariff and Trade (GATT) also came to be liberalized in the Japan-United States negotiations in 1988 [15, 22].

Section 301 of the Trade Act of 1974, revised in 1984, justified retaliations against the unfair practices of foreign trade partners, and the United States Trade Representative (USTR) used the law for the purpose of increasing restrictions over Japanese export activities to the United States In contrast, Super 301 of the 1988 Omnibus Trade and Competitiveness Act justified the United States government opening up more effectively restricted import markets in other countries. USTR under Super 301 designated satellites, super-computers and wood products markets in Japan as high priority negotiating areas. The negotiations brought about some opening of each market, but the tone of the disputes sounded weak, especially because the United States needed Japanese support to negotiate with the European Community (EC) on agricultural subsidies at the Uruguay Round.

The SII agreements may also have a direct impact on opening some import markets. According to the final report of Japan-United States SII talks published in June 1990, the Japanese government agreed to make 430 trillion yen worth of public investments ten years starting 1991; to open 17 public-works projects to bidding by foreign construction companies; to revise the Large-Scale Retail Stores Law; and to apply the Anti-Trust Law more stringently and increase fines [22]. Though the new semiconductor agreement abolished the fair market value system, which has benefited Japanese corporations and increased United States computer manufacturers' costs by about a few billion dollars [33], it included a clause indicating that the Japanese government should make efforts (no guarantee) to increase the share of foreign semiconductors up to 20% of the Japanese market by the end of 1992 [29]. Thus, Japan-United States negotiations have definitely opened up some import markets, but it may take a while before the magnitude of the effects may be known.

According to recent reports based on the Ministry of Finance trade statistics, the United States has been the biggest partner of Japanese imports. Even though the United States share in total imports declined from 34.6% in 1960, to 29.4% in 1970, and to 17.4% in 1980, since then it has been gradually increasing to 19.9% in 1985, to 23.0% in 1986, and to 22.3% in 1990 [13, 16]. However, United States finished product exports to Japan after the Plaza agreement do not give as rosy a picture as the total statistics. Its annual rates of increase from 1986 to 1990 show 23.9%, 0.2%, 33.2%, 19.5%, and 15.5%, while EC rates show 59.7%, 26.7%, 37.1%, 16.7%, and 27.3% [16]. These rates indicate that imports from the EC were increasing more dynamically almost every year since 1986, except 1989, than those from the United States As a matter of fact, the value of EC imports increased from $7.5 billion (52.8% of the United States $14.2 billion) in 1985 to $30.9 billion (95.1% of the United States $32.5 billion) in 1990 [14, 16]. Despite United States pressure to open finished product markets, EC countries, whose luxurious and high-quality goods are in high demand in Japan, are the ones increasing their share in Japanese markets. Hence, even though United States agricultural commodities have quite a significant share in Japanese import markets, its finished products may need to change their image in order to increase these share in Japan. Because of this difficulty, Japanese corporations seem to be opting for some different directions in order to increase interdependence with United States corporations. It is clearly due to the utilization of methods well developed in the Japanese practice of cooperative governance or cooperative techno-governance structures.

Increased Sales Cooperation

Political pressure to increase Japanese imports from the United States does not seem to be functioning effectively. The fact that European goods are succeeding in increasingly infiltrating into Japanese markets may suggest that consumers have a different image of United States finished goods from the European ones. Given this difficulty, the least uncertain way for Japanese corporations to increase imports from the United States is to export their affiliates' goods produced in the United States back to Japan. This is because a firmly developed cooperative governance structure with highly reliable quality assurance can reduce uncertainty for their operations and the quality of products.

Eleven Japanese automobile manufacturers made public statements between December 1989 and February 1990 to increase imports from their affiliates in the United States For example, Toyota Motor announced an increase in its imports to 300 billion yen by 1992 (2.5 times that of 1988). Honda Motor's 1992 imports will be expanded to 160 billion yen (also 2.5 times that of 1988) [12]. Japanese affiliates' automobile exports in the United States totalled 72,000 cars in 1990. Honda Motor exported to Europe and Japan; Nissan Motor to Canada; and Fuji Heavy Industries to Taiwan. Now Toyota Motor plans to export Camry parts produced in the United States from 1992 and complete cars and engines in the near future [30]. As a matter of fact, the most exported car of the United States in 1990 was the Honda Accord. Despite opposition from the United States Defense Department, MINEBEA acquired a former United States military supplier of bearings, New Hampshire Ball Bearing (NHBB). The latter now exports its products all over the world [1].

Also, cooperative governance structure is in a process of being extended beyond its own *keiretsu* in order to accommodate the sales of automobiles produced by United States manufacturers. Mazda Motor is already selling Ford cars; Toyota Motor is to sell GM cars; and Honda Primo is to sell Chrysler's four wheel drive cars [32].

Recently such sales cooperation in other industries seems to be more frequent than ever before. To name a few cases, in 1989 Canon contracted with NEXT to sell work stations in Asia. Kobe Steel provides parts for hard disk drives to PrairieTek, and in return sells them in Japan. Yokogawa Electric now sells Cray Research's supercomputers. NKK has sold Silicon Graphics' products since 1990. Sanyo has sold Micron Technologies' products since 1990. Matsushita Electric has sold Intel's Electric Erasable and Electric Programmable Read Only Memories

(EEPROMs) to its group companies since 1990. These sales agreements are not at all a new phenomenon, but a recent increase, though statistics are not available, seems to be quite drastic [50].

In addition, the new semiconductor agreement is compelling Japanese companies to increase their imports from foreign countries. SONY has already achieved a 4.2% share of all semiconductors used in their production in 1986, and plans to increase that share to 20% in 1991. NEC plans to raise its share to 24% by 1992. However, what is crucial is not simply to increase procurements from United States markets, but rather to promote cooperation in the design phase [31]. Less attention in the past has been paid to the most important factor that could have contributed to the solution of the basic problems. An advantage of Japanese semiconductor producers vis-a-vis customers lies in their strong sense of cooperation at not only the design phase but also the production phase. For example, Hitachi cooperates extensively with Nissan Motor in developing semiconductors used for automobiles; NEC with Mazda Motor and Honda Motor; Matsushita Electric with Toyota Motor and Mazda Motor; Fujitsu and Toshiba with Toyota Motor; and Mitsubishi Electric with Mitsubishi Motors [10]. Therefore, though needs for cooperation may differ by industry, in many cases cooperation in technological aspects is an indispensable process for promoting Japan-United States interdependence. This very much suggests the importance of developing cooperative techno-governance structures between the two nations, which actually is advancing much faster than political negotiations.

Thus, the importation of United States goods seems to be promoted rather through advancing internal procurement from Japanese affiliates in the United States and through developing cooperative sales relationship between Japanese and United States companies. These cases, especially the ones in the semiconductor industry, clearly suggest that the wise use of cooperative governance or techno-governance structures is a crucial factor for promoting much faster importation of United States goods. Now we shall inquire into the concrete examples of Japan-United States technological cooperation.

Increased Cooperative Techno Governance Structures

Japan-United States cooperative techno-governance structures are rapidly developing, greatly owing to the increasing Japanese capability to produce technology itself as well as high technology goods. The estimated non-defense R&D expenditure as a percent of the GNP shows that Japan has already spent a higher percentage than the United States from the early 1970s (1.9% vs. 1.7% in 1971 and 2.8% vs. 1.8% in 1987) [27]. And the Japanese share of total patents granted in the United States increased from 10.5% in 1978 to 20.7% in 1988, while the United States share declined from 62.4% to 52%. The only high technology area where the United States showed an increase was in the pharmaceutical industry. Also, the Japanese shares of both world production and exports of high-tech products nearly doubled between 1980 and 1986; and consequently, Japan came to displace the United States as the world's leading high-tech exporter in 1986 [27]. These figures clearly suggest that it is the Japanese technological success itself that triggered its exceptional treatment of providing military technologies to the U.S.; forced technological cooperation; strong United States government's accusation of the lack of Japanese technological reciprocity; and quite timely and dynamic development of international cooperative techno-governance structures in the private sector.

Though the two countries have initiated thirteen bilateral agreements since 1957 up until 1989, agreements in the 1980s had quite different characteristics from those in the previous period. The advancement of Japanese commercial and military-related technologies shocked the U.S., and led to its initiative to have access into Japanese technologies [7]. United States initiatives resulted in 1) the Japan-United States Agreement on Cooperation in Research and Development in Science and Technology in 1980, 2) the Japan-United States Agreement for the Transfer of Defense-Related Technologies in 1983, 3) the joint Strategic Defense Initiative (SDI) research involving eight Japanese main contractors in 1985, 4) the cooperative development of Fighter Support experimental (FSX) agreement in 1989, and 5) the New Japan-United States Agreement on Cooperation in Research and Development in Science and Technology signed in 1988. The first three agreements focused on creating grounds for promoting cooperative research itself and for utilizing Japanese technologies in United States military products, while the latter two showed rather acute conflicts between the two nations. The first conflict was between United States insistence on the purchase of its present jet fighters and Japanese emphasis on the development of higher-performance and high-technology fighters. It resulted in the joint FSX development project. The second conflict focused on technological cooperation in seven advanced technology areas, but serious disagreements occurred over correcting the imbalance of scientific exchanges, preventing the leakage of sensitive technological information to a third country, and changing the patent system [26]. Japan agreed to make efforts to correct the imbalance of scientific exchanges, but the latter two issues faced discrepancies in the basic interpretations over the public nature of information and a way to systematize the international patent system. Heated negotiations, especially over the joint FSX project, stimulated the rise of techno-nationalism and the exchange of sharp mutual criticisms. Hence, too much attention came to be paid to this issue as if it represents the situation of Japan-United States relations.

Another area that has been contributing to the rise of United States techno-nationalism is mergers and acquisitions by Japanese corporations in militarily sensitive industries. They have definitely generated fear on the part of the United States for the leakage of highly sophisticated and militarily-sensitive technologies and for United States dependence on Japanese corporations. As a matter of fact, the United States Defense Department prevented some Japanese corporations from acquiring United States corporations or forced them to withdraw some investments: in 1981 Kyocera was forced to sell out its subsidiary Xetel; Mitusbishi Kasei was forced to sell a semiconductor and laser manufacturing company, Optical Information Systems, to McDonnel Douglas; Sumitomo Metal Industries had to return the military section of Tube Turns to Allegheny International. In 1984 the Defense Department expressed its discontent over the MINEBEA's purchase of NHBB, but failed to prevent the acquisition; and Fujitsu gave up on the idea of purchasing Fairchild under the Defense Department pressure [11].

While these sensitive issues capture the eyes of people, Japanese companies' supply of military-related technologies to the United States has increased significantly. Carbon fiber fortified plastics (CFRP) with one shape formulating technology is now an indispensable technology for building lighter and stronger jet fighter wings. One fourth of the body of a stealth fighter is made with this material; and General Dynamics is very much interested in obtaining this technology from Japan through the FSX project. It was originally developed for use in fishing rods and golf clubs; and its applied technology to the body of airplanes was developed cooperatively by the Japanese Defense Agency, Mitsubishi Heavy Industries, Fuji Heavy Industries and Kawasaki Heavy Industries. Other indispensable materials are ultra-hard ceramics, ultra-heat-resistant ceramics, and ferrite electric wave absorptive materials [20]. Also very crucial are electric parts such as phased array radars, antenna modules, dynamic and static random access memories (DRAMs and SRAMs), charge coupled devices

(CCDs, electronic eyes in which Japan dominates 90% of the world market), ultra-red ray CCDs, laser semiconductors for the missile guiding system, and flight records borrowed from the credit card system [1]. Definitely Japan is still weak in the body design and engines of jet fighters, but the cost of a jet fighter is said to be 30% for the body, 20% for the engine and 50% for electronics. These figures clearly suggest that Japanese parts supplied to the United States defense industry cover a significant portion of the total cost. Also Xlinks supplies semiconductors installed in Tomahawk missiles, but the company only designs and checks products, 95% of which were produced mostly by Seiko Epson in Japan. But it is undeniable that the Xlinx's comparative advantage in quick and efficient designing with a strong CAD/CAM system enables it to remain as an equal partner to Seiko Epson. In a sense a technological complement is taking place even in military technologies.

In other areas, Ishikawajima Harima Heavy Industries gave technical advice by sending thirty technicians to Pennsylvania Shipbuilding for building a fuel supply ship and for helping the expansion of the air craft career"Kitty Hawk" MINEBEA has advanced bearing technologies, surpassing the United States technological level ten years ago. NHBB, acquired by MINEBEA, continues to supply bearings to United States military [1]. The ignored reality is that even in military technologies much more technological cooperation is taking place now.

Such government-related technological cooperation should be promoted further. In May 1991 the Japanese Defense Agency proposed cooperative research with the United States Defense Department, and offered to share new information on supersonic rocket engine technologies [34]. However, since government-related cooperation contains the danger of stimulating unnecessary emotional and psychological reactions on both sides, it has to be promoted with caution.

What seems to be much more dangerous is the uneven attention paid to the advancement of technological cooperation in the private sector. The September 1984 report of the United States-Japan Advisory Commission stated that hundreds of technological cooperative arrangements exist between United States and Japanese corporations [53]. In reality there are more dynamic developments of cooperative techno-governance structures in the private sector than in government-to-government relationships.

In the semiconductor industry success in developing Very Large Scale Integrations (VLSIs) in 1977 [43,44] enabled Japan to dominate the area of DRAM and to gradually strengthen its competitiveness over other areas of semiconductors. Japan came to dominate 44% (1982), 70% (1982), 90% (1984) and 90% (1988) of the 16K, 64K, 256K, and 1M bit DRAM world markets respectively [4, 28]. When the number of DRAM makers in the United States declined from fourteen companies in 1970 to three in 1986, the Japanese world share of all semiconductors came close to the United States in 1985 [5] and even higher (Japan=48.0% vs. U.S.=39.0%) in 1987 [4]. The United States dependence on Japanese semiconductors has significantly increased. Changes in the world configuration of semiconductor production capabilities, severe international competition, short product cycles of new products, needs for obtaining technologies quickly, and Japan-United States trade disputes all compelled Japanese and United States corporations to extend technological cooperation. Unlike the 1950s and 1960s when Japan was one-sidedly receiving technologies from Western countries, recent technological cooperation rather provides know-how to foreign countries or makes for cross-licensing. Furthermore, foreign investments in Japan came to be quite important not only for obtaining markets in Japan, but also for keeping up with some of forefront technologies in order to remain competitive in the world.

During the 1980s Japanese semiconductor companies had teamed up with 142 partners, of which 100 were American or European. These relationships involved joint ventures, mutual product-sharing, collaborative research or technology-sharing [51]. Texas Instruments (TI) had a cross licensing agreement with Fujitsu to exchange DRAM and Gate Array technologies before 1986, and collaborated with Hitachi to develop 16M DRAM technology in 1988. It now engages in the original-equipment-manufacturing (OEM) of Hitachi's SRAMs, and formed a joint venture with Kobe Steel to produce logic semiconductors in Japan in 1990 [42, 43, 54]. The first collaboration focused on the exchange of advantageous complementary technologies, while the second one was to share the cost and risk of developing new technology. The latter case actually received sharp criticism from the members of SEMATECH, which was trying to develop 16M DRAM technology solely among United States manufacturers. The third collaboration allowed TI to infiltrate the Japanese market with less operation cost and Kobe Steel to venture into semiconductor business. TI could survive in the DRAM area, not only because of these technological collaborations, but also because of its own investments in three Japanese plants. These plants sent 30 Japanese technicians and received 450 United States workers in order to transfer production systems from Japan to the Texas plant [42].

Another United States DRAM survivor, Motorola, collaborates extensively with Toshiba: the former obtained a technical agreement with the latter, produced 1M DRAMs with the latter's licensing in the U.S., and engaged in the OEM of 16 bit microprocessors for the latter in 1987. Motorola and Toshiba together established a joint venture in Japan, Tohoku Semiconductor, and the former engaged in the OEM of 32 bit microprocessors for the latter in 1988. They also agreed to supply each other with discrete integrated circuits (discrete IC), exchanged application specific IC (ASIC) technologies, and cooperatively developed ICs for High Definition Television (HDTV) and Toyota's 16 bit engine control systems in 1990. In order to prevent competition against Motorola in the United States DRAM market, Toshiba's United States plant even changed its production facilities into ASIC production [35, 42, 50].

AT&T, a core company of SEMATECH like TI, also signed agreements with NEC to engage in the OEM of reduced instruction set controllers (RISCs) in 1989 and to jointly develop technologies targeted at the end of the 1990s. From Mitsubishi Electric, AT&T received Gallium Arsenic (GaAs) IC technology in 1990. SONY also provides Advanced Micro Device (AMD) SRAM IC production technology [35].

While TI engages in the OEM of Hitachi's SRAMs, the latter engages in the OEM of high speed SRAMs for and collaborates in the production of semicustom semiconductors with VLSI technologies. Even within Japan Hitachi made quite a big move to contract the OEM of semiconductor production with a Japanese company, NMBS, which may possibly trigger a big reorganization of the Japanese semiconductor industry [39]. Hitachi has also received licensing from Hewlett-Packard for the RISC-type microprocessor technology, and engages in production and sales in Japan.

Between 1981 and 1985, NEC had contracts to expand its cooperative relationships based on existing technologies with Internet Planning, Burroughs, Motorola, and Zilog; had contracts to develop specific applied technologies in collaboration with Anelva, Tektronix, 3M, AMS, and General Electronics; and had contracts to engage in broad collaboration with Intel, Alcoa, Honeywell-Bull, and C&C International [53]. Now NEC, Siemens, and MIPS Computer are cooperatively developing RISC systems for global markets since 1989, while Toshiba engages in the OEM of RISC-type microprocessors for MIPS. In 1990 NEC contracted to engage in the OEM of SRAMs and ASICs for National Semiconductor [50].

Intel also develops microprocessors for Canon auto-focus cameras and Nissan Motor's new engine control systems. Intel and Matsushita Electric also cooperate in developing processing technologies for 16M bit DRAMs and the latter engages in the OEM of ultra-small-size microprocessors for the former. Also Mitsubishi Electric engages in the OEM of EEPROMs and complementary metal oxide semiconductors (CMOSs) for Intel, while it contracts with National Semiconductor to engage in the OEM of 32 bit microprocessors. Kubota has had cooperative research to develop a highly special LSI with C-Cube Microsystems since 1990 [50]. And FSI International formed a joint venture with Mitsui Trading Co. to produce semiconductor surface cleaning equipment in Japan [36].

The new entry of Japanese corporations into the semiconductor business also provides unusual opportunities for foreign corporations to have easy and low-risk access into Japanese markets. For example, TI offered technologies to Kobe Steel and in return obtained new marketing channels. Also Kawasaki Steel formed a joint venture with LSI Logic to produce ASICs in Japan, allowing the latter to enter into the Japanese ASICs market.

In addition, some Japanese corporations acquire foreign entities in order to have quick access to production technologies and markets. Nippon Steel participated in the ownership of Simtek and provided EEPROM technology in 1987. Intel buys all 1M DRAMs and some ASICs from Japanese NMB Semiconductor, which in 1990 obtained 55% of Ramtron ownership and agreed to form a joint 16M DRAM development project [24, 50]. Kyocera and Mitsui jointly invested into Chips and Technologies to enter into the semiconductor market; Mitsubishi Electric acquired Siltec; NKK acquired Great Western for the polysilicon market; and Rohm/Exar acquired Excel for the semiconductor market [51].

In the computer field, IBM and Hewlett-Packard provide, respectively, software and high-performance small-size work-station technology to Hitachi, while the latter provided supercomputer technologies and CMOSs to Cray Research in 1989 and 1990 respectively. Toshiba has also provided SRAMs to Cray Research since 1990, and Yokogawa Electric became the representative of Cray Research in Japan in 1990. Fujitsu has had a joint development project of supercomputer software with KBS2 since 1990. Matsushita Electric contracts joint developments of small-size high-performance computers with Tandy and 64 bit microprocessors for the next generation work stations with Solbourne Computer. Hewlett-Packard also engages in the OEM of work stations for Mitsubishi Electric [50]. Sun Microsystems, which successfully made $1 billion in annual sales after only six years of operations, developed its SPARC microprocessor chips with Fujitsu [51]. And it engages in the OEM of work stations for Fujitsu as well as Oki Electric. Sanyo Electric acquired Icon Systems and Software to enter into the microcomputer market. Kubota also invested into

MIPS Computers and Ardent Computers to enter into the mini-supercomputer market;

International collaborations in the automobile industry are very well known. GM has joint ventures with Toyota Motor and Isuzu Motors. Chrysler has a joint venture with Mitsubishi Motors. Ford Motor has formulated an alliance with Mazda Motor, and the collaborative production of the Ford Escort even resulted the car being called a "global car" [12]. In these alliances Japanese manufacturers provide United States companies with not only Japanese production technologies, but also strength in the compact car market. In some cases Japanese producers also provide United States counterparts sales channels in Japan. Since 1989 much stronger cooperative relationships have started to develop. Mazda Motor requested Ford Motor to produce multi-purpose four wheel drive automobiles in 1990; and Nissan Motor and Ford Motor jointly designed and produced a multipurpose mini-van in 1989. Suzuki Motor and GM also jointly developed a small-size convertible car [50]. Recent United States accusations that Japanese automobile producers in the United States show quite a low local procurement rate triggered a new movement. For example, Toyota announced the expansion of R&D facilities in the United States This is due to the fact that increasing local procurement requires the participation of local firms from the very beginning of the design phase [37]. Japanese automobile manufacturers consider that design and production collaboration is the very beginning of local sourcing, instead of purely looking for local producers in the market. Such corporate behaviors signify that Japanese automobile producers are coping with local demands by extending the use of Japanese techno-governance structures in the United States

The iron and steel industry is another area where technological cooperation is extensively advanced. Within two years of 1979 and 1980 United States and Japanese steel makers contracted 24 technical agreements [23]. Basically, many United States steel makers have given up the business of pig iron and steel manufacturing, and have specialized in highly value-added rolling. Even in rolling NKK provided special technologies to Bethlehem Steel in 1988 and purchased 50% of National Steel's equity interest. Four of the seven largest United States steel makers sold equity positions to Japanese companies or formed joint ventures with them [53]. A joint venture between Kawasaki Steel and Armco enabled the former to have access into the United States market, while the latter obtained new technologies. More recently, cooperation between Nippon Steel and Inland, and between USX and Kobe Steel have been reported.

Increased aluminum usage in the automobile industry is also compelling Japanese steel and aluminum producers to make collaborative agreements with United States companies. Nippon Steel has contracted an agreement with Japan Light Metals which formed a joint venture with ALCAN Aluminum. Kobe Steel and Aluminum Co. of America established a joint venture in Japan for the production of aluminum. Mitsubishi Aluminum and Mitsubishi Trading Co. participate in Reynolds Metals' aluminum smelting venture in Venezuela and have also signed a joint research agreement with NKK, which has strong business ties with automobile manufacturers. Such collaboration enables Japanese corporations to secure raw materials and United States corporations to utilize high quality processing technologies as well as infiltrating Japanese markets. Some United States corporations are greatly benefiting from access into existing cooperative governance structures such as the ones strongly linked among steel, automobile, and electric manufacturers [38].

Even the development of the Japanese aerospace industry with Japanese government's major financing is taking a form of joint development between Japanese corporations and Boeing. The outcome of the cooperative research resulted in the B767X which made the first flight in 1981. Now Mitsubishi Heavy Industries and Kawasaki Heavy Industries cooperate with Boeing in a Japanese-government-sponsored project for developing the next generation airplane, the B7J7 [23].

R&D centers are also found crisscrossing between United States and Japan. TI, LSI Logics, and IBM Japan (Yasu), have R&D centers in Japan for developing semiconductors; Intel for designing integrated circuits; Data General and IBM Japan (Daiwa) for computer research; IBM Japan (Chiba) for software development; Japan Univac for artificial intelligence; DuPont (Yokohama) for full-scale research activities; Imperial Chemical Industries for engineering plastics and optoelectronics; DuPont (Tsukuba) for agricultural chemicals; and Eastman Kodak for photography. Similarly, Kanto Electronics, Kobe Steel, Mitsubishi Electric, Matsushita Electric (Palo Alto, California, and Woodside, Illinois), NEC Electronics, NEC Home Electronics, NEC Memory Design Center, NEC Systems, Ricoh Systems, SONY, Sumitomo Electric, Yaesu Radio and Nakamichi have R&D centers in the United States for developing electronic equipment; Isuzu Motors, Mazda Motor (Detroit and Irvine), Honda Motor, Nippon Denso, Nissan Motor, and Toyota Motor have for automotive research; Asahi Optical for optical disks; Canon for copiers and office automation design; Hitachi for software developments; Kao for haircare, shampoo and rinse; Matsushita Electric for video broad casting systems (Burlington, New

Jersey) and speech acoustics and synthesis (Santa Barbara); NEC Research Institute for human thinking/recognition and knowledge representation; Otsuka Pharmaceuticals for cytology and immunology; and Ricoh of America and Ricoh Scientific Telecommunications Systems for copiers and fax machines [51].

These collaborations are not only to diffuse Japan-United States trade and technological disputes, but more importantly to cope with rapidly changing business and technological environments by sharing with others in technology, financing, personnel, and risks. Essentially, the world is facing turbulent environments of severe international competition, short product cycles, quicker consumer reaction, and stagnating world economic dynamics. Corporations are finding it necessary to create a complex mixture of markets, hierarchies, and collaborative relationships by effectively disaggregating, reintegrating and networking in the international scene. Especially with the rapid technological changes, developing cooperative techno-governance structures is considered to be the most effective way to cope with the current international business environment. Whether institutional linkages are old or new, each one will provide indispensable resources without much delay, or will possibly reduce costs and risks in developing necessary technologies. Though the nature and characteristics of cooperative relationships may differ from superficial to more mature and future-oriented ones, cooperation is becoming more and more indispensable for survival in this fiercely competitive market.

Conclusion

A long history of Japan-United States trade disputes does not seem to ease the tension of the two nations, but rather the disputes seem to be aggravated from export restrictions to Japanese import-market openings, to forced technological cooperation, and even to domestic structural issues. It is undeniable that Japan's imbalance in trade and investment is generating an image of its low international interdependence. Hence, the condition justifies United States efforts to change domestic structures, to open up Japanese markets, and to increase interdependence with other countries. However, the crucial question:"What form of institutional arrangements in the private sector is the most efficient and what form is necessary to the development of future technologies?" is not at all addressed.

Cooperative governance structures of Japanese corporations, which in the past supported their growth and stability, have been facing limitations and challenges from as early as the 1970s. But it is the development of cooperative techno-governance structures out of the old ones that have given flexibility and dynamics to recent Japanese corporate performances. Even in the age of a borderless world [41], Japanese techno-governance structures seem to be proven valid and effective. Basically, imbalance in trade and investment is, to a great extent, due to the triumph of this development and to Japanese success in cultivating a new ideology and system of capitalist production. If so, efforts to increase imports without paying due attention to the structures may not contribute to the solution of the basic problem.

As this paper provides ample evidence, United States political efforts to open up Japanese markets are not necessarily resulting in a significant increase of market transactions. Opted transactions by Japanese corporations are rather an extension of cooperative governance or techno-governance structures to United States corporations. Japanese corporations increase imports from the United States by advancing internal procurements from their affiliates in the United States or by developing cooperative sales relationships between Japanese and United States corporations. Even these relationships, in some cases, require solid technological cooperation from the early design phase.

Japan-United States cooperative techno-governance structures are far more dynamically developed than government-to-government relationships. Unfortunately, the latter often capture more public attention than the former. Especially in the semiconductor industry the former seem to be developing so deeply, diversely, and becoming more complex that the United States accusation of Japan being closed does not sound correct. Similar developments may also be found in automobile and computer industries. However, despite Japanese ingenuity to nurture the new structures, Japan has not succeeded in clearly identifying the shape of ideal cooperative techno-governance structures that are different from the traditional ones. In this point, United States accusations of traditional practices found in cooperative governance structures are quite valid. There is a need for a new set of principles that can promote the fast transformation of the current mixed and murky structures so that a much more efficient form to suit to changes in international environment can be developed. Japan-United States trade disputes, especially SII, are providing quite important stimulation for the necessary, but tortuous process of regeneration and rethinking. However, these disputes are also providing precious opportunities for the United States to examine its own institutional arrangements and to be aware of the importance and utility of cooperative techno-governance structures.

What really underlies the borderless extension of cooperative techno-governance structures is not Japan-United States disputes, though its influence cannot be denied, but rather the drastic transformation of the international division of labor and the rapidly changing business and technological environments. The new environments are characterized by the aforementioned severe international competition, short product cycle, quicker consumer reaction, and stagnating world economy. Corporations are finding it necessary to create a complex mixture of markets, hierarchies, and collaborative relationships by effectively disaggregating, reintegrating, and networking in the international scene. Establishing collaborative relationships in technology is especially considered the most effective way to cope with the current international business environment of rapid technological changes.

If these changes are the natural due course of industrial development, any efforts to hinder the growth of cooperative techno-governance structures retard the development itself. In this point, the United States excessive emphasis on market opening may fail to correct the basic problem. The United States trade negotiators should shift their emphasis from opening markets to promoting the development of cooperative techno-governance structures between the private sectors of the two nations. And they should avoid unnecessarily stimulating the rise of techno-nationalism through government-to-government disputes. For that purpose, the United States government should set up an organization that compiles necessary information and advises United States corporate executives about ways to fully make use of existing Japanese cooperative governance and techno-governance structures.

In contrast, the Japanese government and corporations should together develop an ideal type of and principles for cooperative governance and techno-governance structures. They should be developed in a way that can be, in principle, transferred to any part of the world. Research is very much in need to examine current conditions. It should identify relationships among 1) the nature and characteristics of cooperative interactions, 2) the types of governance methods and structures, and 3) the difference of contingencies.

What are the nature and characteristics of cooperative interactions? They may be differentiated between universal and particular, dynamics-inducing and stagnation-inducing, and stability-oriented and flexibility-oriented characteristics. What types of governance methods are used? Are they market-oriented, hierarchy-oriented, or in between forms? Why are these specific cooperative interactions chosen? Is it because of a certain contingency? And what are the costs and benefits of these cooperative interactions? Answers to these questions will greatly help this creative process. Also setting up a wise men committee between the two nations will greatly benefit the Japanese effort. Once an ideal type is well established, the government and corporations should jointly set up an organization to promote and speed up this tortuous process of transformations.

REFERENCES

1 Asahi Shinbun Keizaibu. 1989. *Miriteku Pawaa*. Asahi Shinbun, Tokyo.

2. Chandler, A. 1977. *The Visible Hand: The Managerial Revolution in American Business.* Harvard University Press, Cambridge.

3. CIM Kenkyuu Group. 1990. *Seisan Kakumei CIM*. Kougyou Chousakai Publishing Co., Tokyo.

4. Denpa Shinbunsha. 1983-1989. *Denshi Kougyou Nenkan*. Denpa Shinbun Hensyuukyoku, Tokyo.

5. Department of Defense, United States Government. 1988."Defense Semiconductor Dependency" Quoted in High Technology Study Group ed., *Beikoku no Gijyutsu Senryaku*. Nikkei Science, Tokyo.

6. Dore, R. 1986. *Flexible Rigidities*, Stanford University Press, Stanford.

7. Dower, J. W. 1989."Miriteku o Meguru Nichibei Kankei no Kiki" *Chuou Kouron* (May) pp 134-149.

8. Friedman, D. 1988. *The Misunderstood Miracle*. Cornell University Press, Ithaca, N.Y.

9. Gerlach, M. 1989."Keiretsu Organization in the Japanese Economy: Analysis and Trade Implication". pp. 141-174 in C. Johnson, L.D. Tyson and J. Zysman eds. *Politics and Productivity*, Ballinger Publishing Co., New York.

10. Ikeda, M. 1990 "Senbetsu/Shuyakuka de Buhin Gyoukai mo Saihen e". *Ekonomisuto* (February) 13:62-65.

11. Inoguchi, T. 1987. *Tadanori to Ikkoku Hanei Shugi o Koete*.. Toyo Keizai Shinpou Sha, Tokyo.

12. Ito, H. 1990."Globalization in Progress at Japanese Auto Industry" *Digest of Japanese Industry & Technology* 257:4.

13. JETRO. 1988. *Nihon no Seihin Yunyuu 1987*. Nihon Boueki. Shinkoukai, Tokyo.

14. JETRO. 1989. *Nihon no Seihin Yunyuu 1988*.. Nihon Boueki Shinkoukai, Tokyo.

15. JETRO, 1990. *Nippon 1990*. Nihon Boueki Shinkoukai, Tokyo.

16. JETRO, 1991. *Nihon no Seihin Yunyuu 1990*. Nihon Boueki Shinkoukai, Tokyo.

17. Johnson, C. 1982. *MITI and the Japanese Miracle*. Stanford University Press, Stanford, Calif.

18. Jones, D.T. 1985."The Internationalization of the Automobile Industry". *Journal of General Management* 10(3):23-44.

19. Keizai Koho Center. l990. *Japan 1991*. Keizai Koho Center, Tokyo.

20. Makino, N. and Y. Shimura. 1984. *Nichibei Gijyutsu Sensou*.. Nihon Keizai Shinbun Sha, Tokyo.

21. Markusen, A. 1985. *Profit Cycles, Oligopoly, and Regional Development*.. MIT Press, Cambridge.

22. Miyasato, S. ed. l990. *Nichibei Kouzou Masatsu no Kenkyuu*.. Nihon Keizai Shinbun Sha, Tokyo.

23. Motoyama, Y. 1986. *Boueki Masatsu o Miru Me*. Yuuhikaku, Tokyo.

24. Nakanishi, T. 1990. *Corporate America Shindan*. Diamond, Tokyo.

25. Nakatani, I. 1990."Effectiveness in Technological Innovation: Keiretsu versus Conglomerates". pp. 151-162 in Gunter Heiduk and Kozo Yamamura, eds. *Technological Competition and Interdependence.* Washington University Press, Seattle.

26. Nakayama, T., et al. 1989. *Kokusai Gijyutsu Senryaku..* Nikkan Kogyo Shinbun Sha, Tokyo.

27. National Academy of Engineering. 1991. *Prospering in a Global Economy.* National Academy Press, Washington, D.C.

28. Nihon Handoutai Nenkan. 1985. *Nihon Handoutai Nenkan 1985..* Press Journal, Tokyo.

29. Nihon Keizai Shinbun, 1991."Kanri Boueki ka ni Hakusha Kakeru Handoutai Kyoutei". June 6, p. 2.

30. Nihon Keizai Shinbun, 1991."Beikoku Seisanhin no Taigai Yushutsu Kakudai" May 11, p. 1.

31. Nihon Keizai Shinbun, 1991."Gaikoku kei Handoutai no Kounyu Kakudai" June 5, p. 11.

32. Nihon Keizai Shinbun, 1991."Beikokusha, Nihon deno Kakuhan Kyouryoku" May 18, p. 1.

33. Nihon Keizai Shinbun, 1991."Shintenkai no Nichibei Masatsu, II" May 25, p. 5.

34. Nihon Keizai Shinbun, 1991."Bei ni Kyoudou Kenkyuu Teian" May 28, p. 2.

35. Nihon Keizai Shinbun, 1991."Nichibei Gyoukai Kyouzon e no Michi". June 8, p. 10.

36. Nihon Keizai Shinbun, 1991."Handoutai Senjyou Souchi de Gouben". June 11, p. 13.

37. Nihon Keizai Shinbun, 1991."Bei no R&D Taisei Kyouka" June 10, p. 11.

38. Nihon Keizai Shinbun, 1991."Kaigai Oote to Teikei Aitsugu". June 21, p 11

39. Nihon Keizai Shinbun, 1991."Handoutai Gyoukai no Saihen Kasoku". June 20, p. 11.

40. Odaka, K., K. Ohno and F. Adachi. 1988. *The Automobile Industry in Japan: A Study of Ancillary Firm Development*.. Kinokuniya Co. Ltd., Tokyo.

41. Ohmae, K. 1990. *The Borderless World*. Harper Business, New York. *Japanese Economic Studies* . 10 (4, Summer):83-101.

42. Ohtani, K. 1989. *Nihon ga Beikoku o Kaeru*.. Nihon Keizai Shinbun Sha, Tokyo.

43. Okada, Y. I990."Technological Development and Growth of Japanese Integrated Circuit Firms: An Exploratory Study" Working Paper at the Center for Japan-United States Relations. International University of Japan, Niigata-ken, Japan.

44. Okada, Y. 1990."Nichibei Handoutai Sangyou ni okeru Governance Kouzou no Hikaku" *Sekai Keizai Hyouron* 3:40-53, 4:59-65.

45. Okada, Y. 1991."Cooperative Sectoral Governance Structure of Japanese Automobile Industry in North America" Paper presented at the 32nd annual meeting of the International Studies Association, March 20-23, 1991, held in Vancouver, Canada.

46. Ouchi, W.G. 1984. *The M-form Society*. Addison-Wesley, New York.

47. Piore, M. and C. Sabel. I984. *The Second Industrial Divide: Possibilities for Prosperity*. Basic Books, New York.

48. Shimokawa, K. 1990."90 Nendai, Sekai Saihensei no Rikigaku" *Ekonomisuto* February 13:46-49.

49. Smitka, M.J. 1989. *Competitive Ties: Subcontracting in the Japanese Automobile Industry*. Unpublished Ph.D. Thesis. Yale University.

50. Takeda, Shirou. 1991."Shijyou no Gurobaru ka to Kigyou no Guroubaru ka". Paper presented at the Conference of the Study Group on Multinational Corporations held in Kyoto, July 5-7.

51. Tatsuno, S. 1990. *Created in Japan..* Harper & Row Publishers, New York

52. Tjosvold, D. 1984."Cooperation Theory and Organizations" *Human Relations* 37 (9):743-767.

53. Uyehara, C.H. 1988. *U.S.-Japan Science and Technology Exchange: Patterns of Interdependence.* Westview Press, Boulder.

54. Wall Street Journal. 1990."Texas Instruments, Japan's Kobe Steel Form Venture to Make Semiconductors". March 20.

55. Williamson, O. 1975. *Markets and Hierarchies: Analysis and Antitrust Implications.* The Free Press, New York.

56. Williamson, O. 1985. *The Economic Institution of Capitalism..* The Free Press, New York.

57. Womack, J.P., D.J. Jones and D. Ross. 1990. *The Machine That Changed the World.* The Free Press, New York.

58. Yamamoto, Y. 1986. *Boueki Masatsu o Miru Me.* Yuuhikaku, Tokyo.

Japan and the Money and Capital Markets
of Asia

Yuichiro Nagatomi
Chairman
FAIR

It is a great honor and pleasure to be invited as the guest speaker to the Conference of the Governors of the Southeast Asian Central Banks (SEACEN) which has a great history of more than a quarter of a century and to be able to meet many distinguished friends from Asia, a region where I am also from. I would like to express my sincere appreciation.[1]

The present world is changing drastically. A historical change, the so called breakdown of the Cold War System, is taking place. This change is mutually interrelated to the structural change of the world's economy.

In North America, the free trade agreement between the United States and Canada has already been signed, and the new agreement between the United States and Mexico is becoming concrete. In Western Europe, on the other hand, EC market integration is under way, and EFTA countries are expected to join the EC in the future.

Under these circumstances, the development of the Asia-Pacific area, particularly the Asian region, is especially significant, and the world's attention is focused on the direction of this region's development.

Let me compare these three regions by using the available figures of 1989. The American region, which includes the United States, Canada and Mexico, has a population of 360 million, and the European region, combining EC countries and EFTA countries, has 370 million. But in the Asian region, adding up the population of Japan, the Asia NIEs, and the ASEAN countries alone, the figure is 510 million.

Nominal GNP at 1989 prices is $5.9 trillion in the American region, $5.7 trillion in the European region, and $3.5 trillion in the Asian region, a figure still much lower than those in the American and European regions.

However, the real growth rate is fairly high in Asia, while those rates in America and Europe are in decline. Therefore, if the Asian region continues to grow at the same pace, it will not be long before Asia catches up and eventually exceeds the American and European countries.

---

[1]Guest speech at the 26th Conference of the Governors of the Southeast Asian Central Banks (SEACEN) January 30, 1991.

Let me give you a calculation of how many years it will take for the Asian region to catch up with the American and the European regions. Suppose that, based on the actual figures for 1989 and several projections, the American region continues to grow at 2.5% per year, Europe at 3.0%, and Asia at 5.0%, Asia will catch up and exceed America in 2011, and Europe in 2015. Since the dollar was strong in 1989, these periods will be shortened if the dollar maintains a lower level than that of 1989 for a long-term period.

The economic developments of the Southeast Asian countries, such as Myanmar, Nepal, Sri Lanka, Vietnam and others, from which we have distinguished representatives here in this SEACEN Conference, will further strengthen the vitality of Asian economic development.

Progress in Cooperation in the Asia-Pacific Region

In January 1980, the late Prime Minister Masayoshi Ohira presented the Pacific Basin Cooperation Concept on his state visit to Australia, based on the findings of Ohira's policy study groups. At that time, I accompanied him and took part in the prime ministers' meeting because, during his term, I was the chief assistant to the Prime Minister Ohira and coordinated his policy research.

The purpose of the Pacific Basin Cooperation Concept is to create a cooperative relationship in the Asia-Pacific region, and to realize a peaceful and vigorous future for the global society through the development of this region.

In the fall of 1980, after Mr. Ohira's death, the Pacific Economic Cooperation Council (PECC) started in Canberra to promote this concept. Since then, the PECC has held meetings every eighteen months in such places as Bangkok, Bali Island and Seoul. I am a standing member of the Japan National Committee for Pacific Economic Cooperation (JANCPEC); and when the PECC's tenth anniversary dinner was held here in Jakarta last September, I was invited and took part in it.

Former Prime Minister Noboru Takeshita also stressed the importance of the Asia-Pacific cooperation on several occasions such as in his policy speech in Jakarta in May, 1989. I also accompanied him as the Director-General of the Customs and Tariff Bureau of the Ministry of Finance on his state visit to Australia and the ASEAN countries.

The Asia-Pacific cooperation has reached the ministerial level. In November 1989, the first meeting of the Asia-Pacific Economic Cooperation (APEC) was held in Canberra, and the second one was held in Singapore in July last year. I attended these meetings as a deputy representative of the Japanese Government, representing the Ministry of Finance.

"The Committee for Asia-Pacific Economic Research" was organized in 1988 at the Foundation for Advanced Information and Research (FAIR) under the direction of Prime Minister Takeshita. This committee has nine study groups with about 170 experts in the ministries concerned, scholars, and private researchers. Based on the mid-term report of the study groups, the first meeting of "The Asia-Pacific Conference" was held in .June 1989 and attended by Mr. Takeshita and people from the Asia-Pacific countries. The second Asia-Pacific Conference is scheduled in May this year, based on the final report of the Committee soon to be released.

FAIR also organized "The Committee for Joint Research on Asia-Pacific Relations." This committee is studying measures to develop the Asia-Pacific region in cooperation with directors of research institutes and professors in Asia, such as Dr. Dorodjatun Kuntjoro-Jakti, professor at the University of Indonesia, and Mr. Jusuf Wanandi, chairman of the supervisory board of the Center for Strategic and International Studies (CSIS) of Indonesia. The first Joint Research Conference on Asia-Pacific Relations has held in April 1988, bringing together the results of the study. The second conference has held in August 1989 and the third conference is scheduled for the fall of this year.

Also established in Japan in order to promote further Asia-Pacific cooperation, is the Cooperation for Asia-Pacific (CAP), which has leading figures in the fields of politics, government, the private sector and academia as its members. The chairman is Mr. Takeshita and the coordinator is Mr. Gaishi Hiraia, chairman of the Japan Federation of Economic Organizations.

Seven Viewpoints for Asia-Pacific Cooperation

Now I would like to explain my seven principles regarding the Asia-Pacific cooperation.

First, we should make this region one of the world's most profitable markets by utilizing its vitality and potential to its fullest extent.

Second we should encourage not only intra-regional economic economic exchanges but also keep markets open to the United States, Europe and all other regions. While it is desirable that the Asian countries strengthen their mutual cooperation for their development, it is counterproductive for the development of this region to create an economic bloc, considering this region's close trade relationships with America and Europe.

Third, by keeping this region the most profitable and open market, it is expected that American and European corporations will be motivated to conduct business in this area.

Fourth, with the positive involvement of American and European corporations, it is anticipated that the U.S. and EC markets will be kept open, that free trade will expand, and that the world economy will develop as one coordinated body.

Fifth, through these activities, corporations of the developed countries will be given opportunities for new investment and financing. On the other hand, the developing countries of Asia, where a young labor force is increasing in numbers, will enjoy increased job opportunities and higher income. These countries are expected to develop from simply a production and export base to mass-consumption societies.

Sixth, in the Asia-Pacific region, there is a great degree of diversity in race, religion, culture, tradition and values. Countries in the region are at various stages of economic development and have different market practices. In order to develop this region, it is important not to try to eliminate differences and enforce conformity by imposing the values of the developed countries, a situation which the developing countries had unfortunately experienced in the past during the modernization of the advanced countries. We must respect the diversity, from which vitality will spring forth.

Seventh, through collaboration between Japan, the United States and Europe for further development of the Asia-Pacific region, economic frictions will be settled constructively and a new world system will be created.

Development of the Economies in the Asia-Pacific Region

Let me now take a look at demographic trends which are said to correlate to the stages of economic development.

The average number of children per woman in 1988 was 1.7 in

Japan, and 1.9 in the United States while in the case of Korea and Singapore, the figures were 1.8 and 1.9 respectively or below 2, which is comparable to the developed countries. Thailand's figure was 2.5, below 3, which is coming close to the figures for the developed countries. Birth rate figures were 3.4 in Indonesia, 3.7 in Malaysia, and 3.3 in the Philippines, all of which are below 4.

The percentage of population under 15 years of age in 1988 was 19.6% in Japan, 21.6% in the United States, 24.0% in Singapore, and 27.3% in Korea, that is below 30%. On the other hand, the share was 34.2% in Thailand, 39.3% in Malaysia, 39.5% in Indonesia and 40.3% in the Philippines,which are mostly reaching the under 40% level. For this trend, the figure in Sri Lanka was 32.1%, in Myanmar 37 9%, in Vietnam 40.0% and in Nepal 42.7%.

Though efforts to raise birth rates are made in the countries where the birth rates dropped under 2, the percentage of the younger labor force is still high, in general. It is desirable to increase job opportunities that correspond to this demographic structure.

In Asia, there are many countries that have been achieving remarkable economic development. It is pointed out that the Asian NIEs have already reached the stage of mass-consumption societies in the second half of the 1970s, and some of the ASEAN countries have been approaching this stage during the 1980s. In this region the concentration of the population in the cities has accelerated. It will be necessary to further improve the environment in the cities, for example, by making tap water drinkable.

The Asian region is often regarded as being just a production and export base and this is often criticized by the Americans and Europeans. However, the Asian region is quickly developing as a big import market as well. In 1988, the total imports of Japan, the Asian NIEs, and the ASEAN countries reached $450 billion, exceeding the U.S. imports of $440 billion. In 1989, this difference widened as the Asian imports grew to $520 billion while the U.S. imports stood at $470 billion.

Furthermore, if we look at West European countries' statistics of annual percentage change of exports by region, the rates of increase in exports to the Asian countries were the largest for most countries both in 1988 and in 1989. This demonstrates that the Asian countries are making great contributions to the world's economic development.

The Asia-Pacific Money and Capital Markets

The Asian region, particularly the ASEAN countries, intends to promote export-oriented industries and actively seek to attract foreign corporations. In response, massive direct investments have been made by corporations of the advanced countries. This has enabled the economies in this region to achieve remarkable progress. For example, Japanese direct investment in the Asian NIEs and ASEAN countries in 1989,was 7.7 billion, and the accumulative total of 39 years from FY 1951 to FY 1989 stood at 37.5 billion.

However, in this region the domestic industries, which are expected to support the advanced export industries, have not been fully developed yet. The export industries depend on parts and materials produced in Japan. This is one of the main reasons why imports from Japan increase. Furthermore, the money and capital markets have not been fully developed yet to sustain the development of domestic industries.

I would like to express my admiration for the intensive efforts which have been made under the leadership of the governors here to rapidly reform their financial markets. Japan would like to cooperate in the development of the markets as much as possible.

Characteristics of Finance in ASEAN Countries

I have been to the ASEAN region many times and exchanged views with finance ministers, central bank governors, and other leaders. In January last year, I was also invited to the SEACEN Governors' conference held in Colombo, Sri Lanka.

I think I could point out the characteristics of the financial markets in the ASEAN countries as follows.

First, profit-taking activities through short-term transactions could be cited as the characteristic of the funds. Although the share of loans with terms longer than 4 years is increasing in Malaysia, bank loans are extremely short-term in general. Even in the case of Thailand where commercial banks have developed, many bank lendings are on a one-month basis. As for long-term financing, it is often done by rolling over one-month lending into loans with a one or two year commitment basis at the longest.

Second, active efforts have been made to develop stock exchanges by promoting the listing of privatized public corporations. Moreover, in

Singapore and Malaysia, computerization of trading was introduced. However, the listing criteria and the standard for stock issues at market prices have not yet been arranged well, due to the lack of sufficient experience in the markets. The market is still insufficient for smooth fund raising, because it is centered mostly on stock listing and trading. Straight bonds and convertible bonds which are very useful means for raising long-term funds are rarely issued. Even in Singapore, warrant bonds are mainly issued.

Third, foreign corporations bring the initial fund for their investments from their own countries. However, they have difficulty in raising their operational funds, and they either have to renew local short-term money or to raise longer-term dollar funds from Singapore or somewhere else, converting them into local currency with foreign exchange risks.

Fourth, the markets have not been developed enough for foreign companies to reinvest their profits and to manage their portfolios in these countries.

Fifth, in order to encourage the growth of domestic industries in this region, it is essential to have long-term capital, which is inadequate at present. Therefore, it is important to promote the following: (a) further development of governmental financial institutions which provide long-term funds, such as the Industrial Finance Corporation of Thailand (IFCT) and the Malaysian Industrial Development Finance Berhad (MIDF); and (b) introduction and development of the private system to provide long-term funds, including those of foreign financial institutions.

Sixth, for the development of this region, Japan is intending not only to supply public funds in the form of ODA but also to recycle private funds. However, with regard to the latter, the market on the receiving end has not been developed enough to absorb such recycled funds. For this matter, too, the development of the financial markets is essential.

Experiences in Japan

I would like to share with you some of our own experiences in Japan as a reference for the development of the money and capital markets in the Asian region.

Before World War II, the securities market in Japan was already sufficiently developed to allow smooth functioning of the interest rate mechanism in the market. This market condition and a decline in the volume of bank lending after the financial depression in 1927 in Japan sharply raised the ratio of direct financing, namely raising funds in the securities market by issuing stocks and bonds. For 1931-36, the average ratio of direct financing stood extraordinarily high at 96.1%.

Around 1936, however, Japan plunged into the period of the regrettable wartime-controlled economy. Funds were severely allocated to the war-industries. The Ministry of Finance and the Bank of Japan implemented strict financial control, and put emphasis on indirect financing in order to allocate funds effectively to the industries. The bond issue market, which had difficulty to allocate funds, was closed. When it was reopened in 1938, selection of issuing companies, volume, timing and terms of issues were all placed under the control of the issuance authority, namely through the Industrial Bank of Japan under the guidance of the Ministry of Finance and the Bank of Japan. The average share of direct financing for 1937-45 was reduced to 27.9%

Allocation of Reconstruction Funds After the War

During the recovery period after the war, the "priority production scheme" policy was introduced, under which industries essential for economic recovery, coal and steel as the first step, then electricity for industries and fertilizer for agricultural productions, followed by marine transportation and textiles for exports, were selected and resources were preferentially allocated to these industries. In the financial market, the Reconstruction Financing Corporation was established as a government financial institution in 1947, and low interest rate funds were intensively allocated to the industries mentioned above.

As a government financial institution, in 1951 the Japan Export Bank (which was reorganized into the Japan Export and Import Bank the following year) was founded to promote exports. In the same year, succeeding and expanding the role played by the Reconstruction Financing Corporation, the Japan Development Bank was established to provide long-term low interest rate funds for the development of the domestic economy, using postal savings as its main funding source. In 1953 the Ministry of Finance began to formulate the Fiscal Investment and Loan Program in order to let the public financing system work to the full.

In the private financial sector, for the purpose of facilitating the effective allocation of funds, the basic scheme of funds allocation during the wartime was maintained, and the securities market continued to be restricted. In the period of 1946-55, the average ratio of direct financing declined further to 17.5%.

Fund Supply for High Economic Growth

In the mid-1950s, the Japanese economy entered the "high growth period" and sustained double-digit growth for most of the period 1959-70. During this period, the Japan Development Bank financial institutions played an important role. At the same time, in the private sector, specialized financial institutions for the purpose of providing long-term funds were nurtured. The Long-term Credit Bank Act was introduced in 1952, and the policy to separate the trust banking business from other banking businesses was decided in 1954. Long-term credit banks and trust banks are different from the ordinary commercial banks, and deposit taking as the source for medium- and short-term lending is restricted. They are allowed, in return, to raise long-term funds by issuing bank debentures or accepting loan trusts in order to secure necessary funds to supply long-term credits.

In 1965, in the middle of the high growth period, the share of these financial institutions in the net incremental funds supplied to the industries were 13.0% for government financial institutions, 14.9% for long-term credit banks, and 15.8% for trust banks. The total share of these three types of institutions, reached 43.7%. In 1980 when the Japanese economy was already in the stable-growth period, the share of these three dropped to 26.7%. These figures show the important role played by these institutions in providing long-term industrial funds during the high growth period.

During the high growth period, the interest rates were maintained at the lower level and the ordinary banks supplied "high-powered growth money" to the industries with interest rates as low as they could, supported by loans from the Bank of Japan. The characteristics during the high growth period in the Japanese economy were:

(a) "Over-Loan", namely the ratio of banks' loans to deposits was much higher than those in the United States and Europe, and

(b) "Over-Borrowing,'namely the capital ratio of corporations was low and they depended heavily on borrowing from banks. These features were often criticized from the Anglo-American viewpoints.

In the process of achieving high growth, efforts to restore the function of the securities market were gradually made, starting in the mid-1960s, for the purpose that control on volume and terms of issues could be more flexible, and the function of the interest rate mechanism could be introduced. However, the results still remained limited.

While bank lending was expanding, the securities market remained a "marginal market for procuring funds." The average ratio of direct financing for 1956-65 was 18.5% and the ratio for 1966-75 was the lowest at 9.6%. These figures show that during this period banks, vis-a-vis the securities companies and manufacturing companies, exerted the strongest influence in the domestic financial market and more generally in the Japanese economy.

Shift to Stable Growth Period and Deregulation

In 1970, the Japanese economy bid farewell to the double-digit high growth and entered into the unstable growth period. Efforts to liberalize and internationalize the money and securities markets started in earnest in 1970, so that the Japanese financial system could adapt to the circumstances in this new period.

Upon my return from the United States in the summer of 1971, after serving as a financial attache of the Japanese Embassy, I was ordered to tackle this task. The influence of banks in the securities market was very strong, and the market was severely regulated with the emphasis on indirect financing. In order to restore the market mechanism in the securities market, the old way of thinking needed to be cut off. To this end, I used and vitalized a new word "capital market" which derives from a German phrase, and a new division called the Capital Market Division was set up in our Ministry of Finance. Under the banner of the introduction of a "capital market", efforts were made to liberalize and internationalize the money and capital markets.

At the end of 1970, the ADB bond was issued as the first yen-denominated foreign bond, but in substance, this bond took on the character of private placement, because a majority of the bond was bought by banks. At that time, since the word "liberalization" was forbidden to be used in our Ministry of Finance, under the name of "making more flexible", the deregulation of the money and securities markets proceeded through introducing new financial goods one after another which were beyond the scope of existing regulations, such as public offering of yen-denominated foreign bonds, foreign-currency denominated private placements, issuance of stocks at market prices, liberalization of coupon rates of convertible bonds and improvements in the bond repurchase market.

In the process of improving the securities market, which had been a transformation of indirect financing, and the Tokyo international capital market being established, fund raising from abroad was on the increase, and the means of fund raising and portfolio management for companies diversified. Companies used to depend largely on bank borrowings during and after the war, and fund raising in the stock market had been mostly in the form of stock issuance at par value to the existing shareholders. Moreover, banks had exercised a strong influence on such stock issues through the approval of capital increase plans of issuing companies and the decision of shares of such stocks to be bought by banks. Then, from around 1972, stock issues at market price and the issues of convertible bonds (CB) started fully.

Liberalization and Internationalization of Money and Capital Markets

Starting in the late 1970s, liberalization and internationalization of the money and capital markets made remarkable progress. The first oil shock took place in 1973, and in 1974 the Japanese economy consequently recorded the first negative growth since the end of the war. In 1975, as a measure against recession, government bonds were issued in large quantity. The terms of issuance were gradually set according to the market conditions, and the size of the secondary bond market grew drastically. The volume of bond trading, which stood at ¥17 trillion in 1972 and ¥52 trillion in 1975, went up to ¥203 trillion in 1978. A large secondary market for government bonds was created.

In 1980, the Foreign Exchange Control Law was amended and international capital transactions were liberalized. In 1984, the Japan-U.S. Yen-Dollar Committee report was published. With these continuous reforms, the pace of the liberalization and internationalization of the Japanese financial markets further accelerated.

As the liberalization and internationalization of the Japanese money and capital markets progressed the share of direct financing in corporate fund raising also increased. While the average ratio of direct financing for 1976-85 went up only slightly to 11.3%; in the second half of the 1980s the ratio increased drastically because of issues of warrant bonds and convertible bonds at home and abroad.

For the period after this, comparable statistics on direct financing ratio are not available, because of the change in the statistical system. If we use the flow of funds account table to calculate the share of direct financing, the average for 1975-84 was 15.1%; and the average from 1985-89 went up to 23.1%, or 28.7% if we include commercial papers which were introduced in 1987.

There are people who predict that this ratio might decline because of the recent fall in stock prices. On the other hand, banks are cautious about extending new loans, facing the stock price fall, the difficulty in making real estate loans and the deadline coming closer for banks to achieve the 8% capital adequacy ratio of the Cook Committee. Against this backdrop, together with high bank lending rates, the issue of corporate straight bonds is increasing rapidly.

In any case, the fundamental difference between the 1930s just after the Great Depression and the present is that, as a result of the completion of industrialization since the Industrial Revolution and the high growth of the economy, big companies have come to hold large amounts of capital reserve and have become much less dependent on banks for equipment and operation funds. This tendency has been further accelerated by the diversification of fund raising measures. If we could use the statistics of substantial industrial funds alone, the share of direct financing would be much higher than the one previously mentioned.

The Emergence of "Excess Money"

In contrast to the period of the Great Depression when the industrialization was still in progress, we now see the generation of massive funds exceeding those required for the real production activities in developed countries where modernization and industrialization have been accomplished. I call these funds "structural excess money". Such funds move freely and swiftly among currency, money, and stock markets beyond country borders and time zones. This is often criticized as a "money game" or a "babble economy".

However, this excess money is not linked directly to real production activities. That is why the Japanese real economy has not been influenced much by the difficulties in portfolio management of Japanese banks and securities companies, due to the stock price fall, and so on.

Recently, there has been some apprehension that Japanese firms may reduce their investment and loans in the Asian region, as the Soviet Union and Eastern Europe are being liberalized. However, I would like to point out three things concerning the activities of Japanese private corporations.

Firstly, they are still trying to estimate the prospects for the Soviet and East European economies, and have not reached the stage of active investment in these regions.

Secondly, for those Japanese corporations intending to invest abroad, there is no major difficulty in funding because they have already accumulated a large amount of financial assets and have diversified funding methods.

Thirdly, Japanese banks and securities companies, after experiencing the recent market turmoil, are seriously trying to redirect their activity from the so called money game to loans to sound borrowers directly linked to real production activities.

Every year, I visit foreign countries to grasp what is actually taking place and to exchange views with leading figures. The number of countries and regions I have visited has reached 77. These trips have strengthened my conviction that the Southeast Asian countries have a strong will to develop, their people are diligent, they have the largest potential for growth and are therefore the most desirable places for investment and loans by the corporations of developed countries.

Conclusion

Generally speaking, the provision of long-term industrial funds is important in order to nurture domestic industries. However, in the early phase of economic development, supply of these funds through the private sector is not adequate. Therefore, as I mentioned before, it is necessary to develop governmental financial institutions which provide long-term funds and to introduce and develop the private financial system to provide long-term funds including those by foreign financial institutions. Development of the securities market as a measure of procuring long-term capital is equally important.

In the Asia-Pacific region recognizing these needs, big efforts have been made. However, if looking at the share of governmental financial institutions which provide long-term industrial funds country by country, while there are some countries like Korea, where the share used to be fairly high, for the ASEAN countries, the shares remain at around the 8% level even in Indonesia where the share is relatively high. I think that further efforts to this effect should be made.

In recent years, the ASEAN countries have actively introduced Japanese financial institutions. Including joint ventures and representative offices, Japanese banks had about 300 activity bases in the Asian region, and securities companies had about 70 bases at the end of 1989.

In order to develop human resources that will lead the development of money and capital markets in the Asia-Pacific region, Japan has decided to provide funds to the Asian Development Bank (ADB), and under the collaboration between the ADB and the Institute of Fiscal and Monetary Policy (IFMP) of our Ministry of Finance, "the ADB-IFMP Training Seminar on Monetary and Fiscal Policies" has started.

This seminar is aimed at heads of bureaus and divisions of the ministries of finance and the central banks in the Asian and the Oceanian Island countries. The first seminar was successfully held last November, thanks to great efforts made by Mr. William R. Thomson, Vice President of the ADB and Dr. Hakchung Choo, Director of the Economics and the Development Resource Center (EDRC). Our Institute accepted 21 persons from 19 countries for two weeks.

The funds contributed by Japan to the ADB for this seminar as well as for Seminars on Fiscal and Monetary Policy Issues in ADB member countries, the International Finance Seminar, and Symposium on Tax Policy and Reforms were ¥61 million for the first fiscal year. For the next fiscal year, we are expecting ¥91 million, though the national budget will be under discussion in the Diet.

Our Institute is in charge of organizing the seminar, in cooperation with the other bureaus of our Ministry, the Bank of Japan, the Tokyo Stock Exchange and government financial institutions as well as with private banks, securities, insurances,and high-tech companies in Japan. As lecturers, foreign scholars such as Dr. Bon Ho Koo, President of the Korea Development Institute, participated as well.

I would like to expand this project further and would welcome the opinions and cooperation from leaders presented here at the SEACEN conference.

In February last year, for the purpose of contributing to the efforts to reform the money and capital markets in this region, our Institute, in cooperation with FAIR, established a "Committee on the Development of Asia-Pacific Money and Capital Markets," while taking fully into considerations the valuable opinions of the ministers of finance and the governors of the central banks in the Asian countries. As an activity of this committee, a "Mission for the Development of Asian Money and Capital Markets" will visit four ASEAN countries in the near future. I would like to ask your cooperation so that this mission will be successful.

I would like to finish my speech by expressing my sincere hope that under the leadership of this SEACEN, the money and capital markets in the Asian region will strongly grow and the Asian economy will prosper. Thank you very much.

Part III

American Perspectives

The Future of U.S.-Japan Technology Relations

Michael W. Chinworth
The Analytic Sciences Corporation

Japan and the United States are wrestling with a complex and contradictory relationship that focuses equally on cooperation and competition. On the one hand, the two countries are tied more closely than ever to one another in important respects. The United States and Japan remain each other's largest overseas markets, and Japan is becoming more "Americanized" to the extent that its companies invest in this country to assume a more visible economic presence. Joint ventures, technology trade and technical exchanges are increasing despite a range of political and economic problems and tensions. On the other hand, there is no doubt that Japan is the strongest economic and technological competitor to the United States for the foreseeable future. The dimensions of that challenge are so great that it has spawned discussions of Japan as a new threat to the United States in place of the former Soviet Union.[1]

Japanese economic and technological success no longer is a matter of dispute. Its industries are highly visible in major industrial sectors. Japan has challenged the United States in one market to another, even those viewed as American strongholds (Japanese beef producers, for example, have begun taking steps to export to this country). A range of issues has developed in part because of that very success that affects every element of the bilateral relationship. Growing trade imbalances, economic tensions, and differences in global interests have led to significant political disputes between the United States and Japan, a situation that is likely to continue for the future. Even the military alliance — and the technological transfers that continue as part of it — is facing transitional period and perhaps a complete re-evaluation. Many fundamental elements in those ties, including the technological aspects, are highly contentious. This could lead, if it has not already, to a widening gulf between the twin elements of cooperation and competition in the relationship as well.

The technological relationship between the United States and Japan is

---

[1]See, for example, "Japan 2000," a draft report by the Andrew Dougherty of the Rochester Institute of Technology, which was supported in part through funding from the Central Intelligence Agency. The CIA subsequently distanced itself from the report, which was highly critical of Japan (Paul F. Horvitz, "CIA Funded Study Says Japan Lacks Global Responsibility," Washington Post, June 8, 1991, p. A5, and Paul F. Horvitz, "CIA Spurns Report That Assails Japan," Washington Post, June 12, 1991, p. A26).

at the center of many of these concerns and will manifest itself across a broad range of fields in the coming decades. The most fundamental is in bilateral economic ties. "Technology" has many meanings and implications, but for the purposes of this chapter, its most important aspect is manifestation of know-how in the form of products and services sold in global markets. Whether it is a component sold in bulk to a computer company for further assembly, or a completed disc player purchased by an individual consumer, basic, applied and process technologies are being exchanged as transactions in international markets.

Japan has been able to build its massive trade surpluses in part because of its growing technological capabilities. While it would be imprudent to argue that the large trade deficits experienced by the United States vis-a-vis Japan mean that the latter is technologically superior to the United States, it nevertheless is not an overstatement to suggest that the gap between the two has narrowed considerably. As Japan devotes more of its economic resources to research and development, it is unlikely that the United States will be able to regain the indisputable lead it once maintained over Japan. Fundamental imbalances in the thrust of technology policies in the two countries will exacerbate these differences further, fostering further political disputes as Japan's technological capabilities manifest themselves in still larger trade surpluses.[2]

Both the United States and Japan view their technology bases in commercial and military sectors as key to their respective competitive position globally and vis-a-vis one another. There are common elements in the technology development policies implemented by the two countries, but there also are fundamental differences that could take the two countries on divergent paths in the technology relationship. Central to the policies in both countries is a major difference in attitudes toward technology sharing and exchanges. Despite Japanese fears of United States "techno-nationalism," the United States retains an element in its technology policies that calls for mutually beneficial transfers and exchanges.[3] The Japanese attitude, to overstate it somewhat, is that the nation's technological strength is central to its ability to survive in an increasingly hostile economic environment.

As economic and technological cooperation and competition continue,

---

[2]This is not to ignore criticisms by the United States and other countries of Japanese practices that have led to closure of or restricted access to its domestic markets for foreign products. These are legitimate issues, but this chapter focuses trends in such areas as allocation of economic resources to research and development because without an ability to sustain the technological base, even an opening of Japanese markets will be meaningless for U.S. producers and the country's economic competitiveness as a whole.

[3]"Techno-nationalism" is a sweeping and still poorly defined notion that generally suggests more strident government policies — usually the United States — that would result in reduced access by other countries but greater political pressures to make leading edge technologies in those countries more available to the U.S.

political ties will face a broad range of challenges differing from those faced in the past. Institutional responses to vent these latent problems have been limited. Japan has responded to growing United States concern over its economic and technology policies through such means as opening major research and development initiatives to foreign participation, while expanding R&D funding to assure continued economic growth. The United States response to such initiatives, however, has been suspicious and counter to its policies of refraining from involving itself in what it has viewed as corporate matters, not areas of government policy.

It is this final point — a fundamental difference in views over the appropriate role of government in technology promotion — that prevents solution of these problems. The United States steadfastly denies that Washington should assume an activist role in technology promotion, particularly in corporate matters. Japan, on the other hand, views government's role as one of furthering technological and economic growth not only to promote domestic businesses, but to assure long term survival. The resulting philosophical clash has concrete influences on the nature of technological development funding in both countries and complicates the hopes for truly cooperative relations in the future. Japan's growing technological strength, however, ultimately will enable that country to pursue an increasingly independent technological path. This could force the United States to form more substantial policies — and of a sort currently in disfavor in Washington — if only to allow government and industry to respond to Japanese challenges and initiatives.

Present Technology Relations

The United States and Japan both are investing heavily in science and technology, but significant differences exist in spending and budgetary patterns that will have implications for the future. First the numbers.[4] Japan's total R&D expenditures reached ¥10,627.6 billion in JFY 1988 (approximately $77 billion at current exchange rates), up from ¥7,180.8 billion five years earlier. Government austerity programs and economic conditions occasionally have retarded growth in R&D expenditures in recent years. Nevertheless, total spending has averaged about 9% in annual increases over the last five fiscal years (see Tables 1 and 2).

United States funding of research and development also has increased, but at a slightly less dramatic pace. Funding for R&D increased 44% through

---

[4]For a summary of Japan's R&D expenditures, see Jon Choy, "1990 Update on Japanese Research and Development," JEI Report No. 37A, September 28, 1990.

the 1980s over the previous decade's spending, reaching $132 billion in 1989 — 2.6% of the nation's gross national product. The rate of increase slowed in the latter half of the decade and, more significantly, federal non-defense obligations declined 3% over the 1980-89 period. In actual performance of R&D activities, the private sector conducts 72% of all research, with universities and government laboratories both contributing about 11% each[5] (see Table 3 and Figure 1).

There are several elements in these figures that suggest that many of the perceived problems in United States and Japanese spending patterns within both countries continue, despite the recognition of their potential impediments. There also are several divergences, however, that have important implications for the ability of the United States and Japan to manage its competitive-cooperative relationship in the future. The first noticeable difference simply is the scale and pace of such investments. The United States outspends Japan by more than two to one in total R&D expenditures, but almost half the United States expenditure is directed to defense. For non-defense applications, then, the expenditures of the two countries are almost the same, and well in Japan's favor in per capita expenditures.[6] While United States spending generally is increasing, Japanese outlays by both industry and government — and especially the former — are accelerating so rapidly that Japan has surpassed the United States in terms of R&D expenditures as a percentage of gross national product (2.9% for Japan compared with 2.6% for the United States). The difference is nearly two-to-one if defense related R&D is eliminated (see Figure 2). The Japanese government predicts that this gap will widen in the next decade, growing to 3.4% of Japan's GNP by 1990 and 5.3% by 2000, compared with 2.9% and 3.4% for the United States over the same period.[7] Higher R&D spending per se does not necessarily translate into greater economic competitiveness, but given the rising costs of future generations of products, it is difficult to argue that companies and nations devoting larger shares of their total economic resources to such research will have a disadvantage, either.

Industry is leading this trend in Japan, accounting in 1988 for 80% of all spending (up from 75.9% in 1983). There is no single industrial sector, from agriculture and construction to pulp manufacturing and communications — that does not have a significant research and development budget. The

[5]National Science Board, Science and Engineering Indicators 1989 (Washington, D.C.: U.S. Government Printing Office), 1989. p. 86.
[6]Science and Technology Agency, "Summary of White Paper on Science and Technology 1990," October 1990, p. 29.
[7]Jon K.T. Choy, "Technological Innovation in Japan and the United States," *The World and I*, November 1988, p. 171-172. The budget for the Technical Research and Development Institute (TRDI) — the research and development arm of the Japan Defense Agency — accounts for just under 5 percent of total government R&D expenditures. Research in private firms accounts for the remainder of total defense related R&D.

Japanese construction industry, for example, expended ¥148.5 billion in JFY 1988 (just under half a percentage point of total sales), an increase of 15.7% over the previous year. The pharmaceuticals industry has the highest rate of R&D expenditures in terms of sales at 6.94%. Manufacturing industries in general average over 3% of total sales in terms of R&D investments, compared with 1.8% ten years earlier.

The United States and Japan in research and development is that the United States has favored basic research over applied research, in contrast with Japan's emphasis on the reverse combination. Although total spending for basic research has increased, it accounted for only 13.3% of total R&D expenditures in JFY 1988, slightly less than five years earlier. In contrast, applied research accounted for 24.3% of expenditures while developmental research represented 62.4% (see Table 4). This has been cited as a source of United States strength and a potential Japanese weakness. Indeed, even in Japan there are calls for higher basic research expenditures (although not necessarily at the expense of applied research budgets). However, it may be the United States that is deluding itself in this regard, since technology is most useful in economic terms when it enters markets as fungible commodities that generate sales and economic growth.

There are other differences. The United States, for example, devotes only token spending to energy research, while Japan allocates nearly 25% of its research to energy. The United States devotes only 1% of its R&D funding to industrial development, compared with 15% for Germany. Life sciences dominate United States university based research, and only 13% of university research is directed toward engineering. In contrast, life sciences receive 34% of funding in Japanese universities, compared to 22% for engineering. All of these statistics have direct bearing on United States competitiveness. They demonstrate in a quick glance another basic problem facing the United States now and in the future: the failure to address its slipping industrial efficiency.

Although Japan has been criticized for its somewhat low basic research expenditures, the commercial emphasis that results in the strong applications orientation of Japanese science as a whole clearly has contributed to its commercial competitiveness globally. The United States, in turn, could be criticized for sacrificing mid-term development and applications in the pursuit of more esoteric and costly basic research. This difference explains in part the growing gap in U.S.-Japanese competitiveness.

This is illustrated in the larger scale efforts of the two countries. Both countries are thinking big in their long term research funding, but with a few differences. Japanese large scale projects have focused on commercial aerospace and nuclear power generation in contrast with massive United States programs such as the superconducting super collider. In addition, there is more of an incremental approach in the Japanese pattern than is evident in United States spending patterns, which appear to be directed toward dramatic breakthroughs instead of marginal but steady knowledge gains and product improvements. It is still unclear if either approach will prove inherently superior to the other, but for now one need only note Japan's growing merchandise trade surpluses and continuing competitive improvements to find a possible answer to that problem.[8]

Private sector spending in both defense and commercial areas are facing hard times in the United States. In Japan, companies continue to devote sizeable shares of their profits to research. Private sector funding of defense related research is uncertain, but both companies and the government have a technology management strategy that emphasizes dual use ("spin on") technologies. Thus, the potential defense technology base within Japan is increasing.[9]

Thus, technology relations are influenced by a number of divergences in technology funding between the two countries. The United States has focused on basic research with a large defense and government funded element, while Japanese funding has been directed primarily to applications supported by commercial industries. The Japanese government role, more often than not, is to minimize risk for industry in funding breakthrough technologies, while individual firms focus on incremental technology advancements. In contrast, United States initiatives seem increasingly focused on high risk, and large scale breakthroughs, requiring greater time and financial resources without necessarily the promise of short- to mid-term applications. Spending in both countries is up, but rising more rapidly in Japan. Finally, there is not a single industrial sector in Japan that lacks a significant research and development component, a distinct contrast with the United States.

Aggressive efforts to license foreign technology supplements Japan's internal funding initiatives. Japan's technology trade still runs a slight deficit, indicating the availability of foreign technology to the country (despite concerns over "techno-nationalism"). In addition, it shows the continued, pragmatic preference to import rather than recreate technology whenever possible. Technology imports totaled ¥366.8 billion in JFY 1988 while exports reached ¥293.7. With a few exceptions, these figures have increased every year since the end of the Occupation era. While Japan might be contributing more to the international community through expanded basic and applied research, its companies nevertheless favor acquiring technology wherever possible, and licensing remains the most popular because of its relative ease and low costs.

---

[8]The budgetary implications of U.S. spending on high risk, large scale projects are explored in Congressional Budget Office, "Large Nondefense R&D Projects n the Budget: 1980-1996," July 1991.

[9]See "Strategic Technology Management in Japan: Commercial-Military Comparisons," Appendix H, in U.S. Congress, Office of Technology Assessment, *Holding the Edge: Maintaining the Defense Technology Base*, Volume 2: Appendices, OTA-ISC-432 (Washington, D.C.: U.S. government Printing Office), January 1990, pp. 175-185.

The same figures, however, indicate that Japan does have more to offer in licensed innovations, a trend that is certain to continue in the future.

Nowhere is Japan's technological prowess demonstrated more than in its trade of high technology products. High-tech product exports for Japan rose from $3.8 billion in 1970 to $31.3 billion in 1980, and more than doubled to $69.1 billion by 1986. In contrast, the United States high-tech product exports rose from $9.0 billion to $44.9 billion and $69.3 billion over the same periods. In other words, Japanese exports of high technology products have risen from an amount equivalent to just one-third of total United States exports to more than total United States high-tech exports in less than two decades[10] (see Figures 3 and 4). It is this trend that has the most direct influence on relations between the United States and Japan, since technology relations ultimately are defined in terms of the products traded between nations.

An Inherent Imbalance

The most important implication suggested by these trends is that the United States and Japan are taking significantly different paths to enhance their technological futures. The United States focus remains firmly fixed on defense, even as defense related procurement declines. (As procurement orders drop, firms will suspend much of their independent R&D, unless other mechanisms are found to support these activities that, absent of large scale orders, simply drain corporate resources in the United States viewpoint.)[11] In

---

[10]Organization for Economic Cooperation and Development, Industrial Outlook Database, July 1988, December 1988 (utilizing OECD definitions of "high technology products;" National Science Board, Science and Engineering Indicators 1989 (Washington, D.C.: U.S. Government Printing Office), 1989, p. 377.

[11]A significant element of the U.S.-Japan technology relationship is in the defense area, where massive technology transfers from the United States to Japan have taken place over the past several decades. While the United States sought those transfers for military and strategic reasons, Japan also recognized their potential economic benefits. This difference in perceptions ultimately resulted in intense frictions over the FSX — an advanced derivative of the U.S. F-16 fighter now being developed by Mitsubishi Heavy Industries, Inc. of Japan and General Dynamics Corp. of the U.S. for the Japan Defense Agency (JDA).

Efforts to rectify the problems resulting from the FSX case have been unsuccessful. Mechanisms established through notes exchanged in 1983 to facilitate military technology exchanges between the United States and Japan have languished, and independent Japanese development efforts as well as the cultivation of closer ties with European suppliers have accelerated since the negotiation of the FSX agreement. While Japan will continue to be reliant upon the United States in a broad range of specialized defense systems and technologies, it is fair to say that the "FSX hangover" (a term used by the U.S. Aerospace Industry Association (Japan) to describe the current state of defense technology relations) will continue to affect U.S.-Japan defense technology ties for the indefinite future. The U.S. and Japanese governments have continued discussions involving five different development projects dealing with components and subsystems. Although it is likely that some research projects will be launched as a result of those negotiations, no agreement has been reached at this writing.

Summaries of U.S.-Japan defense industry and technology relationships can be found in U.S. Congress, Office of Technology Assessment, Arming Our Allies: Cooperation and competition in defense Technology, OTA-ISC-449 (Washington, D.C.: U.S. Government Printing Office, May 1990), Chapter

addition, United States spending patterns are less consistent except for more dramatic programs that demand considerable sustained investments to produce significant results. This is particularly true for the private sector, where an economic downturn has hurt short term research spending and could have a significant impact on future competitiveness.

This stands in contrast with the Japanese philosophy of funding research in order to survive. The quantity of investment in Japan does not necessarily guarantee quality or success, but it is clear from this pattern that industry and government in Japan view R&D investments as central to economic growth that, in turn, is the basis for Japan's long term survival. The 1987 white paper of the Science and Technology Agency (STA) concluded that virtually 50% of all Japanese economic growth in the fifteen years since the oil shocks was attributable to advances in the domestic technological base, compared with 20% at most for the United States.[12] With survival literally serving as the motivation for R&D, Japan will not deviate from the current emphasis of its collective research and development significantly. This could heighten the differences in research strategies between the United States and Japan, with the latter becoming still more directed toward applications, commercial technologies (and "spin-on" applications for defense where feasible), product and process technologies and incremental rather than breakthrough innovations. Given the success of this strategy to date, one must ask whether this will magnify disparities in economic competitiveness between the two countries further.

The practical implications of these trends already is evident. Greater resource allocation to inventiveness will enhance Japanese opportunities for product developments, competitiveness and new innovations. A representative although imperfect illustration of this trend is the number of patents granted in the United States to Japanese affiliated organizations. Japanese firms accounted for only 4.1% of all United States patents granted in 1970. That rose to 20.7% by 1988 (see Figure 5).[13] While there are several explanations for this trend, it nevertheless demonstrates the relative rise of Japanese industry due to competitive improvements resulting in part from its technology strategy. As that trend continues, the potential differences in United States and Japanese economic and trade competitiveness will grow.

4, "The Emergence of Transpacific Collaboration: The Case of Japan," pp. 61-72, Appendix C: "Japanese Defense Policymaking and Industry," pp. 102-110; and U.S. Congress, Office of Technology Assessment, Global Arms Trade: Commerce in Advanced Military Technology and Weapons, OTA-ISC-460 (Washington, D.C.: U.S. Government Printing Office, June 1991), Chapter 6: "Japan's Defense Industrial Policy and U.S.-Japan Security Relations," pp. 107-120.

[12]*Science and Technology in Japan*, Vol. 7, No. 26, June 1988.

[13]Science and Engineering Indicators 1989, p. 356.

Responses to Imbalances in Technology

It is just such a concern that has driven the United States to emphasize "symmetry" in its technological relationship with Japan.[14] With Japan becoming a more potent force in the economic and technological world, there is a growing sentiment in the United States that it must gain access to Japan's technology to the same degree that has enabled Japan to commercialize many innovations first achieved in the United States It may be necessary for the very process of scientific research to undergo substantial transformation in Japan and perhaps in the United States as well, however, for the United States to gain complete symmetry with Japan in technology. For example, Japan's university based research efforts are limited compared with those in the United States and bound by cultural constraints. Universities accounted for only 19% of Japanese R&D expenditures in JFY 1988 (down from 23% five years earlier) even though total spending has increased. Researchers are bound to senior faculty members, who attain their status primarily through seniority, not through demonstrated research capabilities. The result is that junior but potentially promising researchers are denied valuable training and interaction with other members of the international community.

The university system in the United States is where much government funded research is conducted. It also is the community in which scientists from across the world can share information, ideas and experience. While the openness of American campuses is a controversial issue — even internationally recognized institutions have been criticized in Congress for facilitating the diffusion of knowledge abroad while failing to be more concerned with domestic United States competitiveness[15] — they generally are magnets for exchanges through conferences, enrollments and fellowships. However, many United States scientists feel that they will be denied comparable access and benefits until the Japanese university system is reformed. Since most research is conducted in companies in Japan, universities must provide access to research comparable to the degree of openness evident in the United States system. Even if Japanese campuses are relatively unrestricted in access, the cultural quirks of the chair system minimize their usefulness to for-

---

[14]See, for example, "The Scientific and Technological Dimensions of U.S.-Japan Relations," testimony by Dr. Martha Caldwell Harris before the Joint Economic Committee of Congress, December 6, 1990. Dr. Harris is Director of the Office of Japan Affairs for the National Research Council of the National Academy of Sciences.

[15]Representative of the dispute is the Massachusetts Institute of Technology, one of the world's leading academic institutions which hosts federally funded research as well as corporate sponsored initiatives. The controversy over foreign access to research at MIT led to the formation of an in-house commission which concluded that foreign inputs and participation at MIT were as much a part of the Institute's success as domestic ones. See Eugene Skolnikoff, chair, Faculty Study Group, "The International Relationships of MIT in a Technologically Competitive World," May 1, 1991.

eigners, diluting the value of university based research (although one cannot question the technical credentials of their graduates).

More fundamental disparities exist, however, which are attributable more to American arrogance or indifference to Japanese technology than to systemic reasons. The shear numbers of Japanese researchers abroad compared to the dearth of United States counterparts in Japan explains much of the imbalance between the two countries. It also explains Japan's ability to tap United States technology compared to the seeming inability of the United States to do the same in Japan. Over 28,000 researchers visited the United States from Japan in 1985, seven times the number from the United States to Japan. (Almost nine times as many Asian nationals enter Japan annually for research and study as from the United States.)[16]

The large representation of Asian researchers in Japan attests to the potentiality for openness in the Japanese research system (although many of these researchers are in fact students studying at Japanese universities). Nevertheless, in some respects the Japanese system clearly is open to foreigners with sufficient linguistic capabilities to exploit opportunities in Japan. United States corporate, academic and government laboratories, however, do not emphasize routine training and rotation in foreign laboratories sufficiently to take advantage of these potential opportunities. Until they do, the imbalance is likely to continue.[17]

Japan: Absorb and Develop

Japan has adapted to these conditions somewhat, making access to its research more available than before. The Japanese government, for example, sponsors hundreds of United States researchers in Japan annually, still a limited number compared with the thousands resident in the United States alone in any given year, but a distinct step in the right direction from an American perspective. These measures, however, are limited, and the patterns of the past remain in Japan, guiding the course of its research strategy. A strong thread of retaining control over leading technologies while securing access to foreign technologies remains evident in Japanese industry and government

---

[16]Science and Technology Agency, *Kagaku Gijutsu Hakusho* (*White Paper on Science and Technology*); (Tokyo: Science and Technology Agency, 1987), pp. 72-76.

[17]The U.S. government has taken small steps to encourage training of professionals for overseas experience. The U.S Air Force has provided a total of $10 million to four U.S. campuses to support existing or new programs aimed at training American professionals and students for working in and with Japan. The four universities are the Massachusetts Institute of Technology, University of Wisconsin, University of Michigan and Vanderbilt University. The fact that such funding originates in defense appropriations is significant, to the extent that it reflects Washington's concerns over involving commercial government agencies in long term competitiveness issues.

strategies, reflecting again the equation of technological strength = economic growth = long term survival for Japan. Although it is a stereotypical representation, Japan's technology strategy still emphasizes absorption of technology from abroad but cautious distribution of core technologies in return. Companies prefer to export their most advanced technologies as products.

As noted above, Japan's technology trade still runs a slight deficit, but it has narrowed from a 427:1 imbalance in imports to exports in JFY 1960 to a 1.2:1 ratio. Asia is the favored market for Japanese technology exports, receiving 41.2% of all exports in JFY 1988. The United States stands in second place at 28.9% followed by Europe with just over 20%. The picture in terms of imports is dramatically different. The United States and Europe supply virtually all Japan's technology imports, 63.1% and 36.4%, respectively. That figure shows the critical importance of the United States to Japan's technology base and help explains the country's extreme sensitivity to "techno-nationalism." These figures are especially important since they represent commercial — not government — transactions. Furthermore, the move toward greater licensing of Japanese technology implies that businesses are accepting the view held in the United States that technology is a commodity that should be bought and sold like any other. That is a gradual process, however, that might not be moving quickly enough to benefit the United States and other Japanese trading partners sufficiently.

Another Response: International Cooperation

Another reaction in Japan to these divergent trends has been the sporadic effort to foster international collaboration, most recently the Intelligent Manufacturing Systems (IMS) proposal. This proposal demonstrates the difficulties involved when two countries are both intense competitors and potential collaborators. In addition, it represents a basic clash in perceptions involving the requisite role of government in fostering technological and economic growth. For Japan, it is assumed that the government has an appropriate role in fostering industry collaboration in emerging technologies, while the notion of such government backed industrial policy remains controversial in the United States.

The Ministry of International Trade and Industry proposed IMS in November 1989, although the press reported rumors of the program as early as August of that year. Intended as a ten year, $10 billion trilateral research program among Japan, the United States and Europe, IMS anticipated a 60% split of financial contributions by Japan with the United States and Europe contributed 20% each. The Ministry of International Trade and Industry (MITI) established an IMS Promotion Center, which designated the Society of

Manufacturing Engineers (SME) its United States counterpart, well before the United States government had taken a formal position on the question of United States participation in the program. One of the most significant features of the proposal was that it would lead to the establishment of common international standards for new generations of advanced systems, ranging from computer controlled manufacturing systems to international telecommunications networks. A call went out from Japan for proposals from interested parties, with a deadline of early 1990. Initially, the IMS Promotion Center was expected to review proposals, selecting the finalists to get projects under way by the fall of 1991.[18]

IMS was motivated in Japan by several sentiments. The first was a desire to offset international criticism of its closed society and hoarding of technology by initiating and carry the majority of the financial burden for an innovative proposal. MITI intended for IMS, like the Human Frontiers project before it, to demonstrate to the world that criticisms of Japan's technological stinginess were out of place.[19] Another concern was the possibility of being closed out from international markets through the determination of standards unfavorable to Japanese standards.[20]

In some respects, IMS was an extension of common Japanese practices to the international arena, and to this extent, the proposal could be viewed as an effort to become a more active participant in the international R&D community.[21] Sensitive to international criticisms, IMS was an effort to introduce Japanese methods to other countries, although initially it was met with great skepticism. The final possible motive for IMS was to solidify the Western industrial world, of which Japan viewed itself as a member, against

---

[18]For a summary of the IMS proposal and U.S. reactions to it, see George R. Heaton, Jr., "International R&D Cooperation: Lessons From the Intelligent Manufacturing Systems Proposal," National Academy Press, Discussion Paper No. 2, June 1991.

[19]The Human Frontiers program, directed toward biological sciences, has suffered from administrative delays and only now is getting under way. It was first proposed in 1986 at a ¥1 trillion cost with Tokyo supplying half the funding. Funds were not authorized by the Japanese government until JFY 1989 and foreign reception of the program, which envisioned overseas researchers working in Japan as well as directing projects there, was suspicious. The program did not get under way until after an independent foundation was established in France to govern the awarding of fellowships and grants under it. To date, 29 grants have been awarded to researchers from eight countries, selected from 202 applicants.

[20]The HDTV debate in Europe and the United States made many in Japan realize that even though it may have technologically superior systems, they could be closed out of major markets through politically motivated decisions that would have the effect of favoring domestic producers. It may be that MITI sought to preempt this possibility by proposing IMS. Furthermore, with Japan taking the lead financial and administrative role in the project, it would have the opportunity to influence the development of those standards and be assured that it would be part of a final technical standard even though it might not be based on Japanese technology.

[21]Richard J. Samuels , "Research Collaboration in Japan," MIT-Japan Program Working Paper MITJP 87-02, 1987, and Jonah D. Levy and Richard J. Samuels," "Institutions and Innovation: Research Collaboration as Technology Strategy in Japan," MIT-Japan Program Working Paper MITJP 89-02, 1989.

the rising competitive challenge posed by developing nations, particularly those in Asia.

The United States reaction to IMS was something less than MITI most likely anticipated. Rather than jumping on board to a creative, international research program, the United States recoiled in suspicion that MITI was launching an attack on United States technology in the guise of a cooperative venture. Part of the United States reaction was explained by the fact that the country was completely unprepared for the Japanese proposal. Bureaucratic politics delayed the United States response to IMS, with various offices within the United States government competing for jurisdictional authority to interact with MITI. Industry reaction was equally mixed, with many firms viewing IMS as an opportunity to integrate themselves with the Japanese R&D community and government offices, while others interpreted it in its most negative light.[22]

Ultimately, the international political dispute surrounding IMS illustrated the profoundly different points of view regarding the fostering of technology in the United States and Japan. With its adamant free market principles, the United States administration reacted to the Japanese proposal with concern that it would lead to the formation of an "industrial policy" in the United States. Recent administrations have been loath to "pick winners and losers," although industrial policy does not necessarily suggest micro-management of the entire economy. Reaction to the IMS proposal reflected that domestic debate as much as the decidedly mixed feelings in the United States toward cooperating with Japan technologically.

For its own part, the Japanese government was baffled by this response due to its longstanding traditions of fostering cooperation among businesses at the pre-competitive stage. Indeed, much of Japan's economic progress has been attributed to industry-government collaboration (although foreign critics would term it collusion) in such critical industries as electronics, materials, computers, aircraft and other industries. In some respects, extending this approach to the international arena was a logical progression for the government as a whole and MITI in particular.

The reactive position of the United States government and much of industry indicates a possible turning in the technology relationship between the United States and Japan. Rather than simply mimicking United States technology at the commercial level and abiding by United States dictates at the

---

[22]The early 1990 deadline for submission of proposals fell by the wayside as intense negotiations and discussions began among affected governments. By April 1991, the U.S. and Japan, along with European governments, Canada and Australia, agreed to a broad set of principles governing projects, access to the decisionmaking process surrounding IMS, and the sharing of technical data from individual projects. Although far from under way, it appears that U.S. participation in IMS eventually will come to pass. In general, Europe's response — where governments and industry work more closely together and, therefore, would not be alarmed necessarily by a Japanese government R&D initiative — was more favorable than that in the United States.

policy level, Japan has sufficient influence and capabilities to begin setting the tenor of the technology relationship through such initiatives as IMS, which focused on several key Japanese strengths while promising select inputs to shore up critical weaknesses. Japanese capabilities in manufacturing, computers, electronics, communications and other industries were more than sufficient to allow the government make this type of proposal credibly and force other governments to listen. A less technologically advanced nation would not be in a position to make such a bold proposal, not would it be able to imply going it alone — or in partnership with other nations — if the invited participants gave it only cursory consideration. Japan did not, of course, threaten the United States or Europe that it would take such a course, but governments abroad had to respond simply because of Japan's rising technological prowess. With its expanding R&D budgets and continued access to technology from abroad, Japan's capabilities will only continue to grow, promising more IMS like proposals in the future — again, initiated in Japan with the United States in the role of respondent/follower instead of leader. The declining technological position of the United States relative to Japan will only complicate this situation in the future.

United States Responses: A Technology Policy?

While Japan has been attempting to look outward in its research programs and technology relations, the United States has become more introspective, debating the wisdom of unrestricted access to home grown technology and the appropriate means of fostering it. These debates are far from resolved, but the United States government gradually is changing its ways and business and government are moving cautiously toward a new way of assuring continued United States innovation for the future.

As noted earlier, much of the dispute centers around industrial policy. Many United States observers have concluded that the prominent role of government agencies such as the Ministry of International Trade and Industry and the Science and Technology Agency explain Japan's success in absorbing and adapting foreign technology as well as stimulating the development of indigenous capabilities. The organizations guide industry consensus on R&D investments and foster an environment in which firms can collaborate at a basic technology level until left to their own resources to develop innovations into products.[23] MITI's periodic "visions" — expansive discussions of Japanese industrial and technological trends in the future, developed with the inputs of industry and academics as well — are cited as examples of how governments

---

[23]Harris testimony, December 6, 1990.

can influence the private sector positively.

That conclusion, however, is far from universal held in the United States government. For the most part, the executive branch has resisted the call for the creation of a comprehensive industrial policy for three reasons. The first is the potentially distorting effect on the marketplace. The executive in particular feels that funding decisions are best left to the private sector to assure their rationality — an interesting stance given the large federal role in R&D funding. The second reason is the tendency of Congress to seize such programs with parochial pork barrel objectives in mind instead of genuine concerns over the nation's economy. The White House further fears that inefficient industries would be supported for reasons of constituent politics rather than for economic justifications if industrial policy directions were set by the government. The final concern is the potentially distorting influences of a comprehensive industrial policy on international trade, once again citing the damaging effects of supporting failing industries when more competitive international alternatives are available.[24]

What has emerged, and has an official label emanating from the White House, is a United States *technology* policy. In contrast with the notion of picking winners and losers, this approach seeks to eliminate the obstacles to sensible but closely monitored industrial collaboration as well as stimulating general business conditions to foster more extensive and effective research and development in the United States. Outlined by the president's science adviser in September 1990, this policy seeks to "make the best use of technology in achieving the national goals of improved quality of life for all Americans, continued economic growth, and national security."[25] Among the precise objectives of United States policy, the statement calls for a better educated work force, a financial environment conducive to long term investments in advanced technologies, more rapid transformation of technology into products, and the elimination of legal and regulatory barriers that inhibit research and development.

A central element of this strategy is the identification of "critical" technologies that are viewed as central to long term growth in the future. Government offices, trade associations and individual companies have jumped on the critical technologies bandwagon. Included in this list are Department of Defense annual reports on critical industries and technology planning, the Department of Commerce's study of emerging technologies and

---

[24]The U.S. executive branch and successive congresses have refused to use the imbalance in technology relations as justification for either erecting barriers against Japanese firms in the U.S.. Although many critics contend that an industrial policy could aid U.S. businesses facing increasingly stiff international competition, the executive has rejected this as a back door means of supporting failing industries and, ultimately, of undermining the entire economy.

[25]Executive Office of the President, Office of Science and Technology Policy, "U.S. Technology Policy," September 26, 1990, p. 2.

the Council on Competitiveness' report on critical technologies.[26]

Japan has its own exercises in consensus building involving investment in technologies deemed central to long term growth.[27]   Such studies usually are the result of ad hoc panels representing business, government and industry audiences.   While it is debatable if these reports have a dramatic pattern on R&D spending in Japan, there is no doubt that they have contributed to public awareness and a bureaucratic commitment to new generations of technologies.

The situation in the United States is different, however, with much of the United States effort resulting from the encouragement of a handful of figures in Congress.   The efforts are restricted in several respects, however.   The foremost weakness is that they are concentrated in the defense area, where research needs are unique and budgets are highly uncertain.   The Pentagon's emphasis on pulsed power, for example, is not reflected in civilian needs.   By focusing the critical technologies exercises on defense, then, the United States risks distorting priorities.

Another deficiency in the approach of focusing on critical technologies is defining criticality, especially through bureaucratic initiatives.   While congressional mandates to define lists of critical technologies might help produce a consensus over the long run, in the short run they often are little more than bureaucratic political exercises in which representatives of various agencies horse trade their favored technologies with one another.   All too often these technologies are in fact existing bureaucratic missions rather than innovations per se.   The National Critical Technologies Panel report is representative of this problem.   Congress required representation on the panel by the Defense, Energy, Commerce departments, the National Aeronautics and Space Administration (NASA) and three other government offices, in addition to the OSTP.   It is hardly a surprise that the resulting list of "critical" technologies reflects departmental interests and favored programs such as aeronautics, energy technologies (with particular emphasis on nuclear technologies), and applied molecular biology.   While any of these areas could indeed be critical to the long term competitive future of the United States, they are unlikely to draw widespread support as long as they remain nothing more than favored programs.

Washington has taken less dramatic steps that could produce substantial results in the coming decades.   Most important of these have been loos-

---

[26]The reports include: Department of Defense, "Critical Technologies Plan," May 1, 1991, AD-A234-900; Department of Defense, Assistant Secretary of Defense (Production and Logistics), Office of Industrial Base Assessments, "Report to Congress on the Defense Industrial Base: Critical Industries Planning," National Critical Technologies Panel, "Report of the National Critical Technologies Panel," (Washington, D.C.: U.S. Government Printing Office), March 1991.

[27]One such example is the Ministry of International Trade and Industry's *Nihon no Sentaku* (Tokyo: Tsusho Sangyo Chosakai), 1988.

ened restrictions on collaboration among companies, and initiatives to encourage more extensive utilization of government research facilities by industry. The former effort has produced the Microelectronics and Computer Corporation (MCC), a consortium based in Austin, Texas to support research in semiconductors and other advanced electronics areas. Another consortium is SEMATECH, which is directed toward the semiconductor manufacturing industry and is partly supported by Department of Defense funding. Both organizations are too young to be able to claim dramatic impacts on their respective audiences, but they do offer the promise of incremental improvements for domestic industry through shared research, personnel exchanges and other avenues.[28]

The latter effort — more effective utilization of government labs — also is in its formative stages, but has produced promising results through the formation of government-industry consortia. For example, the National Institute of Technology and Standards (NIST) has formed over 300 hundred consortia with industry since changes in federal laws encouraged such partnerships. Private firms have concluded R&D agreements with national laboratories such as Sandia National Labs in New Mexico, which previously were devoted solely to United States government research and were heavily oriented toward defense.[29]

Collectively, these agreements, sanctioned and indeed encouraged by Congress, are known as Collaborative Research and Development Agreements (CRADAs), and could prove to be the vehicle by which the nature of industry-government collaboration in the United States is transformed fundamentally. These efforts are less publicized than the more visible critical technologies exercises, but in the long run are more likely to produce tangible

---

[28]SEMATECH was established in August 1987 and is jointly funded by a group of private sector members and the Department of Defense (the fourteen member companies and DoD each contribute $100 million annually to the organization's budget. Member companies are required to contribute at least 50 % of the organization's $200 million annual operating budget.). SEMATECH is a research and development consortium with particular emphasis on manufacturing technology. SEMATECH's goal is to help the U.S. industry's technological levels to surpass those of Japanese producers in semiconductor manufacturing technologies by the end of 1993. The consortium hopes to produce semiconductor manufacturing equipment and materials necessary to reduce the line width of integrated circuits from current levels of 0.8 microns to 0.35 microns (one micron is a millionth of a meter). Research employee positions within SEMATECH are filled rotating member company personnel through the organization, typically on two-year assignments. One of the first requirements to achieve these goals was the construction of a state of the art fabrication facility. Technology associated with this facility already has been transferred to member companies through workshops, direct inspections and employee work experiences. SEMATECH has been cited as a possible model for other high tech fields where risks are high and/or public benefits are perceived as warranting government-business cooperation. Examples are high definition television (HDTV) and superconductivity. For an upbeat assessment of SEMATECH's progress, see Robert S. Dudney, "Running Hard to Stay Even," Air Force Magazine, September 1991, pp. 18-20.

[29]Brian Robinson, "Sandia First to Sign Industry R&D Pact," Electronic Engineering Times, August 26, 1991.

results for United States industry. While not as dramatic, they are more capable of producing long term, incremental results for businesses in a manner that might be more consistent with business-government relations in the United States than would a MITI like industrial policy initiative. Sustaining interest in them, however, is in part a political problem that Washington cannot afford to neglect.

None of these steps, however, clarifies the United States posture toward cooperative research with Japan. For the most part, they are aimed at enhancing domestic competitiveness — an area that could also strengthen the United States bargaining position vis-a-vis Japan in future ventures, but one whose payoff is in the long term. Indeed, such initiatives as SEMATECH are directed specifically toward United States firms' competitiveness in relation to Japanese companies. Whether they ultimately lead to more extensive technological interaction with Japan remains to be seen.

The Outlook for Cooperation ... and Competition

It is fair to ask what will become of the budding interest in critical technologies, collaborative research initiatives and other concepts in light of Washington's failure to sustain interest in developing and implementing a true technology policy, and the impact on U.S.-Japan technology relations as a result. It has been argued here that the United States and Japan are on divergent paths that will complicate the ability of the two countries to avoid economic frictions that result from these trends. Research and development funding has increased in the United States, but is being outpaced by spending hikes in Japan. Projects are directed toward dramatic breakthroughs rather than incremental improvements that can enhance United States competitiveness immediately, but not dramatically. Finally, the R&D process remains divorced from production, assuring that American competitors — especially those with superior prototyping and manufacturing capabilities — will enter into new markets sooner, thus reaping the economic benefits that assure the ability to fund new generations of research projects and additional improvements in competitiveness.

If this trend continues, the United States will be so concerned with the short term economic ramifications of new Japanese products — mounting trade deficits, faltering manufacturing employment, etc. — that it will be unable to allow extensive cooperation with Japan. Technology relations therefore could take a turn for the worse, with the United States focusing policy efforts on preserving its own technologies, often through market protection. Therefore, the competitive concerns evident in the relationship are likely to continue dominating policy debates — at least in the United States — for the foreseeable future. And Washington could be so concerned with the short term problems associated with those debates that it is unable to develop a comprehensive strategy not only for responding to Japan's challenge, but also enhancing indigenous capabilities to assure long term competitiveness. Increasingly, the government will be forced to address the symptoms of the decline — unemployment and declining industries — rather than the core problem — deficiencies in the United States R&D strategy.

As noted in the IMS debate, institutional and philosophical differences may be the source of additional difficulties, perhaps an even greater impediment to future collaboration than spending and budgetary trends themselves. Japan's IMS proposals clearly indicated that the United States government is unprepared institutionally or in policy terms for collaborating with Japan in larger, commercial research and development initiatives. Many precedents that could lay the groundwork for sustained cooperation and reciprocity in technology transfers could be set through the IMS experience, but such progress is likely to be slow and subject to the vicissitudes of Washington politics.

This is not a certainty, especially given Japan's rising stature as a source of innovation. However, the ultimate outcome of current trends might not be what the United States government currently seeks in terms of business-government relations and preservation of free markets. It would not be surprising if initiatives such as Japan's IMS proposal increasingly sets the pattern for technology relations not only between the United States and Japan, but Japan and the rest of the world. IMS is notable not only for its scope and boldness, but also for the fact that Japan has advanced sufficiently technologically and in broad economic terms to come forth with such a concept. As noted earlier, IMS forced the United States to respond because of the dimensions and potential implications of the proposal. Rather than being on the forefront of global trends, the United States was reacting to a plan conceived and proposed entirely by Japan. This could be the pattern for the future as Japan's technological capabilities expand.

IMS also precipitated an unexpected result that Washington itself has had limited success in achieving, namely, producing closer cooperation between business and government in the United States. The IMS proposal forced businesses and government offices to work together and define common interests in response to what many feared was an effort by Japan to pluck ripe, advanced technologies from the United States and Europe. Washington has discovered that it must in fact work closely with business through this experience.

The irony, of course, is that it has been a Japanese technology initiative that has taken the United States closer to industry-government interactions than Washington has desired to this point. The United States may yet define a set of policies more extensive than its formative technology policy, but it may come as the result of an external Japanese stimulus rather than internal political efforts.

The author wishes to thank David P. Leech and Yukihide Hayashi for their comments on earlier drafts of this chapter.

Table 1: Total Japanese R&D Expenditures, JFY 1983-1988
(¥billions)

Fiscal Year	Amount
1983	¥7,180.8
1984	7,893.9
1985	8,890.3
1986	9,129.9
1987	9,836.6
1988	10,627.6

Table 2: Japanese Government Expenditures, JFY 1990
(¥millions and % of total)

Agency	Amount (¥ millions)	% of Total
National Diet	533	.03
Japan Technology Council	867	.05
Police Agency	1,020	.06
Hokkaido Development Agency	147	.01
Japan Defense Agency	93,068	5.13
Economic Planning Agency	764	.04
Science and Technology Agency	466,623	25.72
Environment Agency	7,882	.43
Justice Ministry	871	.05
Foreign Ministry	6,408	.35
Finance Ministry	1,087	.06
Education Ministry	854,322	47.07
Health Ministry	48,360	2.66
Ministry of International Trade and Industry	233,640	12.87
Transportation Ministry	16,300	.90
Posts and Telecommunications	30,447	1.68
Labor Ministry	4,557	.25
Construction Ministry	5,689	.31
Home Affairs Ministry	555	.03
Total	¥1,814,827	100%

Table 3:   Japan's R&D Expenditures by Source, JFY 1983-88
(percent)

Fiscal Year	Government	Private	Foreign
1983	24.0	75.9	0.1
1984	22.5	77.4	0.1
1985	21.0	78.9	0.1
1986	21.5	78.4	0.1
1987	21.5	78.4	0.1
1988	19.9	80.0	0.1

Table 4:   Japan's Research Expenditures by Purpose, JFY 1983-88.
(percentage distribution)

Fiscal Year	Basic Research	Applied Research	Developmental Research
1983	14.0	25.4	60.6
1984	13.6	25.1	61.3
1985	12.9	25.0	62.2
1986	13.3	24.4	62.3
1987	14.0	24.3	61.7
1988	13.3	24.3	62.4

Figure 1: Japan's R&D Exepnditures by Source, JFY 1983-88

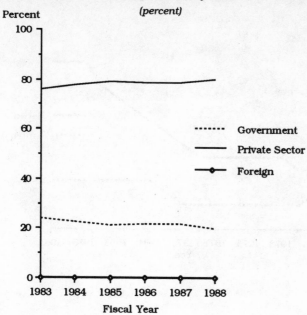

Figure 2: Non-Defense R&D Expenditures as Percent of GNP, 1971-87

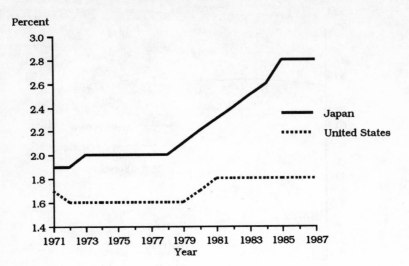

Figure 3: Total Exports of High-Technology Products, 1970-86

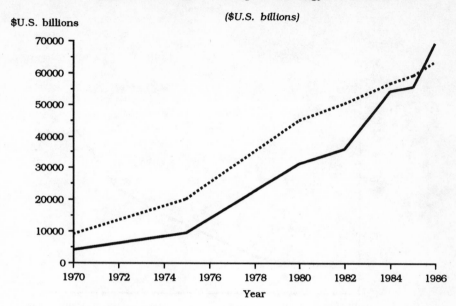

$U.S. billions

(*$U.S. billions*)

Year

```
••••••  U.S. High-Tech Exports
────    Japanese High-Tech Exports
```

Figure 4: Share of Global Exports of High-Technology Products, 1970-86
(percent)

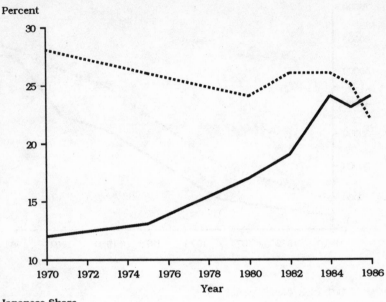

Percent

Japanese Share
U.S. Share

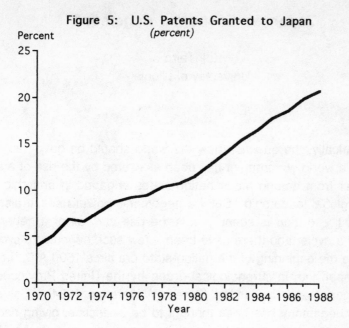

Figure 5: U.S. Patents Granted to Japan
(percent)

Japan as Economic Hegemon?

Koji Taira
University of Illinois

Historically, the question how the world should be governed in the absence of a world government has been answered by the rise of a hegemonic power from among major nation-states engaged in anarchic competition for global leadership. But if a hegemonic power rises, it also falls when its ability to lead is spent. Thus the rise and fall of a hegemonic power spell a cycle, and there have been a few such hegemonic cycles in history since the beginning of the nation-state era circa 1500 A.D.: i.e., the world has been led, in chronological order, by the United Provinces, the United Kingdom and the United States (Wallerstein 1984). For some years, U.S. hegemony has been thought to be in decline, giving rise to a variety of speculations about the next hegemon to succeed the United States.

The decline of the United States is often linked to the rise of Japan. As a consequence, Japan's hegemonic qualifications are being carefully examined by many writers (for example, Vogel 1979, Kindleberger 1986, Gilpin 1987, Kennedy 1987, Makin and Hellman 1989, Taira 1998, 1990, Dietrich 1991). Usually Japan passes the economic test but evokes doubts on other aspects of leadership. Even if Japan passes all technical tests, Japanese hegemony suffers from a lack of legitimacy. It is simply unacceptable to many states, especially to powerful Western states. Taking note of this state of world public opinion, Japan has also settled down to a modest view of its role in the world as a second fiddler beside the United States.

This article is a commentary on the nature and implications of the Japanese strategy for a Number Two role in cooperation with the United States. The greatest benefit that Japan derives from being Number Two is that nationalistic reactions of other states to Japan as Number One may be avoided. Furthermore, a Number Two position is not necessarily damaging to Japan's pride because its history and culture attach appropriate honor and power to such a position. From the American point of view, sharing the burden of leadership with Japan is also an optimal solution, given the economic difficulties of the United States. The military prowess of the United States against the backdrop of looming economic weaknesses smacks of an "imperial over-stretch," arguably the last symptom of a declining hege-mon before a fall (Kennedy 1987).

Economic Qualifications of Japan as a Hegemon

A few basic economic indicators quite clearly imply Japan's great power status.

(1) Japan's GNP per capita is now higher than that of the United States and keeps increasing steadily at higher annual rates. This comparison is based on a straightforward conversion of Japan's GNP into U.S. dollars by the foreign exchange rate. This is an acceptable method of na-tional power comparison, although different methods like purchasing power parity are needed for the comparison of standards of living.

(2) Japan recently was the world's largest net creditor country (1985-1989, though overtaken by Germany in 1990), while the United States since 1985 has consistently been the world's largest net debtor. Currently, Japan is also the world's largest donor of official development aid (ODA) to less developed countries surpassing the United States.

(3)Japan has a large well educated, well disciplined population. Although the population size of Japan is the world's sixth and half as large as that of the United States, the United Nations' human resource quality in-dex places Japan at the top and the United States at the 18th (UNDP 1990). Thus, in terms of the quality-weighted human resources, the numer-ical superiority of the U.S. population over Japan must be severely dis-counted.

Japan's hegemonic economic power, if not already obvious, will convince the worst doubters in a couple of decades, given Japan's supe-rior propensity to save and technological innovativeness. Japan's annual savings are more than enough to keep its rate of growth higher than that of the United States. The balance of savings not used for domestic invest-ment in Japan flows out to the rest of the world as foreign investment. The United States with its chronic shortage of savings relative to its investment requirements is a major beneficiary of Japanese savings exports.

From the interactions of Japan's macro-economics and that of the rest of the world, an unthinkable scenario arises and to think it would be traumatic to Americans. Dietrich (1991) bravely faces this scenario. To summarize his description of it (pp.263-266), circa 2015 Pax Nipponica has arrived; Japan enjoys uncontested dominance in every leading edge industry; Japan's per capita GNP is four times that of the United States; Japan controls the world economy; Japan's Asian neighbors are the second tier nations in the global economic pyramid with Japan at the apex; the United States and Europe belong to the third tier; the third-tier nations are great consuming nations and provide a huge, stable, and profitable market for the ever-increasing flow of Japanese and East-Asian high-tech products.

Fortunately, the benefits to the U.S. economy are also considerable under Pax Nipponica. Says Dietrich:

.. ... our economy is no longer mismanaged because the Japanese are managing it for us. The Japanese now own over 40% of American manufacturing assets [and] ... 15% of American bank assets. Through a combination of strategically placed manufacturing investments and overwhelming financial leverage, Japan is able to move the U.S. economy in concert with Japan's strategic economic world vision (p.265).

There is little backlash from the United States against Pax Nipponica because politicians, academics and journalists are richly subsidized by Japan. Japan has also silenced the complaint of a free ride on defense because a modest percentage of Japan's enormous GNP generates an astonishing level of defense budget.

To those who might consider this scenario preposterous, Dietrich retorts by saying that what had happened to U.S. steel, automobiles, and electronics by 1980 surely would have seemed preposterous if anyone had suggested it in 1955. If the United States wants to avoid the predicament of a fallen giant, according to Dietrich, it needs a comprehensive industrial policy, a strong central state and a top professional bureaucracy; i.e., "there is one way, and only one way, out of our current predicament: fundamental institutional change" (p.xiv).

The end product of the world's economic evolution during the next quarter century as depicted above certainly sounds alarming. What is fortunate about it, however, is that the process of reaching that stage is market-guided and as subtle as the process which has made some of the Japanese industries world-class in the last 25 years. Adjustments to the market forces are incremental and piecemeal. Even though the results of the adjustments over time may amount to a revolution, it only surprises the people after the fact, not during the process in which events are unfolding toward consummation. From this point of view, Pax Nipponica may become a fait accompli before anyone notices it. The Japanese themselves would be astonished to see their country at the top of the global economic pyramid. From the standpoint of their chosen Number Two strategy, clear evidence of their being Number One would be as destabilizing to them as the end of U.S. hegemony to Americans.

The market-guided evolution of the world order as a process of restructuring international relations meets democratic requirements for reallocation of political power and leadership. The question that troubles Americans in this regard is whether the end product of this peaceful evolutionary process ensures the leadership of a country of their choice, the United States. Which country one favors as a world hegemon is much like electing a candidate to a high office in one's own country. The United States has been in the office of world hegemon for half a century. The political instinct compels Americans to prefer continued U.S. hegemony over that of any newcomer. This instinct sometimes drives many American opinion makers into irrational negative campaigns against Japan. Their message that Japanese leadership is unacceptable is often unsupported by reason.

Backlash

Inconsistencies among the negative campaigners (many of whom are so-called "Japan bashers," but not all) as well as their faulty understanding of history indicate that there is no reliable reason for rejecting the hypothesis that Japan, given the opportunity to lead, may have more legitimacy on its side than commonly alleged. A couple of examples may make the point that some critics of Japan are not really thinking, but reacting only emotionally on the basis of whatever hidden private feelings compel them to do so.

Take R. Taggart Murphy, "Power Without Purpose: The Crisis of Japan's Global Financial Dominance" (1989). What is allegedly wrong with Japan's financial power is as follows:

Japan lacks the *ideology* and *political commitment* necessary to fulfill the obligations that go with financial power. To turn sheer financial strength into leadership, a country must be able to think in global terms, to view itself as a world central banker, to sacrifice certain short-term gains to maintain stable financial and trading systems. Japan does not have this world view (emphasis added, p.74).

Britain and the United States were (the U.S. still is, though with decreasing strength) the world's financial leaders. On the ideology and political commitment by which they justified their leadership, Murphy observes:

The political elites in Great Britain and the United States were possessed of a sense of mission. The British elite in the last century fervently believed in their divinely appointed task of spreading Christian civilization and Anglo-Saxon concepts of the rule of law to the farthest corners of the globe. The U.S. Atlanticist elite of the immediate postwar world felt it their mission to prevent the Western democracies from making economic mistakes like the Smoot-Hawley Tariff Act or geopolitical mistakes like Munich *(loc.cit.)*.

Such an unqualified praise of the British and American "missions," as if these were the very embodiments of unquestionable ideals of mankind, can hardly be considered as an objective understanding of history. If these are the examples of "ideology and political commitment" that should go with financial power, any country can generate it out of their sheer national pride or prejudice. If this implies that Japan, to qualify as a hegemon, should emulate the British and U.S. examples, Japanese leadership would only perpetuate historical tragedies of traditional hegemonies. Humanity has the right to expect something much better from the future world order than endless replications of old hegemonic mistakes. Japan's financial power acquired quietly under the guidance of the market forces together with Japan's apparent lack of geopolitical ambition, if this is "power without purpose," is far more humane than the arrogant British claim to the Christianization of the world or the guilty overreactions of the United States to its own Smoot-Hawley fiasco which destroyed the then international economic order.

For another example, one might consider the unusual emotionalism displayed in a lecture by a well-known economist before an academic audience. Dornbusch (1991) describes a likely course of events following "Japan's success and increasing visibility" in this manner (p.21):

It is no secret that there is worldwide resentment against Japan. Among the reasons is the perception of a very closed Japanese society, apparent lack of a genuine and sincere interest in the progress of the world economy, and the sheer envy of Japan's success. ... Japan is an outsider in the western world, and just as it cannot make up its mind to play the game full out, the major industrialized countries and their electorate cannot get accustomed to treating Japan as other than a very distant, rich, and awkward relative who shows up at a family gathering mostly unwelcome and uninvited. ... There is resentment, and there is insecurity and fear in America that we are no longer number one.

These negative reactions to Japan's economic power are clearly based on a lack of understanding of the characteristics of the Japanese economy and society. Even the economists, to whom rationality is ostensibly a supreme value, have not yet outgrown the irrationality of flag-waving nationalism born of the nation-state rivalries of the last 500 years.

The Japanese Ideology and Commitment

Japan, too, has its own ideology and political commitment. Unfortunately these are not fully articulated and expounded, giving rise to misgivings on the part of foreign Japan watchers that Japan has none of them. With some effort and the help of Asian and Japanese studies, however, one may infer from observations what may be called "the Japanese ideology."

To begin with the widely recognized moral foundation, Japan's success in economic development and modernization is often attributed to Confucianism (Morishima 1982). One prominent aspect of the Japanese Ideology must then be a Confucian imperative, which is, to paraphrase, "Put your own house in order first." In a Confucian society, leadership is conferred on the individual who has put his own house in order and demonstrated compliance with other requisite virtues. Leadership should not be aggressively sought after or acquired by stratagems. This Confucian dimension of the Japanese Ideology, then, appears to fit well with how the Japanese have achieved economic self-reliance at home and how it apparently forswears pretension to power or leadership despite its extensive economic linkages with the rest of the world.

A large portion of the world is not Confucian in the logic or process of leader selection. Power politics and nationalist rivalries dominate international relations even where nations' interests would be better served by the market forces. An overt un-Confucian ambition for leadership is recognized as normal. Thus there is a lack of fit between the Japanese ideology and rules of world politics. Fortunately, East and Southeast Asia share varying forms of Confucianism with Japan. Here prewar Japan sinned against its own ethics by over-zealous imitation of Western imperialism. Chastened postwar Japan has returned to the ethical fold of Asia.

The Logic of Number Two

In view of Japan's Confucian modesty, which makes Japan's low profile a virtue, and the widespread misgivings that the rest of the world harbors about the legitimacy of Japanese hegemony, an optimum solution would be for Japan to use its economic capability for the good of the world and to submit to U.S. political leadership which the world apparently accepts as legitimate. It would also be cost-effective for Japan to keep the Pax Americana alive as a world order and to help the United States through economic and technological cooperation. In other words, Japan should "contribute to" world peace and prosperity, but should not attempt to "lead" the world by its own vision and designs. This implies Japan as a Number Two. In Japan, the choice of a Number Two role in this manner is widely accepted (Morita 1988: pp. 222-233; Kuse 1990.)

The acquisition of legitimacy takes time, because it depends upon the gradual transformation of others' perception of the would-be hegemon. Before Japanese hegemony becomes legitimate, world public opinion has to change. During this waiting time, Japan as an apprentice hegemon can improve its knowledge of and involvement in international government. Much has already been learned about ways of managing the global economy from the well-structured hegemony of the United States (Gilpin 1987). The global market forces are watched and assisted by international organizations (GATT, IMF, World Bank, OECD, UN, etc.) In designing, organizing and maintaining these institutions, U.S. leadership has been indispensable. Because of its transparency and objectivity, U.S. hegemony has given rise to theories of hegemony that can be learned and applied by hegemonic candidates.

Today these international organizations collectively constitute a rudimentary form of international government. The hegemon that comes after the U.S. is spared the pains of having to start from scratch. An important part of hegemony today is a leading role in international government through the existing international organizations. A new hegemon can rise through the ranks in the established international order, rather than through "succession war" as in the past.

In terms of economic contributions to the maintenance of the existing international organizations, Japan can clearly afford an extensive involvement in them. But the actual role Japan plays is considerably below the potential. Part of the reason for this discrepancy is historical; i.e., the "grandfathers" who won the last war are still in control. If voting power in international organizations were aligned to various countries' economic weight in the world and their ability and willingness to contribute, it would be strange that Britain, China and the U.S.S.R. are still among the permanent members of the U.N. Security Council (arguably the most prestigious political organ of the world), while Germany, Italy, and Japan are not.

Generally, as world public opinion goes at present, Japan's money is welcome, but its voice is not. Often international organizations forgo benefits from Japan's larger contributions because money translates into voice through rules that tie voting power to the quota of capital subscription. Japan's money was for a long time not welcomed by the incumbents whose voting power was to decrease in the shuffle. Only as recently as in 1990, Japan was "promoted" to the long overdue second rank in voting power in the IMF, equal to West Germany and next to the Number One United States. The political economy of hegemonic transition understandably involves both political and economic considerations even in well established economic organizations. The participation of Japanese nationals in the bureaucracies of world organizations is also extremely low, further disadvantaging Japan through office politics.

There is one international economic organization where Japan is clearly in the leading position, the Asian Development Bank. Whether Japan's position makes any difference may be answered by a comparative analysis of the performances of the ADB and other similar institutions. Unfortunately, such comparative studies are not available. In Asia, Japan's leadership is generally acknowledged. This encourages Japan to be cautiously explicit about its leading role in Asia, though it is still reticent about leadership on a global scale. In the global arena, the United States still is the hegemon. Its political leadership and military power are unmatched. Its domestic economy, however, is debt-ridden and falling behind Japan in growth rates. The world is caught in a peculiar chemistry of Japan's economic power and the political and military power of the United States.

Japan's Political Commitment: Peace

Owing to the unchallengeable military superiority of the United States, the need for military power in the possession of other countries has been considerably reduced. The Gulf War demonstrated how effective the United States was as a military "leviathan." Just as the Hobbsian

Leviathan has pushed brutish, quarrelsome individuals into a consensus on the desirability of a peaceful civil society, the American leviathan has successfully proved the futility of warlike nation-states' obsession with military power as an indispensable means of national security. Once nations are cured of this obsession, enormous amounts of economic resources are released from military expenditures and become payable as "peace dividends?" This simple truth of how beneficial peace is and how easy it is to generate and maintain peace has long eluded mankind. Now it is given the first effective global recognition as a moral, as well as utilitarian, principle that should guide resource allocation in every nation.

A further benefit of global arms reductions, hopefully leading to a total global disarmament, is that the United States itself can now cease to be a military leviathan to ensure peace in the world. The United States now can afford a substantial reduction in its military expenditures and its military power. This leads to a substantial revision of the theory of hegemony as an international government.

An important role of hegemony is the production of international public goods, of which peace is paramount (Kindleberger 1986). Peace as an international public good has been costly hitherto, and the hegemon's qualifications included sufficient economic resources by which to maintain military expenditure and military power. But with a universal peace by consensus among nation-states, peace becomes an international public good without costing economic resources. The hegemon's role must then change from ensuring peace by military threats to a moral leadership to ensure that peace without arms is desirable and possible. Would the United States be able to remain a hegemon capable of maintaining world peace while eliminating, in stages, its military power at the same time?

Global peace results from rejections of arms by individual states. If states really want a lasting peace, a conceivable political action would be a constitutional ban on war as a sovereign act of a state, which would be a quantum jump in the transformation of the conventional, archaic principles of state sovereignty. In this respect, Japan is one of the most advanced countries. Article 9 of the Japanese constitution states:

Aspiring sincerely to an international peace based on justice and order, the Japanese people forever renounce war as a sovereign right of the nation and the threat or use of force as means of settling international disputes.

During the Gulf War (August 1990-March 1991), this peace article of the Japanese constitution effectively prevented Japan from "using force" in conjunction with the United Nations' military action to remove Iraqi troops out of Kuwait. By orchestrating the U.N. action, the United States demonstrated the rights and obligations of a hegemon to ensure peace in the Gulf region. The main point of the U.N.-U.S. achievements is the security of Kuwait's territorial integrity, which derives from a larger principle that every member state of the United Nations is protected by world collective security against invasions by other states. Japan is also a beneficiary of the collective security system and in exchange should contribute to the maintenance and strengthening of this system. In the case of the Gulf War, under its own constitutional ban on military contribution, Japan made a generous financial contribution.

Japan's role in the Gulf War has been subject to intense controversy inside and outside Japan. Many unkind views of Japan's rejection of military participation, despite its financial generosity, have been heard in the West. Ostensibly the type of Japanese contribution most desired by the West was the sending of Japanese troops to the Gulf. Failing in that contribution, whatever Japan did for peace in the Gulf seemed to have no value in the Western eyes. Japan was made a laughing stock of the world for inability and ineptitude to seize upon a great political opportunity to demonstrate its world-leadership capability.

More than a year after August 2, 1990, however, those Western views sound more like irresponsible harassments of Japan than objective assessments of Japan's role or capability in international relations. From a more objective standpoint of political dynamics, what appeared to be a failure of the Japanese *government* was a great success of the Japanese *people* in resisting unreasonable Western pressures. Indeed, the Japanese government was inept and made no principled response to the Western demand. In fact, the Japanese government even appeared to accept as legitimate the Western demand for the sending of Japanese troops to the Gulf. As a consequence, the Japanese government went so far as to try to tamper with the constitution of Japan to make the sending of troops technically right.

The Japanese people rebelled against this illegitimate maneuver of the Japanese government. In the end the people and the constitution prevailed. Japan's refusal to use its troops outside Japan indicate the political maturity and purposefulness of the Japanese people regarding world priorities. To take a stand against Western pressures is an extraordinary achievement on the part of Japan in the light of a long history of subservience to such "external pressures" (*gaiatsu*).

Since Japan's choice of peaceful contributions was a result of intense political debate in Japan, the choice against the use of troops was a victory of Japanese democratic politics in conformity with the Japanese constitution. Furthermore, it was also the choice that Japan's Asian neighbors favored. Large-scale troop movements over Asian waters on the way to, and back from, the Gulf would have threatened Asian peace. Japan's domestic politics and peace in Asia clearly coincided, contributing to the reduction of the lingering Asian suspicion of Japan's geopolitical intentions.

The End of History

The Japanese commitment to peace is also broadly in accord with the long-run historical forces which however enigmatic, have brought history itself to an end. Although the philosophical concept of an "end of History" (Fukuyama 1989) is an update of Hegel with no particular regard to Japan, it has a special significance for the evaluation of Japan's hegemonic qualifications at the present juncture of history.

According to Fukuyama, all the requisite ideas that would put an end to History were produced during the Age of Enlightenment. These were the concepts of freedom, equality, and democracy supported by free enterprise and the market. When democratic polity and market economy pervade the world, History comes to an end in the sense that all thoughts and experiments in search of a better world are exhausted and that history-making clashes of ideals and ideologies, often accompanied by armed struggles, are unlikely. In the last two hundred years, a variety of ideologies promising a better world appeared and disappeared. None of them withstood the relentless growth of democracy and markets over wider and wider areas of the world. The ongoing dismantling of the Communist regimes is the latest testimony to the end of History.

Fukuyama describes the state of the world after the end of History as follows:

The struggle for recognition, the willingness to risk one's life for a purely abstract goal, the worldwide ideological struggle that called forth daring, courage, imagination and idealism, will be replaced by *economic calculation, the endless solving of technical problems, environmental concerns, and the satisfaction of sophisticated consumer demands* (p.18; emphasis added).

Military heroism dies with the end of History and much less glamorous economics become the centerpiece of post-History life. Japan appears to be well suited for a leading role in this state of affairs.

There is one more disruptive legacy of the nation-state era that the world has to subdue: nationalism. While the market forces and technological progress essentially know no geographical boundaries, nation-states are territorially defined. At times "local" sentiments restrain "global" economic forces, as may be seen in clashes between nationalism and multinational enterprise. After all other ideologies and movements are safely defeated, nationalism may still remain as a source of inspiration for the protection of national interest often overriding liberalism which is the bedrock of globalism.

However, as Fukuyama says:

.... the vast majority of the world's nationalist movements do not have a political program beyond the negative desire of independence from some other group or people, and do not offer anything like a comprehensive agenda for socio-economic organization (pp.14-15).

So long as democracy allows free expressions of aspirations and interests of different groups, nationalism is unlikely to stand in the way of global economic forces. It may even thrive as an aspect of cultural diversity that add color and excitement to life after the end of History.

To paraphrase Fukuyama further, as all regions and countries are peacefully integrated by global market forces, the nation-states with their conventional "sovereign" rights will become obsolete as basic elements of world organization. When the concept of sovereignty becomes more hollow, states will increasingly take on the character of administrative units subordinate to a unified world and submit to the rules and procedures of negotiation for the adjustment of differing interests or conflicting rights.

An Interim Role for Japan

Japan has become a hegemonic candidate when a major hegemonic function, "production" of peace, is no longer needed, because the end of History has made peace a sort of "free good" rather than a costly public good that has to be produced and maintained by the hegemon. Other important hegemonic functions are largely economic. They have to do with the creation and maintenance of international institutions embodying principles, norms, rules and procedures consistent with the market forces. The cost of global leadership consists in taking up a major share in the financing of these institutions. The hegemon must also efficiently respond to emergencies arising from imbalances in the balance of payments, shortages of development capital, misalignments of exchange rates, conflicting economic policies of various countries, etc. (Kindleberger 1986).

With the end of History and the likelihood of peace as a global free good, a crucial factor in world governance over a medium term is the quality of U.S.-Japanese cooperation. For a while, there may continue to be intermittent outbreaks of local skirmishes initiated by errant leaders of minor nation-states that are lagging behind the march of History. Today the United States alone has and is willing to use international police power to put down and prevent these international incidents from disrupting global peace. Eventually, democracy and markets will invalidate armed conflicts between nations, giving rise to the primacy of peaceful negotiations for adjustments of national interests.

In the meantime, America as Number One would continue to claim a maximum freedom in the pursuit of its strategy based on its global vision, which is well-known and even credited for bringing History to an end. But Japan's economic power is a critical factor that may make or break the success of America's world strategy. Thus, for its own good, the United States cannot ignore Japan. Neither the United States nor Japan can afford the luxury of a nationalist notion of sovereignty. When production depends on interdependence and teamwork, parties involved must subordinate themselves to super-ordinate goals.

Japan and the United States have complementary strengths and weaknesses, which require closer cooperation for the stability of the world order. American opinion leaders, appreciating Japan's economic strengths, suggest that a closer economic integration of the two countries (*Nichibei* Economy) would generate a more effective hegemony (Gilpin 1987: pp. 336-339). Instead of lamenting the farther fall of the U.S. share in world GNP, which was widespread in the 1970s, American policy makers now link the strategy of the United States to the sum of Japanese and U.S. economies. It is no longer a matter of either U.S. or Japanese hegemony; it is co-hegemony (bigemony) or, a little more generally, a "Pax Consortis" (Chan 1990: pp.102-107).

Conclusion

We reach a rather obvious conclusion. The weight of the Japanese economy is on a hegemonic scale. But the world's need for a hegemonic state to ensure the peace and stability of the world order is one of History-bound concepts and will disappear with the end of History. When all political units, including the nation-states, are thoroughly democratized and disarmed, all political power devolves to the individual. Then all the individuals of the world might wish to reorganize a super-ordinate world community by a new global social contract. The world community may still be divided into geographical units of administration ("former" states). But political competition among these units for hegemony will be checked by internal forces of democracy and the global interdependence of markets. The dialectic of contradictions will finally come to rest under permanent peace and lose its History-making power.

References

1. Steve Chan; Boulder, Colorado: Westview Press, 1990

2. William S. Dietrich; ""In the Shadow of the Rising Sun" University Park, Pa.: Pennsylvania State University Press 1991.

3. Rudiger Dornbusch; "The United States in the World Economy," *Quarterly Review of Economics and Business,* 31, 2 (Summer 1991): pp.3-32.

4. Francis Fukuyama; "The End of History?" *National Interest* (Summer 1989), pp.-3-18.

5. Robert Gilpin; "The Political Economy of International Relations." Princeton, N.J.: Princeton University Press 1987.

6. Paul Kennedy; "The Rise and Fall of the Great Powers". Lexington, Mass.: Lexington Book 1987.

7. C.P. Kindleberger; 1986. "International Public Goods without International Government", *American Economic Review,* Vol. 76, No. 1 (March 1986): pp.1-13.

8. Atsushi Kuse; "Super-No. 2: Nippon" (in Japanese). Tokyo: Shodensha 1990.

9. John H. Makin and Donald C. Hellmann, eds. "Sharing World Leadership?" Washington, D.C.: American Enterprise Institute 1989.

10. Michio Morishima; "Why Has Japan `Succeeded'?" London: Cambridge University Press 1982.

11. Taggart R. Murphy; "Power Without Purpose: The Crisis of Japan's Global Financial Dominance," *Harvard Business Review*, 67, 2 (March-April 1989): pp.71-83.

12. Minoru Morita; "Keizai taikoku no kessei" (An economic power without policy). Tokyo: Nihon Hyoronsha 1989

13. Koji Taira; "Disadvantages of Success: Pains of Behavior Adjustment to Role Changes," *Proceedings of the Symposium on Japanese and Third-World Development*, 1988, pp.22-39. Cambridge, Mass.: Reischauer Institute of Japanese Studies.

14. Idem. "Japan: an Imminent Hegemon?" *Annals of the American Academy of Political and Social Science*, 513 (January 1991): pp.151-163.

15. UNDP (United Nations Development Program); *Human Development Report 1990.* New York: Oxford University Press 1990.

16. Ezra Vogel; *"Japan As Number One"*. Cambridge, Mass.: Harvard University Press 1979.

17. Immanuel Wallerstein; "The Politics of the World-Economy". New York: York; Cambridge Press 1984.

Japanese Multinationals:
An Evolutionary Theory

William V. Rapp
East Asian Institute
Columbia University

Large Japanese multinationals producing manufactured goods are the source of much of the political friction Japan has with other countries.[1] Their continued successful claim on global markets and resources would, from past experience, seem to be a potential source of continuing political economic friction. Japan as a nation has global economic importance, but it is the success of its major multinationals that accounts for much of this, as well as for Japan's ability to provide capital to other countries. Japanese firms, however, need access to world markets — especially the U.S. and European markets — to grow and prosper, particularly in higher value-added products.

It is thus useful to understand these firms' strategic behavior and to predict some of the logical competitive and political economic consequences of the likely continuation, further implementation, and potential success of their strategies. Context is important, so I first examine the possible application of several theories of competitive behavior to the case of large Japanese multinational manufacturing firms. Further, this paper is part of a larger research effort, just beginning, that will examine the competitive dynamics and strategic evolution of these firms.

The three basic theories examined on an integrated basis are: product cycle analysis, cost expectations based on experience, and an evolutionary theory of the firm. The first two have been investigated in some detail for Japan in previous studies by the author and others but the third is relatively unrepresented in the literature or current research. The evolutionary theory presented and utilized here is based on Nelson and Winter (1982).

The next two sections summarize the product cycle and experience based approaches, including how they relate to Japanese development

---

[1] The author would like to thank Columbia University Professors Gerald Curtis of the East Asian Institute and Hugh T. Patrick of the Center on Japanese Economy and Business for their generous support of this project in its initial stages and their thoughtful inputs. He, however, takes full responsibility for any errors of omission and commission which have no doubt crept into this work despite their best efforts.

and multinationals. The main purpose of this analysis is to highlight some essential differences between the postwar competitive experiences of a senior manager in a Japanese multinational manufacturing firm and his U.S. and European counterparts. The evolutionary theory of firm growth and development is taken up in the third section and is integrated with the product cycle and experience approaches, again primarily in a Japanese context. The fourth section examines how some of the features of Japanese MNCs have evolved, these features' contribution to Japan's competitive success, and their effect on future competitive interaction. With this historical and theoretical background, the last two sections look at possible future competitive scenarios, including some of the potential political impacts they imply.

Product and Industry Life Cycles

Japan's economic and industrial development has followed a particular pattern. Products have first been imported from more advanced countries (often called "innovators," indicating a product or technology's origin). These imports were generally from the UK or Europe before World War II and from the United States afterward. As domestic demand developed, the government protected and assisted the domestic industry (import substitution), which grew. Finally, as the industry became more efficient and competitive, it began to export. Japan was aided in this pattern by the fact that more advanced countries like the United States and the UK were at that time becoming less competitive in follower industries. They were moving into technically more advanced industries and products for which their economies had demand, which they had the factories to produce, and which justified the higher wages their workers expected. Once these technologies became known, however, the cost of technical transfer and diffusion dropped, aiding follower countries like Japan to constantly move up the technological ladder.

Having become internationally competitive, exports went first to countries that did not have the industry and where competition from the more advanced countries was on a relatively more even basis, that is, was export versus export. These markets were also generally more price sensitive, so aggressive pricing by follower firms could overcome quality and service deficiencies. Only after building export experience in LDCs and further lowering costs, while increasing efficiency and quality, did Japanese industry begin exporting to the more advanced countries. Such industries in the advanced countries were by that time quite mature, and their products were usually commodities produced in high volume. Price competition was thus again a viable entry strategy, given reasonable quality and service.

As Japan itself evolved, its own more labor intensive, less sophisticated industries and products became subject to the same competitive pressures from the next generation of followers — NICs such as Korea, Taiwan.

This classic product cycle pattern was first observed by Akamatsu (1962) in analyzing the development of Japan's cotton textile industry and the corresponding competitive decline of cotton textiles in the U.S. and UK. He named it the "flying geese" pattern of development.

The initial, import substitution stage would usually be the high growth period for the industry or product. By the time the export stage arrived, domestic growth was usually starting to decrease. Indeed, this development was often part of the motivation for firms to start exporting. Thus, by the time local firms were selling to advanced countries, domestic demand was starting to mature. Exports from that point on became a higher and higher percentage of total production. Porter (1989) notes that when there is a large number of firms, the domestic market is saturated rather quickly and this forces firms to examine foreign markets sooner rather than later. Thus in postwar Japan, where many firms had relatively open access to the available global technologies, and new industries therefore had many entrants relative to domestic market size, domestic markets grew and saturated rapidly. Thus the pressures to export developed more quickly than they did for the innovators. This internal industry pressure was in turn accentuated by the government's promotion of exports in order to earn foreign exchange.

Reflecting another aspect of this process, Japan in the 19th century was producing and exporting very simple manufactures and primary commodities such as copper, green tea, raw silk, and the like. As the country grew and developed, it acquired the technical capability and generated the demand for technically more sophisticated products — initially cotton textiles, then steel, machinery, shipbuilding, automobiles, computers, etc. These more advanced industries were also usually more capital intensive so the build up of capital resources over time aided the process. This kind of inter-industry evolution for the Japanese economy is well-documented (Rapp 1967 and 1975).

Depending on the industry and Japan's overall growth rate, this evolutionary process could take an industry 20 to 40 years to complete. Because the country was constantly changing in terms of its ability to produce and use increasingly more advanced industrial technologies, at any point in time there were industries at different stages of development. For example, the cotton textile industry might be declining, the steel industry might be fairly mature and exporting successfully to a full range of countries, the auto industry might be exporting, but mostly to LDCs, and the semiconductor industry might be in an import substitution mode, while aerospace might still be primarily imports. This is in fact a fairly good profile of Japan's industrial structure in the mid to late 1960s from a classic product cycle viewpoint.

From a firm and strategy development viewpoint, the influence of World War II on inter-industry development was important because it forced Japan to repeat this traditional development pattern in a relatively short time during the immediate postwar period. For instance, by the 1920s and 1930s Japan's cotton textile industry had evolved into the world's most competitive in all export markets, and its steel industry was exporting to LDCs. This process was compressed and repeated at a very rapid rate in the early postwar years. Abegglen and Stalk (1985) note this shift was also reflected in Japan's largest manufacturing firm shifting from Toray (textile producer) in the 1950s to Nippon Steel in the 1960s and 1970s to Toyota in the 1980s and today.

Thus, every Japanese manager, even in fairly traditional or well established industries like textiles and steel, became quite conscious of the economic forces behind the product cycle as it applied to his own industry. Managers also became aware of the substantial cost reductions that were possible because of high growth, the incorporation of new technologies via rapid investment, and constant market expansion.

Indeed, by the early 1970s this development pattern was so apparent that MITI stated it as its formal industrial policy. MITI Vice Minister Ojimi specifically noted: "While certain segments of the industrial structure are being encouraged, there must be modification of those industries where productivity is low, where technology is stagnant and where there is reliance on simplistic intensified use of labor. ... The solution of this problem is to be found, according to economic logic, in progressively giving away industries to other countries, much as a big brother gives his outgrown clothes to his younger brother. In this way, a country's own industries become more sophisticated." Similarly, Takeo Fukuda, then Minister of Finance stated: "Advanced countries must export capital and simple technology to developing countries and then produce new technologies (at home), industrialize these and move out to even higher industrial levels."

These statements anticipate by 15 years Porter's advice that notes the need for countries to move into industries requiring "advanced" factors of production rather than basic factors of production if competitive advantage is to be sustained by a nation's industries. They also represented a view consistently held by the highest economic policy makers in Japan that persists today. In fact, Japan has incorporated this approach into its own foreign aid programs and economic development strategies for various LDCs.

In effect, what had been a pragmatic ad hoc policy to resuscitate Japan's economy after the war became, 25 years later, a formalized model of economic development because of Japan's rapid growth and economic success. In turn, this evolutionary approach was explicitly adopted by NICs such as Korea and Taiwan. Their successes reinforced the model's visibility and acceptance. It should be recognized that by its very nature such a policy tends to dynamically support basic economic forces, and so can be a powerfully self-reinforcing economic growth strategy, at least as one progresses through the follower stage in various industries. But there may be limits to its long-term applicability if firms' intra-industry development goals and the government's inter-industry development goals begin to diverge, as is discussed below.

In any case, based on this view, in the 1970s MITI consciously moved to phase out or de-emphasize the cotton textile industry while promoting the development of the semiconductor industry through projects like the VHISC (Very Highly Integrated Semiconductor) program. This strategic philosophy has persisted into the 1990s with the government's protection and support of efforts to develop Japanese made super-computers and satellites. At the same time, Japan's competitors in Europe and the U.S. have been made forcibly aware of this process of competitive shift, both in the market place and in U.S. and European management literature (see Vernon 1966 and Rapp 1973).

Many executives began to recognize the powerful political and economic forces acting to shift an industry's absolute and comparative advantage from one country to another as being a function of economic growth, changing factor costs, and the declining cost of technological transfer, combined with specific government development policies. They did not on the whole simply accept such a competitive shift as inevitable, however, if it was going to put them out of business. But they were not able in the classical economic tradition merely to move fungible units of capital and labor from producing textiles, steel, and automobiles to producing computers and airplanes. Rather, they had to pursue a mixed strategy that combined resisting, accepting, and following the shift in competitive advantage while on the whole remaining in their basic businesses. Thus, United States and European firms upgraded and diversified.

Some industries asked and generally got their governments to restrain foreign competition. In the U.S., a series of VRAs ("Voluntary" Restraint Agreements) in textiles, steel, television, automobiles, and semiconductors was negotiated over a 20-year period. This was itself in an evolutionary process that confirmed the inter-industry product cycle theory and Japan and the NICs' successful movement into constantly higher value-added industries.

U.S. firms invested in lower cost production facilities offshore, which enabled them to continue to maintain their overall global corporate manufacturing competitiveness and thus retain their markets. However, production jobs were lost to the home country (the U.S.) and transferred to the followers (e.g. Taiwan, Korea, etc.). The product cycle evolution of competitive shift remained in tact. This strategy did have the benefit, though, of frustrating the development of native competitors in host countries and keeping support, sales, and managerial people employed in the U.S. This was a new competitive situation.

The potential to upgrade or expand an existing product line through R&D and technical change is an important and often overlooked aspect of the classic product cycle. (For further analysis of this point see Rapp 1975). That is, in addition to inter-industry product cycle evolution, there also is significant intra-industry product cycle evolution. Synthetic textiles followed cotton textiles; high grade alloy steels evolved after carbon steel; color television came after black and white. Indeed, as Japanese firms have advanced through intra-industry development, and have used up the available pool of easily acquired foreign technology, they have ceased to be followers; they have necessarily become innovators. In fact, those not able to make this shift often start to fall behind competitively and become vulnerable to either foreign or domestic acquisition as in the cases of Isuzu (General Motors), Banyu (Merck), and Fuji Heavy Industries (Nissan).

The response of multinational firms to evolving international competition, especially in terms of overseas investment, has made the product cycle obsolete as a predictor of competitive developments in the eyes of many observers. However, it is still seen as a good description of past events. Indeed, several analysts have modified the classic product cycle to include foreign investment in the cycle profile (e.g. see Gilpin 1975). I shall refer to this as "modified product cycle" analysis to distinguish it from the classic format.

In the history of the Japanese cotton textile industry, for example, foreign investment played no role, and the industry's ability to invest overseas to influence or limit the development of competitors in the NICs and LDCs was extremely limited. This is the classic format. In computers, however, foreign investment in Japan has played a definite role, and FDI is being used effectively by the Japanese in various industries and countries as a competitive tool as well.

There is a big difference between responding to and modifying the strategic outcome of economic forces and eliminating those forces. The basic forces operating to shift competitive advantage from one country to another under conditions of economic growth and development are still very much in evidence. A Korean worker watching the movement of Motorola semiconductor jobs to Malaysia or Nike sneaker jobs to China is every bit as adversely affected by the operation of the product cycle as an unemployed steel worker in Pennsylvania or auto worker in Michigan. The key difference is in the competitive impact on a Motorola or Nike compared to a U.S. Steel or General Motors. This issue of corporate impact and survival compared to national impact is an important one, which is examined in more detail later.

Experience and Cost Declines

From the extensive literature on learning by doing, cost reductions based on experience, and the like, one learns that for a given technology or product, total real costs (net of inflation) for producing, delivering, and selling a product will decline in a fairly predictable manner as a function of accumulated experience (i.e., the total amount of a product that has been produced). Such real cost reductions reflect scale economies, continued product development, improvement in worker skills, improved organizational structures, more sophisticated equipment, etc. For this reason, market share tends to be a good predictor of profitability, and cost reductions tend to take place most rapidly in the early stages of a product or technology's development when growth and accumulation rates are most rapid. [2]

---

[2] See Abegglen and Rapp 1972, Abegglen and Stalk 1985, BCG 1972 and 1975, and Rapp 1973. Porter 1989 (p 66 and 70) refers to the competitive effects of learning by doing and the accumulation

Foreign competitors catch up relatively quickly, long before they have produced an amount equivalent to the leading innovator, because the follower starts on a lower but parallel cost experience curve compared to the innovator. This is logical when one considers that the costs, including time and effort, to develop and introduce a new product are generally quite substantial. On the other hand, the costs of transfer, imitation, and diffusion are relatively lower. Moreover, the older and more mature the industry, the more readily available and cheaper the technology is to all comers.

Also, the follower or new entrant can import and utilize the latest and most productive equipment. In contrast, the innovator is often saddled with older, less productive, perhaps even obsolete, equipment. This situation may both reduce the innovator's average productivity level and make it expensive to respond competitively via new investment. The effect of this phenomena is particularly apparent if there is a major change in production technology. In steel, for example, Japanese firms clearly benefited from the fact that in growing their industry they were able to invest primarily in the new basic oxygen furnace and did not have a large amount of existing open hearth capacity, as U.S. firms did (see Dresser, Hout and Rapp 1972). However, a given industry's technology does to some degree seem to define and drive its organizational structure and potential rate of continuous cost reduction. Therefore, while the follower begins his accumulation of experience from a lower initial cost point, future cost reductions seem to move along a curve that parallels the innovator's. That is, the slope and path of cost reductions seems to be the same. This parallel tracking appears logical in a global industry where technological advances and management or engineering practices are well publicized and are generally available to everyone within a relatively short period of time.

Changes in exchange rates have an impact by shifting the cost curves and therefore relative cost positions. Inflation also has an effect since actual costs and, in turn, market prices are found by multiplying the inflation rate times the real cost level and adding the profit margin. (See Hout and Rapp 1972 and Rapp 1973. The latter provides a simple formula relating the relative rates of growth, the fall in real costs due to experience, and inflation, to changes in cost competitiveness between firms or industries.)

Nevertheless, if exchange rates are operating properly, industries that are growing more rapidly should be gaining both comparative and absolute cost advantage over time. The relation between these phenomena and changes in competitive position as reflected in the product cycle is

---

of small incremental improvements.

quite direct (see Abegglen and Rapp 1972). Such a cost reduction profile over time explains why, when a follower catches up and gets to the innovation stage, further cost reductions occur rather slowly and require substantial additions in experience (i.e., accumulated production) to achieve. It is clearly easier and cheaper to add capacity and reduce costs when one can acquire off the shelf technology from someone else. But in addition, the total size of the business and the total amount produced has grown quite large by that time. So the percentage impact of added sales is declining. A logical consequence of catching up, therefore, is a rise in capital output ratios and a decrease in the rate of productivity improvements by industry. This in turn takes place for a country as a whole as more and more of its manufacturing sector grows up and exits the follower stage. [3]

Therefore, acquiring foreign technology as the major means to grow and competitively develop a firm has become a progressively less viable strategy for large Japanese firms producing internationally traded products. By the time a firm is exporting to the advanced countries, the domestic market is fairly mature and the company is close to the innovation or technological frontier. There are then probably a limited number of new technologies to be introduced. At the same time, foreign firms, often the source of previous technology inputs, are painfully aware of Japanese companies' competitive presence and are not looking to do anything that would further a Japanese competitor's interests. Indeed, Japanese success has been so thorough and spectacular in so many areas that foreign managers routinely project Japanese competition in their industry or product as being possible even if it has not yet occurred. This perception restricts Japanese access to many new technologies, and forces them to develop their own.

Aside from offering an excellent analytical framework for assessing changes in competitive advantage between firms and industries on a global basis, cost-experience effects have had a major impact on the experience and thinking of postwar Japanese managers. Just as almost every senior Japanese manager in a major manufacturing firm has seen the operation of the product cycle in his own industry, so has he seen the rapid reductions in actual costs that came from rapid growth and large additions in productive capacity. This is especially true where the latest imported

---

[3]In fact, Japan's capital output ratio has risen sharply. From 1970 to 1980, it went from 1.34 to 2.23. This compares to 2.10 and 2.53 in the U.S. (see Sato 1987, p 143). By the early 1970s many of Japan's major industries — such as textiles, steel, shipbuilding, automobiles, and TV sets — had passed through the high growth phase and were entering the innovation stage, requiring more investment per unit of output. The trend was accelerated by the Nixon shock and the oil crisis. As these industries represented a growing percentage of total manufacturing, a rising capital-output ratio was almost inevitable. Also, Abegglen and Stalk (1985) point out the corresponding rapid rise in Japanese firms R&D expenditures in both absolute terms and as a percent of sales, pp. 119-147

technology was used from the beginning (e.g. see Gilpin 1975). He also knows the benefits of pricing aggressively, in anticipation of cost reductions, in order to gain market share that will in turn justify further capacity additions. He knows this process will continue to be beneficial until further reductions in price do not expand the market domestically or even for exports (see Abegglen and Rapp 1970). One reason he knows this is because if his firm did not observe this phenomena and operate in this manner, it probably is not currently a major factor in its industry.

In terms of psychology and business experience, American managers have been ill-equipped to deal with competitors having "hands-on" experience of conscious product cycle policies and developments combined with the phenomena of managed cost reductions based on experience and growth in market share. U.S. industries like textiles, steel, and autos were so mature during the postwar period that few if any of their executives had experienced a high growth, rapid cost reduction period. Furthermore, whatever real cost declines did occur with increases in accumulated experience were disguised by inflation that kept nominal or actual cash costs rising. Thus, these U.S. managers were used to seeing costs and prices rise over time, not fall. Cost competitively, U.S. firms were standing still just as Japanese competitors were catching up quickly and were continuing to lower prices to gain market share and further lower costs.

It was during the export phase of this process that Japanese managers discovered the happy coincidence that cost and quality improvements could move in tandem. Traditionally, quality control tended to be something that happened at the end of the production process where statistical sampling techniques were used to prevent defective items from being shipped to the consumer. More frequent samplings, while reducing the chance of shipping a bad product, were also more expensive. In the U.S., because most sales were domestic, producers had extensive after-sales service capability which often was an independent profit center. So the feeling was that any problems could be handled in the field at little or no cost to the producer.

The Japanese exporter couldn't do this, especially in areas like consumer electronics. He was usually exporting to a large, price-sensitive retailer who was only interested in sales and customer satisfaction. Such a retailer had little or no service capability, and didn't want returns which were time consuming to handle. The Japanese manufacturer in turn had no extensive U.S. service network and couldn't afford to have goods shipped back to Japan. At this time, the Japanese were also fighting a global image of producing shoddy products. In sum, the product had to work right out of the box and be virtually free of defects if the Japanese producer was to penetrate the U.S. market.

To achieve this in a cost effective manner led to the development of a "zero defect" manufacturing system. This system was then discovered to reduce total costs because smaller inventory, repair, unusable returns, service, and transportation costs were incurred. In addition, customer satisfaction improved. This situation combined with real quality and price competitiveness to help market penetration and to further reduce costs due to greater accumulated experience. Japanese companies had the self-reinforcing and interactive triple benefit of being preeminent quality manufacturers, low cost producers, and otherwise effective global competitors.

The only U.S. industries where these phenomena were well recognized were computers and semiconductors. Here very rapid growth resulted in very rapid cost reductions and quick product obsolescence. It should not be surprising therefore that it was these industries that were the origin of the experience curve as an analytical framework for managing costs, of 100% automatic testing at different production stages as a way to improve yields, and of the use of offshore manufacturing locations as a way to use product cycles to maintain international competitive advantage (see BCG 1972).

Managing under conditions of high growth makes managers conscious of, and forces them to respond to, some unique phenomena related to cost management and international shifts in cost advantage in order to maintain the firm's competitive viability. The Japanese postwar situation has been somewhat unusual, though, in that this occurred not just at the high tech or venture capital frontier but across a wide spectrum of industries, including some industries that have traditionally been considered quite mature.

Evolutionary Theory in a Japanese Context

This section first sets forth a brief synopsis of Richard Nelson and Sidney Winter's evolutionary theory of the firm, then demonstrates that Japanese multinational manufacturing firms are covered by their theory and that some of the model's predictions have in fact occurred in a Japanese context. Nelson and Winter propose that organizations evolve to accommodate technology, but that organizations also modify technology. The evolutionary development process is thus interactive and involves a lot of trial and error ("searching") as well as learning by doing. Nelson and Winter's evolutionary approach supplements experience curve and product cycle analysis, so both are integrated into what follows.

Nelson and Winter (1982) are concerned primarily with large complex organizations producing a service or product for sale on a repetitive, relatively continuous basis for an extended period on which the company hopes to make a profit. Such a company probably has some history. Large organizations do not usually spring up over night, with the principle exception of government entities (which in any case are not often providing a service but rather are enforcing rules and imposing requirements).

Top management is unable to direct all the day-to-day details, as might be the case of a sole proprietorship. They therefore must delegate.to ensure that decisions are made in a consistent and predictable manner, these managers establish rules and "routines" within which delegated responsibilities can be exercised. Excerpting from Nelson and Winter:

[Routines] include characteristics of firms that range from well-specified technical routines for producing things, through procedures for hiring and firing, ordering new inventory, or stepping up production of items in high demand, to policies regarding investment, research and development (R&D), or advertising, and business strategies about product diversification and overseas investment. ...

In any case, evolutionary modeling highlights the similarities among different sorts of routines. At any time, a firm's routines define a list of functions that determine (perhaps stochastically) what a firm does as a function of various external variables (principally market conditions) and internal state variables (for example, the firm's prevailing stock of machinery, or the average profit rate it has earned in recent periods).

A second set of routines determine the period-by-period augmentation or diminution of the firm's capital stock (those factors of production that are fixed in the short-run). The extent to which actual investment behavior follows predictable patterns probably varies a good deal from one situation to another. In some cases the decision making surrounding the question of whether to build a new plant may not be much different in kind from the decision making regarding whether or not to continue to run a particular machine.... In other cases, the new plant decision may be more like a decision to undertake a major R&D program on a recently opened technological frontier, a problem without real precedent that is dealt with through improvised procedures....

These routine-guided, routine-changing processes are modeled as 'searches.' ... (pp. 14-18).

Consistency and predictability are important for repetition, and repetition is necessary if the firm's output is to be produced on a continuous basis. The decision rules and the routines used to implement them generally are based on historical experience and the feedback from actions undertaken in response to specific events or under certain circumstances. If the feedback was favorable, the action has generally been repeated. If not favorable, the action was dropped or modified. Routines thus incorporate the organization's memory and are often based on the product or service produced as well as the technology used.

In terms of innovation and searches — what they can do next — firms are restricted by their existing organization, technologies, and resource availabilities. That is, they normally look to make organizational or technical innovations or adaptations in the neighborhood of the existing organization and technology. Whether planned or stochastic, innovations represent changes in the company's routines. That is, organizations believe changes in routines are innovations in that they affect and alter the way the organization will operate in the future.

Competitive behavior is continuous and dynamic, and is not an exercise in comparative statics or in moving from one optimal equilibrium to another. In fact, Nelson and Winter explicitly reject the need for maximizing behavior to explain firm action, looking instead to the rules and routines of each firm. Because these rules and routines are constrained by existing organizations and resources, firms are not free to choose from the entire range of possible or potential technologies and organizational forms, even if they had perfect foresight to choose the optimal path at any particular point in time.

In terms of modeling the reality of the Japanese multinational firm, the Nelson and Winter approach seems a sensible one. Japanese corporate behavior is very much a product of custom and history, as the extensive literature on Japanese management practices attests.

For example, up until the 1980s, Toyota always produced cars out of essentially a single location in Japan. Production had followed a normal product cycle evolution from import substitution through export. Indeed, export growth and foreign market penetration had been extremely successful and had further driven down costs and improved competitive market position both domestically and overseas, as expected from experience curve analysis. (See Hout and Rapp 1972, pp. 236-37, who note that

Japan's automobile industry increased its exports between 1964 and 1970 from 15.3% of production to 44.6% while at the same time accumulating experience at a compound rate of 37% per annum compared to the U.S. industry's 3.9%.)

However, in response to a revalued yen, a U.S. VRA, and intense political pressure, top management realized that investment in the United States was inevitable. Toyota's response was an ordered one. First, the company established that its assembly and basic production routines, using mostly imported parts, could work in the U.S. environment. It learned this by forming a joint venture in an existing GM plant in California. This was a comparatively low risk approach involving a relatively small outlay of funds and little commitment to suppliers in Japan.

Having successfully adapted its routines to the U.S. environment, Toyota moved to replicate its organizational, supply, and production processes in Kentucky using some of the staff who had managed the Fremont operation. This move involved substantially more money as well as a commitment to the suppliers it encouraged to invest nearby. But again it was done in stages, with engine manufacture coming after the assembly plant was operating successfully.

The final result reflected Toyota's history and its established routines. That is, the movement of its main keiretsu suppliers to the U.S. to become part of the overall competitive effort was clearly a transfer of Toyota's well-known kanban (just-in-time) system and was a demonstration that it too could be replicated. Having developed managers who could transfer (innovate) Toyota routines to another environment, including its keiretsu and kanban systems, and having gained organizational confidence that it could be done successfully, Toyota undertook additional overseas plant investments, including in the UK. This appears to be a clear evolutionary process.

In addition, considerable analysis (searching) seems to have been done prior to each step, using inputs from prior events as well as changes in the Japanese technology and organizational base that took place during the period. There does not appear to have been any attempt to implement a local solution — such as an American-style assembly plant operation using strictly local parts suppliers — though that was clearly an option. Perhaps the output would not have been considered a Toyota.

The organizations Nelson and Winter wish to analyze are made up of people with different skills, and part of the function of a complex organization is to mobilize and use diverse skills to deliver a product or service. Some skills like computer programming are explicit and people with these skills can be hired or replaced. Other skills are firm-specific, such as knowledge of the company's specific programs or programming methods as well as knowledge of how the organization operates in terms of decision making and personnel interaction. In fact, much of this knowledge is not even articulated. It operates innately in the day-to-day operation of the firm and employees' normal interaction. Such tacit knowledge may be particularly strong in the Japanese environment due to an already very homogeneous culture and population where most managers are male college graduates with very similar educational experiences and tenure with the company tends to be very long. Many firms recruit from the same colleges year after year.

The innate rules on how things should function is often referred to as corporate culture. Here they are called routines and represent the organization's skill base. The more successful and efficiently the routines work, the more successful the organization. But many of the skills that contribute to a firm's success are innate to the firm, such as the knowledge of one's role within Toyota's kanban system or the product and technology knowledge carried by Matsushita's product managers. (A description of how Matsushita uses product researchers to provide program continuity on a global basis is described in some detail by Bartlett and Ghoshal 1988 and 1989.) These skills are thus not readily transferred to or imitated by other firms.

An important competitive implication of this phenomena is that the more critical such innate skills are to a firm's success and the more time it takes to acquire and use them productively within the corporate routines, the more important it becomes to retain personnel. Any corporate or social routine that promotes longer employment tenure then becomes a competitive plus. The extension of this concept to the Japanese permanent or long-tenured employment system seems fairly direct. A natural consequence of long-term employment is a large commitment to both firm survival and the firm's basic business, as employment cannot easily be found elsewhere and it is not easy to bring in top managers from other companies with the requisite skills for diversification. This should lead to a greater degree of corporate specialization, a fact that has been noted by Sheard (1991) and others. [4]

---

[4] Many observers have correctly noted that Japan's permanent employment system has never applied to all workers, perhaps only to the 35-40% of the labor force at large firms and in the government (including former government enterprises such as the railroads and NTT). In addition, from the 1980s, slower growth, declining industries, and an aging labor force have put the system under pressure, especially the linkage of pay primarily to seniority. However, the firms being examined in this paper are those employing the system. Also, the very senior managers within those firms

Porter remarks that countries tend to succeed in businesses that accommodate the demands of top managers and financial markets. In this regard, he notes that compared to Japanese managers, senior U.S. managers stay with their organizations a relatively short time, and the owners of capital buy and sell shares on a relatively short-term basis. Further, because U.S. banks cannot own shares in corporate clients except via certain venture capital subsidiaries, there is a clear divergence between the objectives of lenders and shareholders if a firm runs into difficulties or has a drop in earnings. Both these aspects contrast with Japan's stable shareholder and main bank systems, which seem to promote stability and long-term relations (see Aoki 1990). For these reasons Porter suggests the United States tends to be more successful in higher risk enterprises with substantial short-term payoffs for the individual — venture capital, movies, software, investment banking, etc. (Porter 1989, pp. 111-114). As pointed out by Nelson and Winter and by Bartlett and Ghoshal, a country's success in a given set of industries also depends on the mobility of labor and the real transferability of the skills to another corporation's routines in that or another industry. This is in turn a function of how important innate skills are to the routine operating competitively.

Nelson and Winter explicitly address not only innovation but also imitation. Imitation takes fewer resources than innovation and to imitate successfully one need not perfectly replicate the innovator's routines (i.e., organization and technology). Rather, knowing that the product or service exists, one needs only to create a similar end result that is an economic success. That is, can one compete in the market place without losing money? To do this, it is possible, indeed it is likely, that the imitator will develop original processes and evolve unique routines. This is because it is not possible to constantly check the actual situation of the innovator. Further, the imitator is likely to be facing a different set of economic and competitive circumstances (search environment) than the innovator — who had little or no competition at the time of innovation if it was a new product or service.

Baba (1989), in his analysis of large Japanese manufacturing firms, explicitly sees Japanese industrial growth and manufacturing firm growth in large-scale industries as having been evolutionary in character. He also notes the differences between industry leaders who have usually achieved that position by being aggressive cost cutters (e.g. Matsushita), managerial

---

effectively do have life time employment, either moving up towards president or chairman in their 60s or being seconded to one of the major affiliates as a senior executive after becoming a director in the parent.

followers (e.g. Hitachi), and innovative followers (e.g. Sony). His categorization and assessment are very helpful when examining Nelson and Winter's simulation of the competition between innovators and imitators under an evolutionary perspective of growth and development, including the implications for the Japanese case.

There appears to be a good case for applying the Nelson-Winter approach to an assessment of postwar Japanese economic development and particularly to the role and evolution of what has become the large multinational Japanese manufacturing firm. Quite a number of characteristics support this view.

(1) The Japanese firms being examined are large organizations producing products and services on a continuous and repetitive basis.

(2) They have administrative procedures, organizational arrangements, and decision making processes (routines), many of which are technology based. (The literature here is extensive, see for example, Abegglen and Stalk 1985 or Smitka 1991.)

(3) Top management is unable to directly manage all the details of the organization and has developed extensive systems or routines to create predictable decision-making (e.g. the ringi-system, seniority-based promotion, and an internal board of directors).

(4) Many business practices came into being on an ad hoc basis for one set of reasons, then evolved and had benefits that were originally·unforeseen. When circumstances changed and these practices required modification, the arrangements, rather than being scrapped, were varied according to a firm or industry's competitive condition.

(5) Technologies and products were imitated or borrowed, but the institutional routines used to create them reflected the Japanese industry and individual firm's circumstances.

(6) Such imitation was cheaper than the original innovation.

(7) Most innovations and improvements to various routines have taken place within the neighborhood of the existing routines and have frequently been based on further imitations of changes in available world technologies.

(8) Growth has been more rapid during the imitation stage and has slowed once the innovation stage has been reached.

(9) Accepted routines submerge differences within the organization, so existing practices have a strong inertia and change or innovation in existing routines can be very difficult if it deviates far from current practice. In this regard, the so-called consensus decision-making system is relevant since in order to reach a consensus everyone usually has to compromise.

238

It is thus generally difficult to move far from the norm. Further, the need for a consensus enables "disconsensus decision making" to hold sway too in that any strong holdout can prevent a change from being made. (See Blaker 1977 and Rapp 1986, pp. 21-37 — particularly p. 25.)

(10) The existence of routines in one organization have become components of solutions in other organizations. This last point is clearly seen in the operation of the kanban and keiretsu systems, as well as the synergies between various industries over time.

While the role of industrial policy in Japan's economic development is much debated, there is general agreement that any major impact was prior to 1973 — more particularly, during the recovery of the late 1940s through the mid 1960s (see JEI 1991). Before the 1970s, the Japanese government had both the legal power and a national consensus to take actions to promote re-industrialization and export competitiveness. At the same time, events were occurring that have had a continual evolutionary impact on the development of the large Japanese multinational firm.

First, under the Occupation the zaibatsu holding companies were broken up, with shares in their subsidiary companies sold to the public. However, for the most part, only banks, insurance companies, and other corporations had the necessary funds to buy shares. Thus, cross-share-holdings between affiliated companies was established as well as equity ownership by the main and associated banks.

Second, because of the labor dislocations at the end of the war and the rise of unions and the Japanese Communist Party, there was a real incentive on the part of business and government to encourage both company unions and stability of employment. This was the origin of company unions and the permanent employment and seniority wage systems. (An excellent discussion of this point is Shimada 1987).

However, as Japan entered the high growth phase of the 1950s and 1960s, these structures (routines) bore unexpected fruit. Because of the labor shortages that began to appear in the wake of high growth and the using up of the excess agricultural labor pool by 1957, the only readily available members of the work force were graduates coming out of high school and college. Thus, there was intense competition to recruit them. They were available, cheap, and had good educations. Additionally, given continued rapid growth, firms were going to need more middle and senior managers.

Such hiring practices combined with the seniority wage system led to a reduction in average wage costs for fast growing firms; the more rapid the rate of growth, the more rapid the drop in wage costs. Falling wage costs made rapidly growing firms more cost competitive, allowing them to reduce prices, pick up market share (i.e., grow faster), and hire more workers right out of school. On the other hand, slow growing or mature firms and industries lost cost position and a claim on the available labor resources just as quickly.

Another element of this growth promotion mechanism was that the main bank and bank shareholding system combined beneficially with the "overloan" and indirect finance policies of the government. Dissolution of the prewar zaibatsu together with the hyper-inflation of the immediate postwar years had eliminated the traditional sources of capital for firm growth, and direct financing from the small capital markets clearly could not support rapid industrialization.

To deal with this, the government undertook policies to discourage consumption while encouraging savings to flow to the industrial sector through the banking system. It did this primarily via the Bank of Japan's (BOJ) overloan system: A bank made a loan to a client and BOJ discounted it, putting the bank in a position to lend additional funds to the same or another company. This was clearly a powerful allocation tool in the hands of the government. It could direct funds to chosen industries and even firms by controlling whose paper the BOJ was willing to discount. The system also increased banks' willingness to leverage their balance sheets to fund clients' rapid growth using debt because interest on the discounts with the BOJ was tax deductible, whereas dividends paid on additional bank capital were not. Increased leverage was fine from the companies' viewpoint, too, for similar reasons. At the same time, banks had every incentive to favor firms in which they had significant shareholdings. It was tax efficient for banks because the increased market value of the shareholdings was not taxed unless the shares were sold, whereas earnings on loans were subject to a relatively high corporate rate. Given rapid corporate growth, these shareholdings over time became the source of the banks' large "hidden" reserves.

Overloan also had the somewhat unforeseen competitive effect of uncoupling a firm's increases in sales and market share from growth in its retained earnings because the company did not need to finance from retained earnings the additional assets required to support the increase in sales. In effect a firm could grow using pretax dollars since banks had no real desire to be repaid. Indeed, loans became evergreen, actually increasing over time. Further, because the after tax cost of capital was lower in the high-leverage case, Japanese firms could price lower and grow faster than their U.S. counterparts even if their actual operating costs were higher. [5]

Japanese industry was further assisted from a cost standpoint by another set of circumstances. At the end of World War II, its industry was in bad shape and technologically far behind the West, particularly the U.S. Firms therefore had a strong need to import technology. The government similarly had a strong desire to catch up with the West, to develop an efficient manufacturing base, and to conserve the outflow of foreign exchange. Policies were instituted requiring government permission to import technology given that royalty payments required foreign exchange. The government used this power to force dispersion of imported technology in order that it would benefit a large number of firms and potential exporters.

No technical patent-based monopolies were created. MITI's view was that competition would determine who was the best user of a given technology. Exports and import substitution would be widely stimulated, and profits would not get siphoned off in the form of royalties to foreign firms. MITI also was able to exercise "administrative guidance" so that companies did not get into bidding wars or import old technologies and thereby fall behind a rival. If IBM licensed its computer technology to Hitachi at a certain price, RCA was restricted to licensing its computer technology to NEC at the same price. There were some notable mistakes such as MITI's refusal to give Sony permission to import AT&T's transistor technology, but on the whole the system did what it was supposed to in terms of conserving foreign exchange, keeping the cost of imitation for firms in a given industry roughly equivalent and dispersing the inflow of imported technology. More important for the purpose here, a large number of fast imitators was created.

That is, this situation meant a relatively large number of competitors in a given industry had access to equivalent technology, and virtually all major competitors in all major industries were imitators. Under such conditions, competitive success is highly dependent on the ability to cut costs by making changes (innovations) in corporate routines while closely tracking the technological base. Further, cost savings have to be passed along to

---

[5] This analysis of the interaction of cost, price and increasing market share as a self-reinforcing, beneficial cycle is set forth in some detail in Abegglen and Rapp 1970 and 1972. This behavior only comes to an end when both domestic and foreign markets are saturated and further price declines do not bring forth additional demand. This point is known as "excessive competition" because firms continue to reduce prices anyway in order to use capacity. Such potentially destructive competitive behavior was adjusted for in mature industries in the late 1970s and 1980s through capacity contractions and reductions in employment, often under the guidance of MITI or a MITI-organized cartel. However, these MITI actions usually ended up creating effective quotas based on existing market shares. This meant competitive incentives remained strong to rapidly expand capacity and market share during the high growth phase in order to lock-in the lead position once growth slowed.

customers as price reductions fairly quickly since monopoly rents from controlling supply are virtually impossible.

There is little incentive to invent as long as more advanced technology can be imported and invention remains more time consuming and more costly. Because Japanese firms were growing rapidly and borrowing money aggressively, capital for production expansion was at a premium and funds available for basic R&D, as opposed to development R&D, were small. This is still consistent with the current allocation of research funds by most Japanese companies even though the technical environment has changed towards more internally generated innovation.

The shortage of capital also encouraged allocation of functions that could be delegated to other firms, such as to trading companies or subcontractors. Cross-shareholdings mitigated the business risk of the increased dependence on outside sourcing. The use of the long-term coal and iron ore import contracts that supported long-term project loans funded by offshore banks and foreign raw material producers were a clear innovation of this type. The extensive use of subcontractors from which the keiretsu system eventually evolved was another. It also encouraged the kind of narrower corporate specialization noted by Sheard (1991). Since the main bank was encouraged to lend to associated trading companies and subcontractors as a way of supporting a firm's competitive development, the origins of the bank-related groups was established as well.

However, it was the self-reinforcing nature of the competitive system that really set the corporate routines. Successful firms were the ones that cut costs best and priced accordingly. This could be done by growing aggressively in response to market demand, because this lowered labor costs, allowed the use of additional debt, and brought the latest technology rapidly into the production process.

Ohmae has noted this competitive compulsion (1990 and 1991) observing, for example, that "Japanese managers are victims of their own success and of the habits that success creates. ... If your goal is to beat the competition, you win by narrowing your field of vision and doing more better" (1990, p. 40).

Given the large number of initial competitors in an industry, the market tended to saturate quickly, encouraging exports. To exploit the growth opportunities in export markets, price competition was important — as noted earlier in terms of product cycle analysis. This meant being an effective cost cutter. If you were an effective cost cutter, exports grew rapidly; then, because of experience effects, your cost position — and thus competitiveness domestically — improved as well. Expanding Japanese market share made one even more export competitive, and so on. It is thus hardly surprising that the cost cutters in Baba's analysis emerge as Japan's industry leaders, whereas in the U.S., innovative firms are usually more at the forefront.

In Japan's competitive environment, tracking the development of known technologies through aggressive investment policies and pursuit of market share even during economic downturns became the reinforced and established routine. As industries reached the technological frontier after 1973, though, some attention had to be paid to innovation even by the price cutters. This is also exemplified by Bartlett and Ghoshal (1988) in their analysis of Matsushita, the pre-eminent cost cutter among consumer electronics firms. However, the innovators that survived had to pay more attention to cost control, which shows the continued emphasis in the Japanese competitive environment on reducing costs and lowering prices.

Even aside from the particular dynamics of the Japanese market place, emphasis on cost control and cost reduction has a definite general business logic, especially if you are risk averse. If you are the low cost producer, it is unlikely you will be driven out of business. Indeed, many bankers, when assessing large project financings for commodity products, look for the entity to be among the 25% most efficient operations worldwide from a cost standpoint. This is meant to assure project survival in case there is a severe drop in commodity prices — on the presumption that less efficient producers go out of business first. Although firms generally don't have very good control over prices and markets due to competition, they usually have some ability to manage costs. Thus, cost minimization may be the best way to achieve company profit maximization. In any case, it has made sense in the Japanese competitive context during the postwar period, and this is what matters in understanding Japanese management routines.

This conclusion is supported by the results of Nelson and Winter's competitive simulation comparing the outcomes under different economic conditions for innovative firms versus fast imitators. The worst situation for innovators — in which their share of industry capital and market share drops the most during the period being examined — is when the fast imitators show no restraint when achieving profitability but instead continue to expand investment and market share aggressively. The situation is even worse when bank credit is readily available, so that the fast imitator is not dependent solely on operating cash flow to expand. While this model was developed from purely hypothesized decision rules or corporate routines, the correspondence to the Japanese case could not be more direct.

Nelson and Winter also observe that slow technical progress (i.e., slow development of indigenous technologies as compared to rapid adoption of others' technology) should result in less industry concentration — that is, more competitors. This seems to be an accurate paradigm for Japan.

The model applies in both the science-based technology case, which most approximates Japanese industry prior to 1973 when a broad spectrum of world technology was readily available to Japanese firms, and the cumulative technology case endogenous to industry growth, which applies more as Japanese companies became more dependent on their own resources to advance the technological frontier. Nelson and Winter note:

> "The results that show a tendency for firms that do innovative R&D to lose out in a competitive struggle with skillful and aggressive imitators are particularly provocative, and illustrate a possibility not much discussed in the literature. Nor has there been much discussion differentiating the kinds of regimes for technical progress under which the social costs are slight (science-based industries) or heavy (cumulative technology industries) when firms that invest in innovative R&D are driven to the wall or out of business." (p. 350).

The implications of this observation for U.S.-Japanese relations, with Japanese firms seen as continually exploiting U.S. inventions, is fairly clear and will be addressed below. But first it is worth looking at some other interesting results from Nelson and Winter's simulation. When R&D is profitable, innovators can grow with the imitators, but small firms tend to get eliminated (p. 350). This seems consistent with the Japanese case, where there appear to be a larger number of large firms in both the innovative and imitator categories in key industries and where venture capital is almost non-existent. Indeed, most Japanese venture investors — whether investing in U.S. or Japanese start-ups — generally only invest once the product has been developed, produced, and sold. From a U.S. viewpoint, this is mezzanine or third-generation risk capital. But it is consistent with the Japanese view of risk aversion, and their historical experience of buying or investing only in proven technologies. They can then track and improve it. In this manner even the innovation or technology selection pattern has become a routine for most large Japanese manufacturing corporations, reflecting their historical experience and what they consider to have been a source of competitive success. "The rules are what they are because they have evolved that way over time" in response to real economic forces and competitive conditions. Those economic forces and competitive conditions have of course initially been Japanese. The routines developed to deal with them have then been successfully adapted to the international environment in the form of export growth and subsequently foreign direct investment. Hence the emergence of the competitively successful large multinational Japanese manufacturing firm.

Successful routines have an inertia and self-reinforcing aspect. Once established they are difficult to change unless there is a reason such as a competitive or political compulsion. Even then, they are highly likely to be modified to accommodate the situation rather than be scraped. This view appears particularly applicable to the Japanese corporate environment. In response to the changes in foreign exchange rates and the VRAs of the 1980s, for example, large Japanese exporters of manufactured goods — particularly cars, machinery, and electronics — at first absorbed much of the resulting cost increases in order to preserve market share. They then moved to develop sourcing and production facilities in both their advanced country markets and in the NICs and LDCs, depending on the product and industry. In this regard they were responding to the effects of product cycle developments (see Marston 1990).

Another factor also was in evidence. Once one firm in an industry moved abroad, almost all firms in that industry did as well. A foreign investment by Toyota could perhaps be interpreted as reducing the perceived risk of assembly abroad for Mitsubishi. A more important motivation, however, seems to be competitive compulsion. If Toyota is successful, Mitsubishi is hurt. Toyota will increase market share and improve its penetration of the U.S. and other markets. This improves its global profitability and cost position, including in Japan. The increased volume of imported parts may lower its costs (experience curve effects), or Toyota can spread the cost of designing and developing a new model over a larger number of units on a global basis. Further, if Toyota were to eventually export from the U.S., experience curve effects could make it a stronger cost competitor in both the U.S. and Japanese markets. Finally, Mitsubishi is facing the same adverse circumstances due to the VRA and the appreciation of the yen Toyota is, and this is the logical way to go to reduce costs and to be competitive.

Concurrently, steel companies began to see the import of Korean steel into Japan and an erosion of their competitive position in the U.S.A while their major automobile customers were moving production to the U.S. Machinery manufacturers saw similar phenomena not only in autos but also in electronics. Therefore, they felt a compulsion to come to the U.S. While machinery and parts manufacturers could establish new plants rather easily, steel makers could not, due to the time and cost involved, including environmental regulations, of establishing a greenfields facility. Japanese tire and chemical companies faced similar situations. Thus, for these industries acquisitions (partial or total) and strategic alliances became the order of the day. These relationships universally involved substantial capital inflow to the U.S.A., introduction of more modern equipment, and innovation in the U.S. companies' organizational and production routines.

Ironically, even companies like Armco, which had always been on the technological and value added forefront of the U.S. industry, were forced into this type of arrangement because they no longer had the capital for modernization. For Armco, the reason was a disastrous diversification into insurance and real estate because it was dissatisfied with the returns from steel.

While a primary motivation of the Japanese producers was to continue to serve their major automobile clients as they shifted production to the United States, the factors of competitive compulsion acted as well. That is, there was a concern that if they did not satisfy a major client's needs in the U.S.A., another Japanese competitor might via its U.S. venture. Having established a satisfied customer contact, that competitor might then use it to access the client more widely. (In a sense the Japanese did something similar to U.S. steel companies when they were unable to supply the market in the 1950s and 1960s due to strikes. They developed satisfied U.S. customers during the strikes who never fully returned to the U.S. steel suppliers even after the strikes had ended.)

This can happen because the permanent employment system and constant job rotation of managers in large Japanese firms means everyone knows everyone else. So the man buying steel in the U.S.A. may have had, or may in the future have, the job of buying steel in Osaka. In any case, he knows the man buying steel in Osaka. They may be from the same college or even friends. Given the proper introduction, a good steel marketing man could begin to develop the kind of relationship that might lead to orders, especially if the product had already been bought and shown to work in the auto company's U.S. cars.

The excellent management coordination and continuity of Japanese corporate networks exposes firms to this type of competitive risk. For this reason, Japanese firms tend to operate defensively as well as offensively, even offering products and services at a loss to maintain client control, though they make every attempt to minimize the cost of doing so.

Another possible example of this strategic thinking at work is Bridgestone's acquisition of Firestone. Not only was it felt they overpaid, they had to put in another $1 billion to modernize the company after they bought it. However, the production of 2 million cars was moving to North America, and Bridgestone had the dominant share of the tires used when those cars had been made in Japan. Its major Japanese rivals already had presences in the U.S. market, and Bridgestone could not build its own plant due to pollution regulations. From a Japanese viewpoint, they had no choice but to pay whatever it took. Of course Bridgestone was confident that over time it would be able to substantially lower the costs of Firestone's operations by introducing Japanese routines. The move from Akron is probably a part of this process.

From these examples one begins to appreciate that perhaps the competitive routines of Japanese multinationals are even more a function of continued competition among Japanese firms as they have moved from the import substitution stage through the foreign direct investment stage than of competition with major foreign corporations. Future routines will evolve similarly and will be a function of competitive pressures combined with likely economic, political, and other developments that affect their situation. Some of the relevant pressures and considerations that will have an impact on Japanese managers are listed in Table 1.

Table 1
Pressures and Considerations Affecting Japanese Managers

(1) The over-riding consideration is corporate existence, and it will remain so despite shifts in national comparative advantage, exchange rates, capital costs, industry competitiveness or other conditions. The senior executives' own survival and benefits — there is really no alternative employment available to them — demand nothing less. Their lifelong commitment to the firm, its customers, its employees, its suppliers, and its bank compel this as well. This is the origin of Ohmae's "companyism."

(2) The yen will continue to remain strong and may get stronger. Further, the natural shift in cost competitiveness will continue towards the NICs in many major product areas.

(3) Pressure from the U.S.A. to reduce the balance of payments deficit will persist.

(4) Japan's aging labor force and low birth rate will combine with continued growth to make the current labor shortages even more acute, especially for technical personnel (engineers and scientists).

(5) The need to constantly upgrade technology on an intra-industry basis will continue due to pressures from Japanese and foreign com-

petitors, as well as customer requirements. Competitive success and firm growth since the war has depended on continual access to and adoption of constantly improving technology. It is also one way to counter the shift in cost competitiveness towards the NICs while dealing with higher wages due to labor shortages and a stronger yen. The "information age" is a reality, and technology is a key component of it.

(6) Because all Japanese producers in an industry face similar external pressures, and the managers have similar backgrounds, the competitive compulsion is such that followers will almost always follow the leaders if they can. In terms of foreign direct investment in already mature markets like autos in the U.S.A. and Europe, this could lead to overcapacity and the transfer of "excessive competition" abroad. But government action has always served to preserve market share. Therefore being the most aggressive investor and lowest cost producer still may be the appropriate strategy and will be pursued until it is demonstrated to be unsuccessful.

(7) Technology transfers to the NICs and LDCs will be monitored carefully and if possible will be via one's own affiliates. The NICs will try to emulate Japanese experience and develop their own global competitors, who will try to evolve with the product cycle.

(8) The Japanese market is quickly saturated, but it is large and an important place to introduce products. Maintaining or growing market share domestically and abroad is still relevant, especially since Europe and North America are forming economic mega-states in which Japanese MNCs must fully participate in order to be globally competitive. Customers will also be participating in these markets and must be supplied. All this requires Bartlett and Ghoshal's (1988) global management and local action.

(9) The Japanese government has achieved its long-term goal of catching up with the West and has been weakened by a series of scandals. It has no strong ability or desire to exercise authority over the actions of Japanese MNCs outside Japan.

(10) The Japanese government's primary industry concerns are continued inter-industry development, e.g., countering U.S. satellites and supercomputers in Japan. Their major economic problem is the growing transfer payment claims on Japanese resources from an aging population.

Given these types of considerations and emerging economic factors, it is logical for large multinational Japanese manufacturing firms to try to develop strategic routines to manage the product cycle, which is what appears to be happening. For example, as higher quality products are used by Japanese auto assemblers, such as very thin, light-weight one-sided zinc-coated sheets, U.S. auto producers are forced to upgrade too, and the product is only available from Japanese-affiliated U.S. steel firms. This strategy also has the effect of denying the NICs the U.S. market share that would normally have come to their firms with the operation of the classic product cycle as the U.S. industry matured and became uncompetitive. The Japanese market is protected also to the extent Japanese customers constantly upgrade their requirements, and the NICs do not have the ability to build experience and lower costs based on U.S. market penetration.

A similar phenomena can be observed in TVs where the Japanese have not only maintained U.S. production, but by exporting large-screen sets from the U.S.A. to Japan and elsewhere have effectively created a cost base that has kept the NICs out of this market segment. Upgrading to high definition TV may be an extension of this routine.

Japanese MNCs have also undertaken extensive investment in the NICs: Sanyo TVs from Korea, Canon cameras from Taiwan, etc. Their manufacturing investment in Malaysia, Thailand, Korea, Taiwan, Indonesia, et al, has grown enormously. To the extent this modern capacity prevents development of local competitors in what would have otherwise been vulnerable mature products produced in Japan, the Japanese MNCs may have frustrated the replication of a Korean Toyota, a Taiwanese Matsushita or an Indian Toray. In this they have created Gilpin's modified product cycle evolution. Just as importantly, they have co-opted many of the available "advanced factors" in those countries, who in Porter's vision could provide the basis for those countries' long-term industrial competitive advantage in some sector.

Many economists would argue that a host country is benefiting from the training and addition of these factors to the labor force, so there is no cause for concern. However, balanced against this consideration is the worsening competitive situation for their native firms if Japanese MNCs are successful in translating their long-term employment routines to their local subsidiaries. They will then be able to retain and build on the benefits of these newly developed advanced factors. No wonder the Koreans are constantly complaining about the unavailability of the latest technologies from Japan.

Capturing such advanced factors, of course, not only helps the Japanese firms' competitive position by making it more difficult for competitors in the NICs to develop, but Japanese MNCs are also alleviating their own shortages of home-country technical personnel. Similarly, investments in U.S.-based laboratories and software acquisitions are also part of strategic routines developed to supplement the availability of Japanese resources or, in some cases, their complete absence in Japan.

In the process they are initiating a new type of competition, which will no longer be just for global market share based on superior Japanese (primarily manufacturing) routines. The competition will be for key global resources, particularly the kinds of advanced factors Porter considers the basis for sustained competitive advantage. U.S. scientific personnel in areas of competitive interest to large Japanese manufacturers are a clear objective. The U.S. laboratories announced by major Japanese auto, electronic, and pharmaceutical firms all point in this direction. Investments in venture capital funds and the large number of patents filed worldwide each year do too.

Autos seem to demonstrate many of the routines being pursued. In the upscale market, Japanese firms are taking advantage of the recession to offer high-quality cars at a good price without backing off the lower end of the market. This looks like a modified repetition of their traditional approach of first building experience in Japan, then entering export markets that are price sensitive where they can compete head to head, i.e., their exports against the European exports in the U.S. luxury import market. This strategy seems to have been successful. While Cadillac and Lincoln have helped U.S. producers hold a steady 50% share of the U.S. luxury market, it is European marques that have lost out to the Japanese — declining from a 32% share in 1987 to 24% in 1990 and 20% in the first half of 1991. Indeed in the face of a shrinking overall luxury market and their own falling sales, Peugeot and Sterling actually abandoned the U.S. market in 1991.

In the regular car market, the Japanese are building capacity to maintain or improve market share and are extending their keiretsu and kanban systems to the U.S.A. and Europe to achieve superior cost position. This raises Ohmae's concern about excess capacity in what are two mature, slow growing markets and, in turn, a possible industry shakeout. This situation could have adverse competitive implications for U.S. and European firms if the Japanese are in fact the low cost local producers.

This may become quite clear-cut in the U.S.A. if they introduce the computerized ordering system they already use in Japan. This is now potentially possible given their U.S. manufacturing base. If customers can order a car to their specifications in the expectation of three-week delivery, the implications are profound for reducing the cost of dealer inventories (financing and space), end of year sales, and rebates — while at the same time increasing customer satisfaction. Further, dealer networks could be expanded dramatically since any service station with a CRT and a couple of demonstration models becomes a potential outlet.

This shows the potential competitive effect of "disadvantaged factor" analysis. The high cost of land and the shortage of space encouraged Japanese manufacturers' drive to reduce inventories at all points in the design to delivery process. This is already well-known in the just-in-time delivery system for manufacturing, but another aspect is computerized customer ordering because in Japan there is little room for extensive showrooms or dealer inventories, and what exists is expensive. However, once such a system is developed, the cost of diffusion even overseas drops dramatically. An example of how computerized ordering has been used by a U.S. consumer durable goods maker and its dramatic impact on cost position is reported by *Fortune* (1991, p. 48). A program for side-by-side refrigerators cut the order-to-make cycle time by 50% and inventory costs by 20%, while increasing product availability by 6%.

In this sense, a nation's firms may gain a global competitive advantage because a routine developed in response to a set of factors in the home country would not be justified on the basis of factor costs in a competitor's country. However, having been developed, similar costs in the latter country can still be saved, creating a cost advantage.

To appreciate the competitive importance of this potential cost advantage, one must also recognize that U.S. and European firms have no concept of "excessive competition" in their local markets. They have previously experienced it only in terms of Japanese imports, against which they got help from their governments. Japanese industrial history is replete with examples that indicate that any government solution to "excessive competition" that might arise would likely be based on market share. In some cases the economic rents received by firms under such government restraint systems have been quite large and are a direct function of market share. So there is no reason to exercise restraint in terms of growth and pricing. Therefore, the Japanese auto makers have taken aim at the U.S. van market, even though they know Chrysler has half of that segment and desperately needs to hold it for corporate survival. The initial reaction has been a somewhat unusual banding together by the U.S. companies and a joint dumping suit by the Big 3.

In addition, any restraint by one producer could benefit its Japanese competitors. This benefit to a competitor in an important product or market over time could give that competitor a sustainable and growing competitive advantage. High growth situations are especially risky as Japan's postwar economic history has amply demonstrated. This development could thus ultimately threaten a person's job and even the survival of their firm. Therefore the possibility of achieving a consensus on corporate restraint, i.e., not aggressively seeking growth in market share by rapid investment and lower prices, seems remote. Someone fearing possible adverse competitive consequences would strongly resist the change in routines. To forego a competitive reality for an abstract concept would not make sense. This is why these intensely competitive routines persist.

The current routines of introducing more upscale cars, investing abroad, transferring Japanese manufacturing methods, cooperating with supplier firms, using Japanese bank loans for finance, etc. have all been quite successful. Therefore, the feedback mechanism says keep doing them. This is why Ohmae's exhortation to be restrained is a bit unrealistic, though his observation that U.S. and European competitors will have to deal with excessive competition in the market place, for which they may not be fully prepared, seems quite accurate (1991). After all, Japan's experience is that in the case of excessive competition, it is the low cost producer who wins.

On the other hand, Ohmae's concept of restraint would, if practiced, appear to have a favorable impact, at least according to Nelson and Winter's simulation. They note that restraint exercised by the fast imitators has much more favorable outcomes for the innovators. This is also true for the case when imitation is difficult (Nelson and Winter 1982, p 342). But neither of these two conditions seems to hold in the Japanese competitive environment.

Finally, it should be recognized that the auto producers are continuing to build on and to extend major inter-industry synergies begun first in the 1950s and 1960s in steel and ships. At that time, to lower the cost of steel making, Japanese mills needed to lower raw material costs, particularly the transport component. Because ship capacity rose less quickly than construction costs, building larger coal and ore carriers was a good way to do this. Ordering progressively larger ships significantly lowered raw material costs and thus steel costs. It also made possible the building of very large blast furnaces at port sites, introducing further economies of scale. Shipbuilders were large users of steel, so this lowered their costs and prices, thus favorably influencing raw material import costs for steel, and so on. (A more detailed discussion of these phenomena can be found in Dresser, Hout and Rapp 1972 and Rapp 1973.)

The interactive ratcheting down of costs and prices was further benefited by Japan's switch from coal to imported oil for power generation.

This created a large demand for VLCCs and ULCCs, which helped create experience and growth for both steel and shipbuilders. In addition, to the extent steel and shipbuilding were large consumers of power, they benefited from and contributed to a declining cost of power. Building on this very favorable domestic market situation, Japanese steel and ship producers were able to extend this beneficial competitive routine to exports. They were aided in this by the reduced cost of freight for finished steel exports in larger ships. This demonstrates with a vengeance Nelson and Winter's observation of how one firm's routine can become part of another's solution.

The auto producers were able to build on and contribute to this synergistic relationship in two ways. First, they had a ready supply of high quality, low cost steel, making their cars more competitive. Their rapid growth furthered and interacted with this development. Second, when they had gained enough experience to enter the export market, they needed an efficient way to transport cars in volume. Enter the specialized car-carrying ship which eventually lowered the cost of shipping a car from Japan to the U.S. west coast to below what Detroit could do via truck and/or rail. This interactive set of routines is continuing in the development of new quality steels for autos and the steel companies' U.S. investment presence. Also, to the extent Japanese producers can use the same car carriers for exports from the U.S.A. that they use for imports, they can cover their transport costs on the basis of a roundtrip rather than a one-way passage. This will further lower the cost of delivering cars from U.S. and Japanese production locations, improving cost positions in both markets.

A new leg is emerging in this set of interactive industry routines which, from a competitive point of view, requires consideration. This is the increasing marrying of electronics, especially consumer electronics, with the automobile. The development of high performance car stereos, phones, faxes, electronic maps, electronic fuel injection, climate controls, cruise controls, and so on, testifies to this. Many of these systems are being pioneered in Japan, home of the world's dominant consumer electronics producers. Japanese auto producers have been particularly aggressive about introducing such equipment and features into their upscale and luxury models. The close working relation between these two groups and the overwhelming worldwide presence of Japanese consumer electronics would thus appear to give Japanese auto producers another synergistic routine that will become an integral part of their global strategies for the 1990s. To the extent these strategic routines are successful, the Japanese consumer electronics, steel, and shipbuilding industries will benefit as well.

Based on these and similar observations of current competitive behavior, and given the expected contextual considerations presented above, a number of strategic decision rules and corporate routines are likely to operate for Japanese MNCs in the future, based on existing technologies, past behavior, and competitive successes. These are listed in Table 2.

Table 2
Expected Japanese MNC Strategic Decision Rules and Corporate Routines

(1) Firm survival and success will continue to be the over-riding goal due to limited and unattractive alternative employment opportunities combined with effective permanent employment for top management.

(2) Cost control and cost minimization in manufacturing (especially to economize on capital costs per unit of output, including working capital such as raw materials, work in progress, and finished goods inventories) will be a key to competitive success. Routines developed as a function of the previous capital shortage and a shortage of physical space have continued to prove effective globally. Improvements in cost position and quality go together. Quality and cost position assure corporate survival if there is a shakeout.

(3) Strategic growth and investment will not be constrained by debt or balance sheet considerations, because of the persistence of indirect finance (even direct finance in international capital markets often ends up in the hands of main banks, insurance companies, and other stable shareholders). In addition, the use of foreign debt can be used to hedge exchange risks and reduce taxes.

(4) Technological development is of paramount importance to firm survival but will be pursued primarily on the basis of access to proven technologies. Progress will be on the basis of incremental improvements, including synergistic routines for product improvement from major suppliers. This view is based on their experience of profitable growth via broad-based technology acquisition, constant development, and a low risk of failure.

(5) Long-term employment will facilitate global management due to a firm's ability to invest in and benefit from extended training and worldwide job rotation.

(6) Maintaining or increasing global market share via aggressive investment and pricing strategies will remain important in order not to lose competitive position.

(7) One's posture vis-a-vis other Japanese competitors is global and

needs to be defensive as well as offensive.

(8) Domestic capacity additions, foreign investment, corporate relationships, trade, and acquisitions are strategic weapons to be used in achieving overall corporate objectives rather than something to be pursued for their own sake. For example, a Japanese MNC will not normally make an acquisition just to earn a high rate of return.

(9) There is a need to manage the flow of technology abroad and to control competitors' access to technological resources.

(10) Risk is to be avoided due to the lack of good employment alternatives, consensus decision-making, and the availability of proven routines and technology.

(11) Innovations should stay close to one's existing business as this is what one has the routines, resources, and technology to support. It is also less risky.

While one cannot predict with certainty what the competitive outcome of following these rules and routines will be, and no simulation has yet been performed, still some reasonable judgments are possible. One can observe, for example, that past derivatives of these rules have worked pretty well, and they seem to be working competitively in the current environment too. Japanese companies control TV and other mass-market consumer electronics worldwide. There is only one very weak U.S. TV producer left, and it has teamed up with a Korean manufacturer. U.S. consumer electronics seems confined to the super quality niche market. Only in PCs is the U.S.A. really holding its own. In autos, despite the recession, Japanese car makers are picking up share in the U.S.A. and Europe, especially in the luxury models. Here they may have even been helped by the recession as yuppies feel poorer. So $40,000 for a Lexus looks better than $80,000 for a Mercedes. The rise in European exchange rates against the yen and the 10% U.S. luxury tax on the cost of an automobile over $30,000 that falls disproportionately on the relatively more expensive European imports may also have helped.

Transplants in autos, consumer electronics, tires, construction equipment, machine tools, zippers, chemicals, instant noodle manufacture, soy sauce, etc. are reported as going well. Some top foreign scientists are being attracted to the Japanese MNCs' new laboratories. They have signed many technology-sharing agreements with major foreign competitors as well as numerous small high tech firms. The main Japanese companies (cost cutting leaders and innovators) seem to be setting the competitive agenda in each industry, and the other Japanese competitors in that industry appear to be following. Therefore, there appears to be a general, if modified, reworking of the routines described in this paper. Particular strategic routines of course vary with the firm, industry, product, point in the product cycle, local competition, government policies, etc. What is going on in the NICs or Europe will thus be different than what is happening in the U.S.A. though they will clearly be related.

Many analysts, policy makers, and non-Japanese competitors might view the foregoing as more of the same. What is different about the currently evolving Japanese multinational competition?

First, it is now local. The presumption that if Japanese MNCs invested abroad they would face the same cost factors as local producers is now in doubt. This means the assertion that local producers would then face a "level playing field" and could easily win at home is also in question.

Second, there was a feeling the Japanese would be constrained to the same availability of capital and debt as local counterparts, so their capital costs and capital structure would be similar. Further, they could not afford to expand overseas capacity rapidly. Actually, however, the use of debt raised from Japanese banks at favorable rates, as well as equity-linked Euro-financings, have enabled them not only to finance increasingly large investments but to hedge foreign exchange exposure, reduce their taxes, and lower their overall cost of capital. The keiretsu system has permitted them to spread investment costs and the risks of overseas production as well. It has also facilitated the speed of entry and establishment of overseas production capacity on a greenfields basis.

Three, potential exports from the U.S.A. or Europe create the opportunity for both added experience curve benefits at the offshore production location and political leverage by helping a country's balance of payments.

Four, the use of Japanese-related suppliers may offer opportunities to spread development costs on a global relationship basis as well as to manipulate transfer prices to achieve cost advantage in a particularly competitive market.

Five, the objective remains market share and cost minimization even at the new production location. Japanese MNCs may not hold their offshore production locations to any particular profit goal, but rather will look at a model or product line's global profitability. This type of approach to internal accounting and cost management can create serious price to performance problems for local producers that are totally dependent on the local market or that look at each individual model's profitability in discrete markets.

Six, they may actually have, or will achieve, local low-cost production status.

Seven, in some markets there is now excess capacity compared to likely future demand. This may lead to aggressive pricing and a market shakeout, which is normally favorable for the low cost quality producer.

Eight, acquisitions and capacity additions will be made for strategic reasons, not for project-specific financial returns. This means Japanese firms may be willing to pay more for key resources, expecting to recoup the additional amount by minimizing future costs through the effective introduction of Japanese cost-cutting routines and by increasing future market share.

Nine, because production is now local, the political options open to local competitors are fewer and more constrained. When it was jobs in Osaka versus jobs in Michigan or the Midlands, the political equation was easy and trade restraints were possible. Jobs in Kentucky versus Michigan, or the Midlands versus Paris, is not such a clear political equation. In the NICs, local joint venture partners are also interested in maintaining their profitable situations. Japanese firms thus now have local political constituencies, which can be amplified by their customer relationships. This was discovered in the Toshiba case when U.S. firms dependent on Toshiba chip supplies gave Toshiba support in conversations with their Congressional representatives. Further, the traditional solutions of exchange rate changes or VRAs will not work with respect to efficient local producers.

Dealing with this new competitive environment may be wrenching for many non-Japanese competitors if it requires changes in established corporate routines. Diversification is no panacea either. This is shown by Armco's and U.S. Steel's experiences moving into businesses they didn't understand at a tremendous cost in management time and corporate resources that could have been better focused on meeting the competition in their basic business. The effects of diversification into unrelated businesses not only hurt the companies involved, it helped their foreign competitors, thus compounding the U.S. companies' difficulties.

There are policy concerns arising from the further evolution of the large multinational Japanese manufacturing firm, and people should be thinking about and assessing them.

It is important to note that there are potential areas of direct political friction between the Japanese MNCs and the Japanese government emerging from this suggested scenario. Having caught up with the West and achieved an increasing standard of living for its people, the government of Japan's current foreign policy seems more oriented towards assisting future world development than mediating between major Japanese multinationals and their foreign hosts. In addition, the government bureaucrats' power levers have been somewhat diluted while the resources and independence of the MNCs have increased.

Furthermore, government officials are continuing to promote their own successful development routine of inter-industry evolution in areas like space, supercomputers, and bio-engineering. The major Japanese MNCs, though, have no intention of being phased out of their basic businesses and are decidedly more interested in intra-industry evolution. Since industrial policy involves creating a differential access to resources for the favored industries, government policy clearly would aim to take resources from established mature industries like automobiles and transfer them to fields like aerospace. (A more detailed discussion of these phenomena can be found in Dresser, Hout and Rapp 1972 and Rapp 1973.) Those resources could be financial or just as importantly scarce technical personnel. Automobile manufacturers, however, might well like to use those same financial resources and advanced factors to develop additional models and markets for their luxury cars or to build additional capacity overseas. The potential competition between the government and the MNCs is apparent due to these different industrial objectives and the rival claims for the available strategic resources and the advanced factors needed to achieve those objectives.

The Japanese government also will be facing larger and larger transfer payments over the next several decades to support an aging population in terms of pensions and medical care. They will expect Japan's major corporations to assist in meeting these social obligations. Those corporations, whose growth will be overseas, will have an increasing responsibility to their overseas work force compared to their Japanese work force. Given developments in the North American, European, and Asian markets, the bulk of their economic interests may also soon lie outside Japan. These areas, too, have aging populations, though not as rapidly as Japan's. Thus, it is not clear to what extent they will be willing or able to shoulder the burden the government may have in mind for them. Worldwide tax issues will loom large for Japanese MNCs in the coming years as they try to hold onto resources for their own growth. These conflicts over the access to, and use of, resources will not only be with foreign governments but with their own, as everyone tries to claim a piece of an apparently wealthy and growing Japanese MNC pie.

Past policy attempts by the governments of Japan's trading partners to confront competition from Japanese MNCs have been mostly inadequate or counter productive. Yen appreciation helped force overseas investment and made the investments relatively inexpensive. Also, by lowering the investment cost relative to the size of the total corporation, its reduced the relative level of perceived risk associated with these investments. Having established successful international investment routines, large multinational Japanese manufacturing firms are now using them to further build global market share. Foreign exchange effects were thus absorbed short-term and invested around long-term. Additionally, near term pressures to improve productivity at home eventually got transplanted as routines that improved cost competitiveness at overseas facilities.

Quotas and VRAs not only taxed U.S. and European consumers via higher domestic prices, they transferred the financial benefits abroad in the form of economic rents to the foreign producers (e.g. Japanese MNCs), who used the funds to grow and develop the next generation of higher value added products. As the Japanese MNCs expected, quotas were allocated on the basis of existing market shares, so they reinforced the success of the leading cost cutter's competitive routines while giving it the resources to start the process again on the next generation of products or via overseas investment or both. One anomaly in this process in the case of automobiles was for Ford, GM, and Chrysler who had finally made investments in Japan (Isuzu, Suzuki, Mazda, and Mitsubishi) as a strategy to counter increasing Japanese competition globally.

Yet, they were actually hurt by the way the VRA and quotas were administered, even if they were somewhat assisted by reduced Japanese competition in the U.S. marketplace. This is because the quotas were allocated to the Japanese producers by U.S. export market share which helped the market leaders and their related companies. The U.S. affiliated companies' share was fixed and limited by the VRA at a relatively low level as they were the weaker Japanese competitors. Indeed, this was one reason the U.S. companies had been able to invest.

But given the way the VRA was administered, the weaker producer were denied a chance to improve their own or their parent's position in the global market place which would have come at the expense of the stronger Japanese firms on a compounding basis due to experience effects. The stronger firms of course represented the real competition then and in the future. In sum, the effect of the auto VRA was to strengthen the stronger Japanese producers financially and in terms of global market share. At the same time, it sent a negative signal to the U.S. firms in terms of using this competitive routine (i.e. a Japanese affiliate) as an aggressive counterstrategy since it reduced its potential effectiveness in Japan and overseas as well as the parents' return on their investments.

Only under an auction system, in which the economic rents are captured by the local government and everyone has equal access, do quotas make competitive sense as a government routine. This also permits foreign MNCs the chance to team with weaker Japanese competitors as a reasonable counterstrategy. Such an approach not only denies leading Japanese competitors the added financial resources to facilitate their move into next generation products, it introduces an element of risk into the strategy of aggressive expansion. That is, the leading Japanese MNCs might not get the quota share needed to operate at full capacity or would in any case have to pay for it in competition with other exporters, foreign importers, and financial speculators. In the past they have gotten this quota as a free good or as an effective reward for their aggressive investment and cost cutting behavior. The auction approach could help to break the success feedback mechanism with respect to this routine.

Past government policies to manage the political economic consequences of Japanese competition have not worked well. However, given the potential for increasing competitive pressures, coupled with the potential for real competitive success, the environment now seems ripe for non-Japanese firms to press for political relief, despite Japanese manufacturers' local constituencies.

Successful local manufacture by Japanese firms has raised new political issues over taxes (due to the local subsidiaries' high debt and implicit corporate guarantees), transfer pricing (affecting taxes and customs duties), technology access and control (often defense related but also important to the NICs for their own development), invention versus exploitation (where Japanese firms are perceived as benefiting unfairly from their commercial exploitation of U.S. ideas and inventions), antitrust (keiretsu transplantation shutting out local suppliers), national origin (EEC and U.S., including "screwdriver plants"), local-government subsidies to Japanese transplants (U.S. and EEC), reverse dumping cases (Brother versus SCM), and treaty relations within the North American and European common markets.

Europeans are being forced to address some tricky considerations in the current Japanese-EEC auto talks which from a competitive strategy viewpoint are logically stuck on whether local production should be considered part of the overall long-term quotas. This is the true competitive nexus between the European and Japanese industry. It would certainly be appropriate if the U.S.A. were engaged in a similar sort of debate.

The U.S. government — Congress and executive branch — has generally practiced ad hoc, piecemeal protectionism even while the executive branch has preached free trade, and worked for it in many areas. In short, the government has eschewed having a coherent overall policy that would still address the particular problems of specific industries or sectors of the economy. This aversion stems in part from the fear that such a coherent policy would evolve in to an industrial policy. An industrial policy is in turn seen as antithetical to the Administration's strong belief in the benefits of unfettered market forces and an open economic system in determining the allocation of economic resources. What they fail to realize is that those benefits may never materialize if other countries and their industries manage their policies and allocation of resources in such a way as to gain the benefits but to not pay the price in terms of jobs and global market share of such an open system.

But the compelling real world logic of Nelson and Winter's evolutionary theory argues that the macro economy is composed of the results of micro decisions. If certain micro units are important enough, they can and will affect the overall results of the economy. Therefore, paying attention to the details of specific industries can be important even if one takes the view that whatever happens in the marketplace is OK. At least one would then have an appreciation of what results are likely, and whether one wanted to live with the political economic implications. As one Japanese diplomat said during President Bush's recent "job mission" to Japan: "the devil is in the details."

For example, a decline in the competitiveness of local firms reduces profits and wages, and thus taxes. It also increases expenditures for unemployment, welfare payments, and relocation. This all has an adverse impact on savings rates. If a VRA is pursued as a remedy, it not only does not solve the long-term competitive problem, it raise prices, thus increasing inflation and also reducing savings. Financial resources are transferred abroad, further adversely affecting long-term industry competitiveness and the profits needed for investment and growth. Indeed, Nelson and Winter note in their simulation that profit growth affects capital availability over time. So, given these micro conditions, one might expect such a loss in global competitiveness in key major industries to lead to a decline in the savings rate, a decline in real wages, a balance of payments deficit, a weakened capital stock, and a growing budget deficit. Conversely, the country whose firms are becoming more competitive and gaining global market share should see the reverse. This looks like the U.S.A. and Japan beginning in the 1970s.

Being aware of the situation does not involve picking "winners and losers." The discussion here is about the impact of Japanese competition on real industries, employing real resources, whose performance have an important outcome on a country's total economic results. The other country's government has done the picking, and what is being suggested or requested is counter-targeting (i.e., offsetting the effects of another government's actions) or even compensatory targeting (i.e., offsetting past actions no longer occurring but whose residual competitive impact is still felt).

Conclusions

What has been described is a successful past, present, and quite possibly future competitive scenario for large multinational Japanese industrial concerns based on the likely continuation of certain corporate routines. These successful routines are primarily found in a select number of companies producing a limited number of products in a few industries. The most immediate area of real concern, therefore, is among competitors who find it difficult to respond adequately to these successful routines and secondarily for firms who may find it difficult to do so in the future.

To the extent these difficulties are due to inadequate understanding of the routines being used, the analysis presented may be a useful tool for searching for and innovating new strategic routines. The analysis presented and evolutionary theory both note that while Japanese corporate strategy and decision making have many common factors, in fact each competitor, each industry, even each product is different and must be considered in its own context, particularly its place in the product cycle. There is no single solution to the competitive challenge. Rather, a series of searches and innovations in a complex of routines is required.

The competitive context (selection environment) will change over time, given changes in outside conditions and innovations among all the competitors. Taking these considerations into account is a complex and fuzzy task. Searching for and innovating a set of competitively successful routines requires a lot of analysis and discussion within and perhaps between affected corporations. Indeed, cooperative options are clearly being explored in several of the relevant industries, including between Japanese firms and foreign firms (e.g., Ford-Mazda, Toshiba-Motorola) and among Japanese firms (e.g., Isuzu-Subaru), even as they compete in other areas.

Such activities will be quite detailed and specific, but will vary with each competitor according to its strengths, weaknesses, and existing or potential resources.

Resources include various forms of corporate relations and government assistance. This policy analysis approach thus offers no comprehensive design because of the important policy fact that there are no grand designs or comprehensive cure-alls. Innovating a competitively successful routine will evoke a competitive response from leading Japanese competitors in an industry or product area, and they are likely to pull other Japanese competitors along with them. They clearly have the resources and the resolve to stay for the long haul. In reaction to this response, the new routines will then probably require additional modifications, and so on.

Potential broader social and political concerns arise from the industries and firms under consideration being generally large and economically important to the nations concerned. They have political influence both directly and indirectly. They are large employers, often of unionized employees, as well as big purchasers of goods and services. They are suppliers to government, sometimes defense related. In some countries, the government is a significant shareholder, even the major shareholder. Therefore, if pressed competitively, the impact is highly visible to business leaders, senior politicians, and the whole population. The likelihood of their seeking, even being offered, political assistance seems apparent.

To the extent firms can develop competitively effective routines on their own, they may not need or want such assistance. But there are going to be cases where that will not happen. In these cases, governments will need to evolve new sets of routines or innovations to deal with the specifics of each situation. From this viewpoint Harley-Davidson and Sematech offer better models, at least in a U.S. context, than VRAs such as were developed for textiles, steel, TVs, autos, and semiconductors (unless the benefits are subject to some sort of auction system). Nor would another devaluation of the dollar help much, since most leading Japanese manufacturing firms effectively insulated themselves from that kind of situation based on routines developed in response to the last round of exchange rate cuts.

This political economic process will naturally involve engagement with the Japanese government on trade, industrial policy, and economic issues. Both governments themselves have long evolutionary histories with respect to such discussions as various sets of "successful" negotiations have been frustrated in the details of the implementation stage (see Rapp 1986). These will no doubt color their approach to dealing with new issues.

In their approach, Nelson and Winter's view all this as quite natural.

One expects government and industry to modify routines to deal with changed circumstances while maintaining their overall objectives. They also note: "that the `private enterprise' of agriculture is vastly different from the `private enterprise' of aircraft manufacturing. And both of these sectors are substantially and differently shaped by public programs. The unique organizational characteristics of a particular sector ought to come to the fore in the analysis of policy towards that sector" (1982, p. 364).

Americans have to get beyond the idea of the quick, permanent, or general fix. They must address the fact that competitive issues are inherently specific and ongoing and will probably be the main source of friction between Japan and the rest of the world into the next century. There also needs to be some attempt to get ahead of the problems rather than examining options when the competitive situation may already have deteriorated badly. (Actions with respect to satellites, supercomputers, and telecommunications thus look better than those in textiles and semiconductors.)

These realities seem to be better recognized in Europe and the NICs, as seen in the current negotiations over the Japanese automobile industry's presence in the European market and Korean pressure for better technology access. Further, Americans need to reexamine the posture that all firms and industries are of equivalent value from a national perspective. That is, the notion there is no fundamental difference from a policy or security viewpoint between a GM or Intel and a McDonalds or Budweiser should be seriously questioned. In fact, this attitude needs to be thought through and discussed openly if only because it is clear that other countries and governments don't feel the same way and are pursuing or have pursued different routines with adverse outcomes for U.S. companies and workers.

At the same time, not just other governments and firms need to rethink their current routines. The Japanese should begin to recognize that their major corporations are pursuing certain tracks that affect their well-being, not only because of reactions abroad but also because of future competing claims on resources. In addition, the recent financial scandals demonstrate that business as usual (acting according to previously accepted routines) can lead to actions that not only don't play well abroad but don't play well at home either. Problems aren't disappearing with the old solutions of *tatemae* and bureaucratic foot dragging.

Perhaps most importantly, Japanese need a new set of goals to substitute for growth and catching up with the West. Without a new vision, it will be difficult for the LDP and the bureaucracy to innovate the appropriate set of new routines even on an evolutionary basis. In this regard Japan may be facing some of the same concerns in the 1990s about the congruence of national interests, objectives, and benefits with respect to Japan's multinationals that Gilpin (1975) raised about the U.S.A. and its multinationals in the 1970s.

Unfortunately, given the apparent success of the current Japanese routines both in government and business, any fundamental change is unlikely. This makes it all the more difficult for other governments to successfully manage any friction between their constituents and Japan over the growing competitive impact of large multinational Japanese manufacturing firms. The government of Japan is likely to see it as the foreign government's problem, the result of competitive inadequacies of the other country's firms and government. Japan's government may indeed claim it has no control or influence over Japanese corporations' actions. Still, no matter how valid these points are, when major portions of an economy and jobs are at stake, such an approach projects a rather rocky future for Japan's relations with the world.

Fortunately, many non-Japanese firms are seeking to develop appropriate routines to remain or become competitive. To the extent they succeed, Japan's relations as a country may actually be smoother than they would be otherwise.

BIBLIOGRAPHY

1. Abegglen, James C and William V Rapp, 1970. "Japanese Managerial Behavior and 'Excessive Competition'." *The Developing Economies* 8 (4) pp. 427-44 (Dec).

2. Abegglen, James C and William V Rapp. 1972. "The Competitive Impact of Japanese Growth." In Jerome Cohen, editor, *Pacific Partnership: United States-Japan Trade.* Lexington MA: DC Heath.

3. Abegglen, James C and George Stalk, Jr. 1985. *Kaisha: The Japanese Corporation.* Basic Books.

4. Akamatsu, K. 1962. "An Historical Pattern of Economic Growth in Developing Countries." *The Developing Economies* 1 (March-August), p 4-25.

5. Aoki, Masahiko. 1990. "Toward an Economic Model of the Japanese Firm." *Journal of Economic Literature* 28 (1) p 1-27.

6. Baba, Yasunori. 1989. "The Dynamics of Continuous Innovation in Scale-Intensive Industries." *Strategic Management Journal* 10, p 89-100.

7. Bartlett Christopher A and Sumantra Ghoshal. 1988. "Organizing for Effectiveness: The Transnational Solution." *California Management Review* 31 (1) p 1-21.

8. Bartlett Christopher A and Sumantra Ghoshal. 1989. *Managing Across Borders.* Harvard Business School Press.

9. BCG (Boston Consulting Group) 1972. *Perspectives on Experience.* Boston MA: Boston Consulting Group.

10. BCG (Boston Consulting Group Ltd.) 1975. *Strategy Alternatives for the British Motorcycle Industry.* London: Her Majesty's Stationery Office.

11. Blaker, Michael. 1977. *Japanese International Negotiating Style.* Columbia University Press.

12. Cusumano, Michael A. 1988. "Manufacturing Innovation: Lessons from the Japanese Auto Industry." *Sloan Management Review* 30 (1) p 29-36.

13. Dertouzos, Michael L, Richard K Lester, Robert M Solow and the MIT Commission on Productivity. 1989. *Made in America: Regaining the Productive Edge.* MIT Press.

14. Dresser, James van Jr, Thomas M Hout and William V Rapp. 1972. "Competitive Development of the Japanese Steel Industry." In Jerome Cohen, editor, *Pacific Partnership: United States-Japan Trade.* Lexington MA: DC Heath.

15. Fransman, Martin. 1991. "Economics and Innovation: The Knowledge-Based Approach to Japanese Firms and the Relevance of Economic Thought." August 1991 paper presented to the Wallenberg Symposium on Economics and Technology, Marstrand, Sweden.

16. *Fortune.* 1991a. "Why Japan Keeps on Winning." July 15, p 76-81.
Fortune. 1991b. "How Jack Welch Keeps the Ideas Coming at GE." August 12.

17. Gilpin, Robert. 1975. *U.S. Power and the Multinational Corporation.* Basic Books.

18. Hout, Thomas M and William V Rapp. 1972. "Competitive Development of the Japanese Automobile Industry." In Jerome Cohen, editor, *Pacific Partnership: United States-Japan Trade.* Lexington MA: DC Heath.

19. JEI (Japan Economic Institute) 1991. "Industrial Policies in Search of a Model: Comparing the Experiences of Japan and the United States." JEI Report 29A, August 2. Washington DC: JEI.

20. Krafcik, John F. 1988. "Triumph of the Lean Production System." *Sloan Management Review* 30 (1) p 41-52.

21. Marston, Richard C. 1990 . "Price Behavior in Japanese and U.S. Manufacturing." National Bureau of Economic Research, *Working Paper Series* 3364.

22. Nelson, Richard R and Sidney G Winter. 1982. *An Evolutionary Theory of Economic Change.* Harvard University Press.

23. Nelson, Richard R. 1991. "Why Do Firms Differ, and How Does It Matter." June 1991 Draft Paper. Columbia University.

24. Ohmae, Kenichi. 1990. *The Borderless World: Power and Strategy in the Interlinked Economy.* Harper Business.

25. Ohmae, Kenichi. 1991. "The Fallacy of Doing More Better." *Across the Board,* March, p 40-43.

26. Patrick, Hugh T. 1986. "Introduction." In Hugh T Patrick with Larry Meissner, editors, *Japan's High Technology Industries*, University of Washington Press.

27. Porter, Michael E. 1989. *The Competitive Advantage of Nations.* The Free Press.

28. Rapp, William V. 1967. "A Theory of Changing Trade Patterns Under Economic Growth: Tested for Japan." *Yale Economic Essays*, Fall, p 69-135.

29. Rapp, William V. 1973. "Strategy Formulation and International Competition." *Columbia Journal of World Business*, Summer, p 98-112.

30. Rapp, William V. 1976. "Firm Size and Japan's Export Structure: A Microview of Japan's Changing Export Competitiveness Since Meiji." In Hugh T Patrick with Larry Meissner, editors, *Japanese Industrialization and Its Social Consequences.* University of California Press.

31. Rapp, William V. 1986. "Japan's Invisible Barriers to Trade." In Thomas A Pugel, editor, *Fragile Interdependence*. Lexington MA: DC Heath.

32. Rapp, William V. 1975. "The Many Possible Extensions of Product Cycle Analysis." *Hitotsubashi Journal of Economics* 16 (1), p 22-29.

33. Sato, Kazuo. 1987. "Savings and Investment." In Kozo Yamamura and Yasukichi Yasuba, editors, *The Political Economy of Japan: Volume 1 — The Domestic Transformation*. Stanford University Press.

34. Sheard, Paul. 1991. "The 'Structural Impediments' View of Japanese Corporate Organization: A Critical Evaluation of the Recent Debate." *Proceedings Seventh Biennial Conference,* Japanese Studies Association of Australia, vol 1, p 19.

35. Shimada, Haruo. 1987. "Japan's Industrial Culture and Labor-Management Relations." 1987 Unpublished research paper.

36. Smitka, Michael J. 1990 Oct. "Business-Business Relations: Auto Parts Sourcing in Japan." *Japan's Economic Challenge*. U.S. Congress, Joint Economic Committee.

37. Smitka, Michael J. 1991. *Competitive Ties: Subcontracting in the Japanese Automobile Industry*. Columbia University Press.

38. Vernon, Raymond. 1966. "International Investment and International Trade in the Product Cycle." *Quarterly Journal of Economics* 80 (2), p 190-207 (May).

39. Womack, James P, Daniel T Jones, and Daniel Roos. 1990. *The Machine That Changed The World*. Maxwell Macmillan International.

America and Japan's Role
in the Post-Cold War World

Martin E. Weinstein
University of Montana

There is very little evidence suggesting that fundamental or dramatic shifts in Japan's basic strategy and foreign policy are imminent or likely during the next one or two years. Consequently, in looking at Japan's strategic and foreign policy options, I suggest that in addition to examining the recent and current foreign policy debate, we also attempt to peer into the next ten to twenty years, the 1990s and the first decade of the 21st century. Given the rate and extent of change occurring in the international system, especially in the Soviet Union and in Europe, and the Iraqi invasion of Kuwait, it is more likely than at any time since the late 1940s and early 1950s that fundamental changes in the international system will occur during the next decade or two, which could compel Japan to change its strategy and foreign policy.

Japan's strategy and foreign policy, including both its security policies and its foreign economic policies, have been highly successful and stable since the late 1940s and early l950s, when they were formulated and defined. The success of these policies has generated an enormous inertia and an enormous reluctance to depart from them, until and unless it becomes clear to the Japanese government and the voters that it is necessary to do so. Although the Persian Gulf crisis generated an unprecedented level of international criticism of Japan, and the Japanese are now much more aware of the need to enlarge their international role, it is still not clear what the nature and scope of their response will be.

Japanese Policy Since World War II
The Yoshida Strategy

What are the defining characteristics of this highly successful policy? What is the baseline from which we begin our speculation about options and possible changes in the future?

Ever since the late 1940s, and indeed even back to the 1860s and

1870s when the Meiji oligarchs began Japan's industrialization, there has been a clear perception in the Japanese government that:

(1) the building of a viable and then a competitive industrial economy and a stable, effective political system has been the primary objective of national policy; that

(2) the achievement of these goals is very heavily contingent on foreign policy; and that

3) the security and economic dimensions of foreign policy are inextricably linked.

It has been clear to Japanese officials since early in the modernization process that given its geographical position and resources, the success of Japan's industrialization would depend on access to overseas raw materials (and in the 20th century, especially energy), and to overseas markets. The particular lesson of World War II, which was engraved very deeply on the national psyche, is that Japan cannot achieve this necessary access to the world economy by the use of military force. The Japanese concluded, therefore, that they must avoid as much as possible any military role in international politics, and that they must rely on peaceful, non-military means to build their economy and to make a decent life for themselves.

By the late 1940s and early 1950s, Japan's conservative foreign policy makers, especially Shigeru Yoshida, who served as Prime Minister from 1948 to 1954, had concluded that in the bi-polar, United States-Soviet dominated international system, the best foreign policy for Japan was:

(1) to become an ally of the United States (not a military dependent), and

(2) to base Japan's economic future on the relatively free, open international economic system that the United States was constructing — most especially on cooperative economic relations with the United States itself, which would be a major source of raw materials and a major market for Japanese manufactured products.

It is worth noting forty years later that while Japan's reliance on American raw materials has declined somewhat since the 1950s, it still relies heavily on American farm products, timber and coking coal, and in the 1980s, Japan's exports to the United States reached record levels, approaching 40% of total exports.

Prime Minister Yoshida's strategy was rooted in the belief that the alliance with the United States would protect Japan against the Communist, Soviet threat to its military security and political stability. Within the secure, stable strategic-political framework provided by the security treaty, and by the United States nuclear deterrent and naval and air preponderance in the

Pacific and over the world ocean and trade routes, the Japanese would be able to concentrate their energies and organizational skills in the 1950s on the task of economic reconstruction, and then on the goal of becoming a highly efficient, competitive industrial economy.

Recent Events Shake the Premises of Success

As we know, this foreign policy was highly successful — perhaps too successful. By the end of the 1980s, however, the basic premises of the Yoshida policy were being called into question by two related developments in Japan's external environment. First, the Communist, Soviet threat appeared to be diminishing to the point where it could cease being the negative force binding the United States and Japan into a security alliance. At the same time, Japan's successes in building a competitive, industrial economy were generating potentially dangerous levels of resentment, fear and antagonism toward Japan in the United States. As a consequence, Japan bashing became popular in the Congress and in the media, and the U.S. government began moving toward protectionist economic policies directed against Japan — such as the Super 301 provisions of the 1988 Trade Act. This mounting antagonism, and the creeping protectionism which accompanies it, threatened to undermine the GATT and the relatively open international systems of trade and finance upon which Japan's prosperity and security depends.

Obviously, these two related, to some extent mutually reinforcing international developments call into question the basic premises and elements of the foreign policy that has served Japan so well since the Korean War (1950-53). Equally significant has been the call from abroad that Japan take on a larger role in the international community to a level commensurate with its economic power. At no other time was this more clearly stated, and Japan's actions as closely monitored, as during the 1990-91 crisis and hostilities in the Persian Gulf.

Japan's apparently lethargic response in the Gulf was in reality an abortive policy initiative encumbered by protracted legislative debate on issues of constitutionality, and exacerbated by the inability of a prime minister with a weak power base to win a timely consensus on either the allocation of funds or the dispatch of Self Defense Forces (SDF) personnel overseas. The result was predictable: criticism from the international community, led by the US, that Japan was shirking its international responsibility and reaping the benefits of the "allied" military action, to which Japan contributed money, but not men.

The image of a Japan that reacts slowly and timidly only when forced to by an international crisis, or of an economic power that lacks geopolitical power, is indeed difficult to overcome, at home as well as abroad. "Tokyo would not have been criticized so harshly, if it had acted at the same time as Washington, or at least more promptly than it did," stated Professor Shin'ichi Kitaoka in the April 1991 issue of *Chuo Koron* , "but because we were so slow, we always seem to be acting reluctantly in response to American pressure."[1] Following Japan's pledge on March 1, 1991, of an additional $9 billion to the Gulf effort (beyond the $4 billion previously promised), an editorial in the *Nihon Keizai Shinbun*, Japan's leading financial daily, accurately concluded that because the Japanese government had moved so slowly, its willingness to pay for as much as 20% of the cost of the war "was not really appreciated,"[2] even though an earlier report in the same paper cited official American appreciation of Japan's "generous and timely support," as expressed by Presidential Press Secretary Marlin Fitzwater.[3] Similarly, when a minesweeping group of six ships and approximately 500 Marine Self Defense Forces personnel were dispatched to the Gulf in April, 1991, the editors of the *Yomiuri Shinbun* wondered in their headline: "Will U.S. Dissatisfaction be Mitigated?",[4] while an article in the *Asahi Shinbun* noted the low priority given Japan by Secretary of State Baker in his meetings with individual leaders of the allied nations' foreign ministries.[5]

If nothing else, however, the events in the Persian Gulf may have heightened domestic awareness in Japan of the necessity of increasing its international role. In November 1990, before hostilities actually broke out in the Gulf and before criticism of Japan reached its peak, an *Asahi Shimbun* poll showed that public opinion ran very strongly against any Japanese involvement beyond economic support. As many as 78% of the respondents opposed the dispatch of SDF personnel to the Persian Gulf,[6] and 55% even rejected a plan for using SDF forces to transport Gulf War

[1]Masamichi Inoki and Shin'ichi Kitaoka , "Rekishiteki sokyo toshite no senso" [The Gulf War and Pacifist Japan], *Chuo Koron* , April 1991, p.103.
[2]*Nihon Keizai Shinbun*, March 2, 1991, p.2.
[3]*Nihon Keizai Shinbun*, January 27, 1991, p.12.
[4]*Yomiuri Shinbun*, April 25, 1991, p.2. [In Japanese, "Beino fuman yawaraguka"].
[5]*Asahi Shinbun*, March 15, 1991, p.2.
[6]*Asahi Shinbun*, November 6, 1990, p.3.

refugees.[7] By June of 1991, however, only 13% of those polled in a survey conducted by the *Mainichi Shinbun* were opposed to SDF participation in U.N. peace-keeping operations following the 1991 war,[8] and an *Asahi Shimbun* poll showed that 64% had come around to the view that "it is now necessary for Japan to play a much more active role than before in settling international disputes".[9] Of course, one can argue that the Japanese public was more willing to consider SDF participation in a U.N .operation in June 1991, because the danger of imminent hostilities had passed. However, it is probably also true that the protracted barrage of intense foreign criticism of Japan's policy of limiting its involvement in the Gulf to funding while avoiding the fighting, also contributed to this shift in public opinion.[10]

The Current Foreign Policy Debate

The media in Japan is as open and free as any in the world, and the print media in particular is an extremely rich source in studying politics and foreign policy. Groups of journalists from each of the major national news-papers, organized into press clubs, have attached themselves to the prime minister, each of the powerful ministries, and to the powerful faction leaders in the political parties, who serve in the National Diet. Politics and foreign policy are covered in extraordinary, generally accurate detail and with ex-tensive analysis. Moreover, there are in Japan monthly, intellectual jour-nals, such as *Chuo Koron, Bungei Shunju* and *Ushio,* in which foreign policy intellectuals of all political persuasions, from Marxists to right-wing nationalists and everyone in-between, criticize policy and tell the govern-ment what it should be doing. Based on a study of several hundred news-paper articles and several dozen journal articles and books on foreign pol-icy published between 1988 and 1991, and interviews with senior Japanese foreign policy officials, there appears to be virtually no evidence that Japan is planning to fundamentally or even substantially change its foreign policy. These materials did indicate, however, that there is widespread awareness in Japan that the alliance with the United States is in danger, that its future is less certain than ever before, and that substan-tial, even fundamental changes in national and foreign policy may become

---

[7]*Asahi Shinbun*, February 5, 1991, p.3.
[8]*Mainichi Shinbun*, June 23, 1991, p.6.
[9]*Asahi Shinbun*, June 19, 1991, p.15.
[10]*Asahi Shinbun* , May 9, 1991, p.2.

unavoidable within the next decade or two.

One of the effects of the alliance's apparent vulnerability and uncertain future is that its Japanese critics have lowered their voices if not changed their minds. When, in the 1950s and 1960s, the United States had a position of unchallengeable economic and military strength, and when the reliability of its guarantee of Japan's security was hardly questioned, a slight majority of the Japanese voters consistently told polisters that they did *not* support the Security Treaty. In those long ago days, there were many Japanese who believed that the Americans had too much military power, were excessively anti-communist and trigger-happy, and that to keep the United States from behaving recklessly, it was wise not to support the Security Treaty. Most of those critics were actually content to have Japan protected by the United States, and polls indicated that approximately 80% of the Japanese then believed that the United States would come to Japan's defense if it were attacked or threatened with attack.

Following the rapprochement with China in 1972, the defeat of the United States in Vietnam in 1975, the apparent weakening of U.S. naval and air strength in the Pacific relative to that of the Soviet Union, and the increase in trade frictions, Japanese belief in the reliability of the American security guarantee dropped to about 20% in the 1980s. It is not surprising that under these changed conditions, many former critics of the Security Treaty decided it was now necessary to strengthen the credibility of the treaty by supporting it.

It should not be surprising, therefore, that during the last few years criticism against the United States-Japan Security Treaty and the alliance has dropped to an all-time low. By the mid-1980s, a variety of opinion polls showed that between 70-80% of the Japanese voters had become supporters or had a favorable view of the alliance. During the general election in the fall of 1989, Ms. Takako Doi, at the time the new, more pragmatic leader of the Japan Socialist Party (JSP) (the English version of its name since changed to "Social Democratic Party of Japan"), bowed to public opinion by declaring that if the Socialists won the election and formed a government, they would *not* abrogate the United States-Japan Security Treaty. They would, instead, study the treaty and perhaps recommend some revisions. Since the JSP had been calling for abrogation of the treaty since the party was formed in 1954, Ms. Doi's change of line created dissension among her party cadres. A number of the more persistent, left-wing Socialists have publicly disagreed with the Doi position. Nevertheless, the effect of Ms. Doi's change was to sharply reduce and divide the most harsh and consistent critics of the alliance.

At the same time, on the center and right of the political spectrum there has been a lively debate about the future of the United States-Japan alliance. The Toshiba Incident in the summer of 1987, the Trade Act of 1988 which led to the Super 301 actions of 1988-89, and the FSX controversy have been given much more coverage and attention in Japan than in the United States. Moreover, critics of Japan in the Congress, such as Representative Richard Gephardt, Senators Lloyd Bentsen and John Danforth, and among intellectuals, such as Clyde Prestowitz and James Fallows, probably have a larger more attentive audience in Japan than they do at home. The natural and expected result is that many of the Japanese who have been publicly supporting and explaining the alliance for several decades have begun to wonder aloud about what has to be done to keep the alliance alive, or whether it can be saved at all. An examination of several representative writings indicates the variety of analyses and views in this new genre.

Save the Alliance Even at the Cost of Wrenching Economic and Social Changes in Japan.

Seizaburo Sato, who recently retired as a professor of international relations at Tokyo University, is one of the leading and most outspoken advocates of preserving the alliance with the United States. In March of 1990, professor Sato published an article in *Chuo Koron* [11] in which he pulled together many of the ideas and arguments of those in and outside the Japanese government who believe that while the alliance has entered a period of instability and vulnerability, Japan has a vital stake in keeping it alive. To preserve the alliance, Sato argued, Japan should make dramatic and substantial changes in its own foreign economic policies as well as in its domestic social and political structures.

Sato believes that there is a tendency in both Japan and the United States to act as though the Soviet threat has disappeared. In his view, while the Soviets are clearly in a period of confusion and decline, they still have enormous nuclear and conventional military forces, and depending on how their current crisis is resolved, these forces could once again become a serious threat to both Japan and the United States. He concludes therefore, that it is shortsighted and irresponsible to talk and act as though the U.S.-Japan Security Treaty were obsolete.

---

[11] Seizaburo Sato, "Jidaino henka ga yori kyokona domeio motomeru" [Changes in the Times Call for Still Stronger Alliance], *Chuo Koron* , March 1990.

Professor Sato then goes on to argue that even if the Soviet threat does, in the future, virtually disappear, the U.S. and Japanese economies have become intertwined and interdependent, and that the economic dimension of the alliance is fundamentally beneficial to both partners, and to the entire world economy. He believes that the economic costs of abrogating or abandoning the present high levels of economic interaction and cooperation would be staggering. If Japan and the United States start fighting trade wars, and indulge in protectionism and techno-nationalism, Sato expects that not only the Pacific region but the entire global political-economy would be dangerously destabilized.

Professor Sato's prescription for preserving the alliance is that Japan should take the lead in eliminating whatever restrictions remain on trade and investment. He advocates that Japan move quickly to reorganize its distribution system and business practices to make them more accessible and attractive to Americans. On the issue of technology, he urges Japanese to make available to the United States whatever superior technology it may have developed, especially if this technology has military applications. Sato urges Japan to "offer its best technology to America. . . and help Americans to build the best possible FSX fighter."[12] (The FSX is an advanced, experimental jet fighter based on the F-16, which is being jointly developed by General Dynamics and Mitsubishi Heavy Industry. It is to be manufactured in Japan for the Air Self-Defense Force in the late 1990s.)

Japanese (and perhaps Americans) Underestimate the Danger of their Economic Quarrels .

Although this is essentially a variant of the Sato approach, it is worth examining because it indicates the seriousness and depth of concern among Japanese conservatives over the future of their relationship with the United States. Hisahiko Okazaki has thoughtfully expounded this theme. He is a senior diplomat who has served as ambassador in Saudi Arabia and Bangkok, and who is well known in Japan for his many books and articles on foreign policy and strategy. In the January 1990 issue of *Bungei Shunju* , Mr. Okazaki published an article entitled, "What Can Japan Learn From Holland?"[13] In this article Mr. Okazaki presented a scholarly analysis,

---

[12]*ibid.*, p.134.

[13]Hisahiko Okazaki, "Oranda ni 'nihon' ga mieru" [literally, The Holland that Can be Seen in Japan], *Bungei Shunju* , January 1990.

drawing heavily on British sources, of the causes of the Anglo-Dutch wars of the late 17th century (first war, 1652-54; second war, 1665-67 and third war, 1672-78).

In these wars, Holland was defeated by Britain, and lost much of its overseas holdings and influence, as well as suffering severe economic damage and dislocation. The main point that Okazaki makes is that the Dutch did not expect war and persisted in believing that Britain and Holland were basically friendly, compatible countries beset by economic frictions and quarrels, which would be peacefully resolved by mutual, enlightened self-interest. After all, Holland and England had fought together against Spain and the Habsburgs in the Thirty Years War. They were both Protestant states in a century when religion was as important as ideology was to be in the 20th century. Both countries were proud of their commercial, trading and manufacturing skills and viewed themselves as rational and enlightened rather than passionate and military. The Dutch firmly believed that even after the defeat of the Catholics and the decline of the Spanish threat, they and the English would continue as friendly trading partners, if not close allies.

Nevertheless, Okazaki draws on the writings of British historians to show that in the late 17th century, Holland's trade surpluses with England, together with its technological successes and its banking skills, generated such resentment and jealousy across the Channel that enlightened English self-interest gave way to Holland bashing and protectionism that did as much damage to England as to Holland, and which finally led to war, which did much more damage to Holland.

Okazaki cautions that there are many differences between the Anglo-Dutch relationship in the 17th century and the current U.S.-Japan relationship. But he concludes his article by asking:

> Was there some way that Holland, itself a model economic superpower, could have avoided conflict with England while maintaining its security interests and continuing its prosperity? If so, where did the Dutch take a wrong turn? Did they have a plan to avoid this wrong turn? Answers to these questions may provide Japan with vital information by which to chart its course for the years ahead.[14]

Save the Alliance, But Only As an Equal Partnership

Shintaro Ishihara, a novelist and a Liberal Democratic member of

---

[14]*ibid.*, p.305.

the National Diet, has gained a certain notoriety in the United States as a consequence of the unauthorized translation and distribution in the summer of 1989 of a book of essays he co-authored with Sony chairman Akio Morita, entitled *A Japan that Can Say 'No' to America*. The controversy surrounding the initial appearance of this book seems to have led Mr. Morita to disassociate himself from it. However, an authorized translation of five of Mr. Ishihara's original essays, together with six additional pieces was published in early 1991 by Simon and Schuster, entitled *The Japan that Can Say 'No'*. [15]

For several decades, Ishihara has run for political office on two foreign policy planks. He has supported the U.S.-Japan alliance, but he has wanted Japan to stop being "subservient" to United States demands and "bullying." He has argued, long before the revisionists and Japan bashers appeared in the United States, that unless the growing economic and technological equality and interdependence of the the two countries is matched by more equal influence and control over alliance policy, Japanese resentment and American arrogance are likely to destroy this highly successful and mutually beneficial relationship. Several of Ishihara's older essays in this vein appear in the new book, along with more recent pieces on the FSX controversy.

In the FSX essays, he expressed great irritation at those Congressmen and critics in Washington who attacked U.S.-Japan co-development of the FSX as a technological give away to Japan, which would endanger the United States aerospace industry. Ishihara wrote that Japan should have responded to those charges by developing the FSX itself. Probably the most controversial and inflammatory point he made was his contention that the Pentagon depends on Japanese chips to control its strategic missiles, and that if Americans continue to bash and bully Japan, Japanese should consider the possibility of selling their chip technology to the Soviets as well as to Americans. This, he argued, would awaken Americans to the reality of their technological dependence on Japan, and get them to talk about power-sharing as well as burden-sharing.

Ishihara's threat of selling chip technology to the Soviet Union faded quickly as the Soviet Union slipped into deeper economic and political weakness during 1990-91. Whatever one thinks of Ishihara's approach, it should be noted that while his arguments imply that the treaty is dispensable, he does not call for the abrogation of the Security Treaty, and repeatedly states his support for the alliance as a partnership of equals. It seems

---

[15]Shintaro Ishihara, *The Japan that Can Say 'No'*. (New York: Simonand Schuster), 1991.

to me that the greatest difficulty in Ishihara's approach is that it is not clear what he wants to do about the military inequality between Japan and the United States. Sometimes he seems to be calling for Japan to become a military as well as an economic superpower — a message that raises as much fear within Japan as it does outside.

On economic questions, Ishihara's views overlap with those of Sato. He urges that Japan drastically reform its distribution system and transform itself into a leading free market, free trading country. He believes that the Japanese consumer will benefit from such reforms, and he is confident that Japan is strong and competitive enough to thrive in this role. However, he contends that unless the United States undertakes whatever reforms are necessary to regain its financial solvency, to rebuild its industries and to educate its people, the American economy will continue to drift into ever greater difficulties, thus endangering the bilateral relationship with Japan and the entire world economy.

The Alliance Cannot Be Saved Because the United States Does Not Need It Anymore.

In January 1990, Soichiro Tahara, a well-known writer on politics and foreign policy, published a brief article in *Ushio* [16] in which he summed up the views of pessimistic conservatives who are supporters of the alliance, but who believe its days are now numbered. In this article, Tahara agreed with almost everything Professor Sato was to say in March, except that he was convinced that Americans had only put up with the U.S.-Japan alliance because of the Soviet, Communist danger, and that Americans were prematurely concluding that the Russians were no longer a threat. Therefore, he wrote:

> The United States needed Japan as an ally in the Cold War, and learned to tolerate us, even though our manufacturing success disrupted the American economy. But what will become of Japan if the Berlin Wall comes down, and if the Cold War disappears? The answer is obvious. Japan will become unnecessary. Unless Japan develops its own positive, acceptable strategy about what kind of a role it should play in the world.... America and many other countries as well will turn more and more against us. [17]

Mr. Tahara's prescription for dealing with the post-alliance world is

---

[16]Soichiro Tahara, "Nichibeianpojoyaku wa ippotekini haki sareru"[The US-Japan Security Treaty will be Abrogated Unilaterally],*Ushio*, January 1990.

[17]*ibid.*, pp. 67-68.

not a foreign policy as such, but rather a proposal for Japan to become the model of a successful, industrial, urban country, which he believes will elicit the respect and admiration of the world, including the United States. For Mr. Tahara, the essence of Japan's foreign policy problems is not the existence of powerful and potentially hostile military states, or economic disputes and frictions, but that there is something about Japan and the Japanese that makes them disliked and unpopular. He seems to believe that if Japan makes itself into a model industrialized, urban state, it will dispel suspicions and hostilities, will become universally respected and liked and thus will have no need for alliances.

Japan As an Economic Hegemon

Although a number of non-Japanese writers have argued that Japan will overtake the United States as the world's leading economic power, and will establish a *Pax Nipponica* early in the next century, it is not easy to find respected Japanese writers who take this position. It is, however, an option that bears examination. One of the more intriguing forecasts of Japanese economic hegemony has been written by Koji Taira, a Japanese economist, who is on the faculty of the University of Illinois. Professor Taira edited and contributed to the January 1991 volume of *The Annals of the American Academy of Political and Social Sciences,* entitled *Japan's External Economic Relations: Japanese Perspectives.*[18] His article, entitled "Japan, an Imminent Hegemon?", is the only one in the journal that focuses on the possibility of Japanese hegemony.

The first point to be noted is that Professor Taira expects that the post-cold war world will be a relatively peaceful one, in which military politics will be almost entirely superseded by economic politics. In this world, he argues that Japan will achieve a hegemonic position based not on its capital surplus alone, which he believes will soon shrink, but based primarily on its unique organizational skills. He believes that it is organizational skills that have enabled Japan to attain the flexible, just-on-time manufacturing technology which has made it into the highest quality, most cost efficient manufacturer in the world. Professor Taira predicts that Japan will maintain its manufacturing lead well into the next century, and that Japanese manufacturing firms will continue to build plants world-wide. Japanese manufacturers, therefore, will assume leading positions in the

---

[18]Koji Taira, "Japan, an Imminent Hegemon?," *The Annals of the American Academy of Political and Social Sciences,* January 1991.

American and European economies, as well as many other parts of the world. Since he also believes that there is and will continue to be a close, cooperative relationship between government and industry in Japan, he concludes that it is only natural that the Japanese government will use Japan's manufacturing and economic preponderance to serve Japan's political as well as economic interests. In Professor Taira's view, (which he shares with writers such as Emanuel Wallerstein and Robert Gilpin) an economic hegemon is necessary to maintain a relatively open, orderly global economy, and Japan's economic hegemony will be benign and beneficial.

Professor Taira, in tune with Paul Kennedy's *The Rise and Fall of the Great Powers,* notes that Great Britain and the United States achieved their hegemonic positions partly as the result of lengthy, destructive wars which demonstrated their economic strength and staying power. He believes, however, that Japan will achieve hegemony in a peaceful environment without any dramatic confrontations. It will accomplish this feat by maintaining an unassuming, cooperative, non-threatening posture in its foreign policy, while publicly continuing to treat the United States as the leading global superpower. According to professor Taira, the *tatemae* (outward show) will be a United States-Japanese partnership with the United States as senior partner. The *honne* (hidden reality) will be quiet Japanese control and manipulation of this partnership behind the scenes. Taira believes the United States will be satisfied to appear to be in charge, while Japan will be satisfied to quietly run things.

My own view is that it is most unlikely, in view of the paranoia already demonstrated in the Congress and the media, that Americans will tolerate any form of Japanese hegemony, economic or otherwise. If the United States does not regain its economic vitality and self-confidence, I expect we will resort to protectionism and techno-nationalism, even though this will damage our own economy and the entire international economic system.

Creating a Japan-United States-European Community Partnership to Shape and Maintain a New World Order — the Foreign Ministry Position

In Japan, Foreign Ministry bureaucrats are frequently criticized for being excessively conservative and unimaginative. Indeed, their harsher critics have characterized them as mere caretakers of the alliance with the United States. Although they are undoubtedly constrained by their official position in publicly expressing their views, the Foreign Ministry pitched into the public debate last May, with a rather bold article in its house journal, *Gaiko Forum,* by its highest career official, Vice-Minister Takakazu Kuriyama.[19]

Mr. Kuriyama's sober view of the post-cold war world (published months before the Gulf crisis and the stalled negotiations in the Uruguay round of trade talks), was that unless new global security and economic systems are soon created to replace the rapidly disappearing bipolar, American-Soviet structure and the GATT-IMF structure, the world was in grave danger of drifting into instability and violence, and/or destructive trade wars. He made the point several times that in the 1990s, the United States will not have the economic strength to either act as the world's policeman, or to take the lead in promoting a system of global free trade and investment. Since the United States (GNP $5 trillion), the European Community (GNP $5 trillion) and Japan (GNP $3 trillion) together produce about two thirds of the world's total goods and services ($20 trillion), he concluded that the best hope for the future lies in their forming a tripartite partnership that will make and implement the rules of a new international order.

Mr. Kuriyama was deeply aware of the antagonism developing against Japan in the United States, and his proposal for a global triumvirate was intended to help defuse the bilateral tension by transcending it. He also wrote that while Japan had reached a position of great wealth and influence in the 1980s, its economic achievements and prowess were frequently exaggerated in America and in Europe, as the 5-5-3 GNP ratio indicates. Nevertheless, he urged that Japan must now take an active role in the triumvirate.

Since Japan is constrained by its constitution and by public opinion from assuming any military responsibilities, he proposed that Japan make its contribution by becoming the world's leading free trader and importer — playing an indispensable economic role which the United States no longer seems willing or able to perform, and which Europe is not yet prepared to assume. Mr. Kuriyama points out that since it failed so disastrously in its efforts to play the role of a great power before World War II, it is crucial that Japan now allay any suspicions about its intentions by continuing to be peaceful, unassuming and non-threatening. Japan, he writes, should develop "the foreign policy of a great power without appearing to be a great

---

[19]Takakazu Kuriyama, "Gekidono 90 nendai to nihongaiko no shintenkai" [The Great Upheaval of the Nineties and the Evolution of Japan's New Diplomacy] ,*Gaiko Forum* , May 1990.

power" (taikokutsura o shinai taikoku no gaiko).[20]

Although Mr. Kuriyama indicates that "idiosyncratic nationalism" will become an increasingly serious threat to world political stability and peace in the 1990s, and that economic order and prosperity depend on political order and peace, it is not clear how the triumvirate would constitute a global security system, and what roles each of the partners would play, *except* that Japan could make no military contribution. The reader will have no doubt have noticed that both Taira's "hegemon" and Kuriyama's "great power" bear a striking resemblance in their functions and disguises. The principal and crucial difference is that while Taira expects the post-cold war world to be relatively peaceful and in no need of a military security system, Kuriyama sees a serious potential for political instability and violence, but makes no clear proposal for coping with it.

In the historical context of this essay, and set against the climate of recent opinion in Japan reflected in the articles we have examined, it is easy to understand why Prime Minister Toshiki Kaifu's government was unable to play any military role in the Gulf War, and limited itself to a monetary contribution of $13 billion, which was expected to cover about 20% of the cost of the war. As noted, critics within and outside Japan have argued that Prime Minister Kaifu's weak position in the ruling Liberal-Democratic Party, combined with his unassertive personality to prevent him from using the Gulf War as an opportunity to give Japan a more prominent, clearly defined foreign policy. I believe that it was most unlikely that any of the prime ministerial candidates would have made a significantly different policy. Moreover, among foreign policy officials and within the foreign policy community, views were sharply divided and ambivalent. Writers such as Seizaburo Sato spoke out strongly for Japan to be more supportive of the the United States in the Gulf, and for Japan to play some kind of a military role within the framework of the United Nations. Soichiro Tahara argued that President George Bush had decided upon a war in the Gulf without first consulting Japan, and that Japan's national interests in the flow of oil and political stability in the Middle East would have been better served by a policy of containing Saddam Hussein. Many Japanese officials publicly took a position close to Professor Sato's, while privately they leaned toward Tahara's views. There was a feeling among officials that Washington's idea of the New World Order was a system in which the United States makes the decisions and Japan pays the bills — and gets criticized for not doing more.

---

[20]*ibid.*, pp. 15-17.

Before moving on to look at the possibility that changes in the international environment will compel Japan to change its foreign policy, it should be noted that within the government and among most foreign policy officials there is even more caution and uncertainty about future foreign policy than among the writers and publicists. Officials are working to preserve the alliance with the United States, and while they are aware of the strains and cracks in the relationship, they believe that for them to plan or speculate about alternative future foreign policies would undermine their work. Moreover, they believe that at this juncture in history the future is so murky and uncertain that contingency planning makes little sense. They are basically intent on shaping the future along the lines of Takakazu Kuriyama's US-EC-Japan concert system. They believe that while the end of the Cold War is not going to quickly and automatically solve all the world's problems, it is an opportunity for the United States to channel more of its attention and resources to economic revitalization, and for the advanced, industrialized nations to coordinate their efforts to patiently and persistently help the poorer nations, including perhaps the Soviet Union and former satellites, to build better lives for their people. As long as these goals seem attainable, they see no need to devise alternative policies.

Three Scenarios for the Future

The foreign policy debate in Japan indicates that there is a keen awareness of the factors that are threatening to make the Yoshida strategy inappropriate in the coming decade. There is a sense that Japanese foreign policy has to be more responsible and more active, but that responsibility and activity seem to be limited almost entirely to economics. Although the Japanese themselves do not appear to be planning and preparing to make a new security or defense policy, if during the next ten to twenty years the bipolar international security system continues to unravel, and if the global economic system breaks into regional blocs, Japan will have to adjust to the new environment. For purposes of discussion, let me suggest three future global futures and the impact they are likely to have on Japanese foreign policy, especially on the security component of foreign policy, which has been most resistant to change.

Scenario A : The Soviet threat continues to decline, the United States substantially reduces its conventional naval and air presence in

East Asia and the Western Pacific, while United States-Japan relations continue to be basically cooperative within the framework of the security alliance, despite the trade imbalance and economic frictions. The decline of the Soviet threat could take place in the context of economic development and peace in Russia and Eastern Europe, or it could occur in an economically distressed and violent regional environment. As long as the United States-Japan-NATO system holds, and the world economy remains intact, with high levels of trade and investment flowing between the United States, Japan, the European Community and the rest of the world, the global outlook will be relatively good. Either the West will be able to assist in economic development in the former Soviet empire, or it will be able to contain whatever threats might emanate from this region. This scenario assumes that the United States economy becomes sounder and more competitive, and that Japan and the European Community continue to move in the direction of open, freer trade, services and investment.

In this case, Japan would probably have to assume responsibility for its own conventional defense, while the U.S. nuclear deterrent would continue to offer protection against Soviet or other nuclear threats. Assuming that the Soviet conventional threat in Asia will continue to diminish, Japan could assume responsibility for its conventional defense with gradual, moderate augmentations to its present force levels, especially its air, naval and short-range missile forces, that would not be seen as threatening by its neighbors. This is basically a scenario for moderate, incremental change within a relatively stable, less threatening international environment.

Vice-Minister Kuriyama's proposal for Japan-United States-European cooperation would fit easily into this world. However, while the triumvirate would preclude wars among the great powers, it could not always prevent wars among the lesser states. The Gulf crisis suggests that the effective control of local wars will be difficult and could disrupt the tripartite system, unless it becomes a military-security as well as an economic partnership. Although the Europeans and Japanese went along with American policy in the Gulf, they have probably sent the message to the United States that they expect to be consulted in the next crisis, and not simply called upon for support after the key decisions have been taken in Washington.

Scenario B : The Soviet threat continues to decline as postulated in A, but economic quarrels, protectionism, techno-nationalism and trade wars lead to an end of effective United States-Japan security cooperation as the United States withdraws from military positions in East Asia and the Western Pacific, including the Philippine bases. In this scenario it is likely that U.S. relations with the European Community will also deteriorate and that NATO will come apart. This would lead to the reemergence of a traditional, multilateral international system, with the United States, the Soviet Union or Russia, Japan, the European Community and/or a unified Germany and China each operating on their own, outside the relatively cohesive alliances we have had since World War II. As long as none of these powers is perceived as militarily aggressive or threatening by the other major powers, this scenario could also lead to a relatively peaceful international security environment, albeit at lower levels of economic activity than in Scenario A.

Japan would probably respond to this environment by:

(1) attempting first to continue in its present non-nuclear, lightly armed posture, and then, if necessary,

(2) by building some kind of minimal, perhaps non-nuclear deterrent and augmenting its conventional air and naval forces, stopping short of an arms build-up that would cause military tensions with China, Russia or the United States.

Considering how difficult it would be to accomplish this build-up without generating tensions and instability, I believe Scenario B to be possible but unstable and extremely difficult to maintain.

In order for this kind of international system to survive, and in order for Japan to pursue this kind of independent but non-threatening security policy, the five powers would probably have to operate along the lines of the Concert system that prevented major wars in Europe from 1815 to 1914. They would all have to eschew ambitious foreign policies and be willing to negotiate and compromise whenever potentially disruptive disputes arose among themselves, and at the same time be prepared to cooperate on an *ad hoc* basis to intervene to keep conflicts among the lesser powers from disrupting the system. Again, the Gulf crisis suggests how crucial and difficult this kind of cooperation would be. In fact, the 21st century analog of the 19th century European Concert system would probably have to be much more like Scenario A .

It is important to understand that while the break-up of the global economy does not necessarily lead to political conflict and war, the economic and ecological costs of a system of uncoordinated, competing spheres of national influence or regional blocs will be very high, and the potential for conflict in Scenario B is much greater than in Scenario A. The European Concert system in the 19th century coincided with the early development of national manufacturing economies, and was supported by the relatively free movement of international trade, investment, currency and people.   In the far more interdependent global economy of the 1990s, the break-up of the global trading and investment system would be likely to leave the Soviet Union, Eastern Europe and the lesser developed economies of the world in desperate straits, which will tend to push all of us into Scenario C.

Scenario C: The United States-Japan alliance ends as a result of economic quarrels as postulated in Scenario B, but after several years of economic decline and political disintegration there is a nationalistic, militaristic, authoritarian backlash in Russia.   Russia has thousands of advanced nuclear weapons and is using its conventional forces to re-conquer and impose its authority on the various national groups within the Soviet Union — rebuilding the Russian empire. It has no intention of reviving the cold war with the United States, but it is determined to prevent encroachments on its empire by a unified Germany, by China or Japan. It pursues detente with the United States, but takes advantage of the end of the United States-NATO-Japan coalition to assume a tough, truculent posture toward Japan, China and/or Germany (perhaps allying with one of these against the others). In this anarchic, violent world, in which the global trading and financial systems have collapsed or badly deteriorated, it is likely that Korea would again find itself the cockpit for rivalry between Russia, China and Japan.

In this kind of environment, Japan would probably see no alternative to protecting itself by becoming a major military power, both nuclear and conventional. This would be a dangerous, unstable world, and Japanese rearmament would aggravate the danger and instability.

Implications for the United States

It is difficult to conceive of a future international environment in which the United States would gain any substantial, lasting benefits by ending its alliance with Japan. If the Soviet threat does continue to diminish and we enter a relatively stable, less dangerous post-cold war world, then the continuation of an effective U.S.-Japan alliance enhances that stability and promotes higher levels of economic activity and cooperation. This is the most beneficial scenario for the United States as well as for Japan.

Scenario B suggests that minimal American security interests could be met in a relatively, peaceful post-cold war world without an alliance or close cooperation with Japan, but the world of Scenario B is less stable than in A, less prosperous, and less likely to deal effectively with international economic-ecological and political issues. If Scenario B deteriorates into some variant of Scenario C, and I think it will be prone to do so, then we will have exchanged the nasty old days of the cold war for a nasty, new world that will be at least as dangerous.

List of Authors

Michael Chinworth, Senior Analyst, The Analytic Science Corporation, Arlington, Virginia, U.S.A.

Wolfgang Hager, Professor of Economics and Euro-Consultant, Brussels, Belgium

Manfred Kulessa, Lecturer for East Asian Economy, University of St. Gallen, Switzerland, Furstenbergstrasse 20, Bonn 2, Germany 5300

Theodor Leuenberger, Dean, Department of Economics, University of St. Gallen, St. Gallen, Switzerland

Akio Morita, President, SONY Corporation, Japan

Yuichiro Nagatomi, President, FAIR, Toranomon Central Building, 1-7-1 Nishi-Shimbashi, Minato-ku, Tokyo 105, Japan

Yoshitaka Okada, Professor of Sociology, International University of Japan, Yamato-machi, Minami Uonuma-gun, Niigata 949-72, Japan

William Rapp, Senior Research Fellow, East Asian Institute, Columbia University, New York, N.Y., U.S.A.

Dieter Schneidewind, Member of the Board, Wella AG, Berliner Allee 65, Darmstadt, Germany 6100

Hellmut Schütte, Professor, Euro-Asia Center, INSEAD, Fontainbleau, France

Koji Taira, Professor of Economics and Labor Relations, University of Illinois, Urbana IL 61801, U.S.A.

Andreas van Agt, Ambassador, Delegation of the Commision of the European Communities, Washington, D.C., U.S.A.

Thilo von Brockdorff, Secretary General, Japanese-German Center, Tiergartentstrasse 24-27, Berlin 30, D-1000 Germany

Martin Weinstein, Director, The Mansfield Center, The University of Montana, Missoula, Montana 59812, U.S.A.